LOUIS I. KAHN
BEYOND TIME AND STYLE

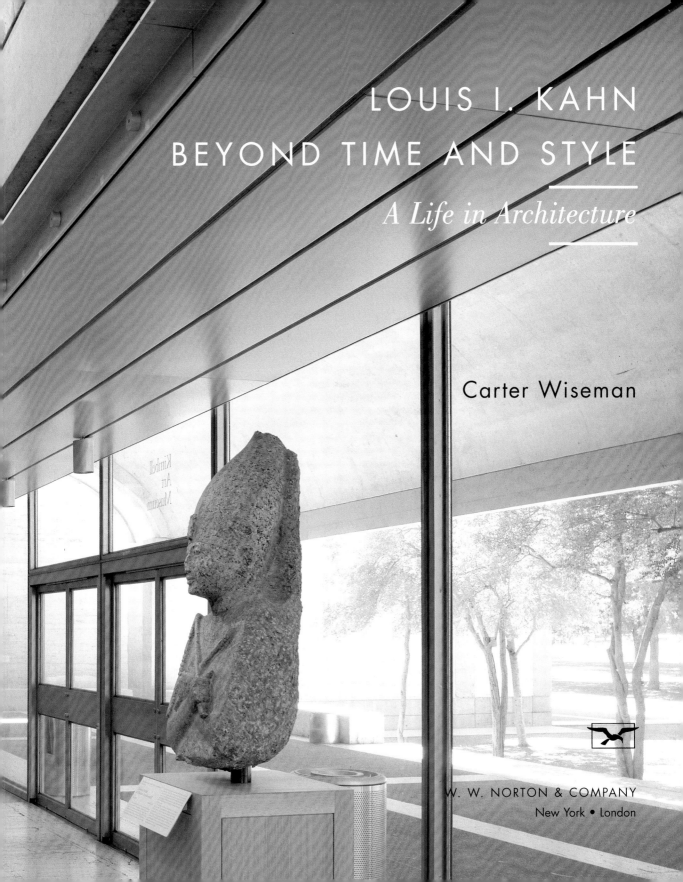

LOUIS I. KAHN
BEYOND TIME AND STYLE

A Life in Architecture

Carter Wiseman

W. W. NORTON & COMPANY
New York • London

TO E., E., O., AND D.

For information about permission to reproduce selections from this book,
write to Permissions, W. W. Norton & Company, Inc., 500 Fifth Avenue,
New York, NY 10110

Manufacturing by Friesens through Four Colour Imports, Ltd., Louisville, KY
Book design by Abigail Sturges
Production Manager: Leeann Graham

Library of Congress Cataloging-in-Publication Data

Wiseman, Carter.
   Louis I. Kahn—beyond time and style: a life in architecture / Carter Wiseman.
      p. cm.
   Includes bibliographical references and index.
   ISBN-13: 978-0-393-73165-1 (hardcover)
   ISBN-10: 0-393-73165-0 (hardcover)
   1. Kahn, Louis I., 1901–1974. 2. Architects—United States—Biography.
3. Architecture—United States—20th century. I. Title.
NA737.K32W57 2007
720.92—dc22
[B]
                                                            2006030936

ISBN 13: 978-0-393-73165-1
ISBN 10: 0-393-73165-0

W. W. Norton & Company, Inc., 500 Fifth Avenue, New York, N.Y. 10110
www.wwnorton.com

W. W. Norton & Company Ltd., Castle House, 75/76 Wells Street, London W1T 3QT

0 9 8 7 6 5 4 3 2 1

CONTENTS

INTRODUCTION

The building at 1501 Walnut Street in Philadelphia is a five-story structure in a vaguely Neoclassical style. To the street it presents a shiny black stone veneer on the ground floor and, to the left of the front door, several small nameplates identifying the tenants. The lobby is cramped, and the elevator is old and very slow. Until June 24, 2004, passersby would have had no reason to associate the building with some of history's greatest works of architecture. But on that day, a metal plaque was unveiled on the sidewalk in front of 1501. It reads, in part: "Louis I. Kahn (1901–1974). Among the foremost architects of the late 20th century. Trained in the Beaux-Arts method at the University of Pennsylvania, Kahn redefined architecture through the extraordinary use of mass, light, and structure. A Penn professor, his office was here."

For nearly two decades, the top two floors of 1501 Walnut gave birth to such Kahn masterpieces as the Salk Institute for Biological Studies in La Jolla, California; the Kimbell Art Museum in Fort Worth, Texas, the Government Center in Dhaka, Bangladesh; and the Yale Center for British Art in New Haven, Connecticut. These buildings may not be as well known

The unassuming front door of 1501 Walnut Street in Philadelphia, Kahn's last office, and the one where he created his finest buildings. CARTER WISEMAN

to the public as Le Corbusier's pilgrimage church at Ronchamp, in France, or Frank Lloyd Wright's Guggenheim Museum, or Mies van der Rohe's Seagram Building. But most critics and scholars now agree that Kahn's buildings are in the same category of quality as those by the earlier Modernist masters.

What accounts for this gap between high quality and renown? For one thing, Louis Kahn was not a public figure in the way Wright, Le Corbusier, and Mies were. He did not indulge in capes and porkpie hats (Wright), owlish glasses frames (Le Corbusier), or large cigars (Mies). Another reason is that Kahn had a late start professionally, and died relatively young, at seventy-four, only twenty-one years after his first major building was completed. Moreover, his designs were not spectacular. Wright's Guggenheim was as controversial as it was good; Mies brought corporate skyscrapers to their pinnacle; and Le Corbusier continued to inspire followers with his sculptural virtuosity well after his death. Kahn's architecture—a subtle blend of history and modernity—is an acquired taste that must be developed over time.

Kahn was further handicapped by both circumstances and timing. Nevertheless, his was a quintessential American saga. Born just after the turn of the twentieth century, he was hardly a candidate for stardom. He was a poor Jewish immigrant. His face had been badly scarred in a childhood accident. Educated in architecture at the University of Pennsylvania in the faltering tradition of the French École des Beaux-Arts, he graduated just as the Depression, the arrival of European Modernism in America, and World War II were putting an end to the architectural world he had been taught to admire. And once his moment came, in the early 1950s, he found his most receptive environment to be institutions of culture and higher learning rather than those of commerce, limiting both his fees and his exposure. Because his most productive period spanned only slightly more than two decades, his output was understandably limited.

But as time has passed, the names of many of Kahn's most prominent contemporaries—Wallace Harrison, Edward Durell Stone, Paul Rudolph, and Philip Johnson among them—have slipped in stature, while Kahn's has risen steadily. More than a score of books have been written about Kahn's work. The first important one was by Vincent Scully, the Yale art historian whose pioneering 1962 monograph identified Kahn's architectural talents and presciently located Kahn among the best of his generation. Many other perceptive studies have followed, exploring Kahn's work in depth from the points of view of art history, architectural design, engineering, and technology. Some scholars—most recently Sarah Williams Goldhagen, Thomas Leslie, and Robert McCarter—have concentrated on the historical, social, and theoretical dimensions of Kahn's work, seeking to establish the meaning of Kahn's legacy. His writings, paintings, drawings, and speeches have been collected and critiqued, sometimes with an almost reverential appreciation for what some have seen as a spiritual or even mystical dimension in his thinking. For his 2000 book *Louis I. Kahn: Unbuilt Masterworks*, MIT's Kent Larson used computers to analyze and represent with provocative power what many of Kahn's unbuilt projects might have looked like had they been completed.

Yet questions remain about the nature of the man and the artist Kahn became, as well as how he actually brought his art into built form. Not the least of the reasons is that much of his personal life was a mystery even to many of those who knew him well. Indeed, Kahn seemed able to maintain multiple and parallel intimacies, both professionally and personally.

Working for Kahn was for many young architects an unforgettable experience. For some, that experience would remain the high point of their professional lives, even though they later went on to distinguished careers themselves. Like so many charismatic figures, Kahn was able to give people who were receptive to him the feeling that he cared only—or at least primarily—about them. And that was no doubt true, at least for the moment when Kahn was most receptive to those people, and until he had absorbed what he needed from them.

The effect extended well beyond the office. Kahn had what in retrospect seems to have been an almost compulsive need to associate with women who were both physically and intellectually attractive. When he met his future wife, she was planning to earn a doctorate in psychology.

The architect at work.

Throughout his mature life, Kahn conducted affairs with numerous other women, usually professional employees. But these liaisons were not mere office romances. Kahn seemed to be drawn irresistibly to women who could join him in his aesthetic quest. One, Anne Tyng, a forceful advocate of geometry in architectural design, bore him a child, Alexandra, in 1954, only to see Kahn move on, both romantically and artistically. Another, Harriet Pattison, a gifted landscape architect, in 1962 bore another Kahn child, Nathaniel, who would make a film that explored his father's life with such effect that it was nominated in 2004 for an Academy Award. It is a measure of the multilayered nature of Kahn's relationships that he and his wife never separated, and that many of the other people—both female and male—with whom he was close retained their loyalty to him despite what might have rightly been considered emotional betrayal. Yet some of Kahn's closest colleagues never knew that he was even married. Moreover, his own children did not know until long after his death that Kahn was not the name their father was born with, or that he was not born where he said he was.

This combination of supreme artistic achievement and personal elusiveness has allowed something akin to a cult to develop around Kahn's legacy. In his later years, the architect was given to pronouncements that verged on the cryptic. The most famous of them reflected his insistence that materials should be consulted about their use: "What does a brick want to be?" Kahn famously asked his students. Whether profound, obscure, or deliberately provocative, such remarks fueled an enthusiasm among some of Kahn's followers that amounted to worship, setting his built achievements almost beyond reproach, and therefore even further from lay accessibility.

However, those who worked most closely with Kahn knew him as a thoroughly down-to-earth practitioner, an architect who actually relished making changes to his original designs and solving problems that would have exasperated lesser talents. He told colleagues that he dreaded finishing a building, because he felt that completion meant the end of the design process. Unlike some of his better-known contemporaries, who expected their clients to accept their work without question, Kahn rejoiced in the extended process of creation, often working on designs well into construction or even after a client had officially withdrawn from a project.

Kahn never ceased to search for sources—ultimately, where architecture began and how its most lasting qualities could be honored anew. And for that reason—which was so apparent to all those who looked carefully at

Kahn's life and work—his failures at the personal level were often accepted, if not always forgiven. Louis Kahn, it would seem, was committed to a goal that exceeded the talent, the grasp, and perhaps even the understanding of most of those who knew him. And in that, he shared a tortured but triumphant tradition in the arts, creating work that would remain beyond the reach of conventional analysis or quantification. It was art of the highest order, but it was made at a high cost to those who shared in it.

This book, concentrating on a selection of Kahn's most successful built work, is an attempt to bring the architect forward as an individual—deeply complex as a man, supremely talented as an artist and designer, mesmerizing as a teacher, and a monumental figure in the history of architecture.

CHAPTER ONE

ARRIVAL

ESTONIA, THE NORTHERN LIBERTIES, AND PENN
1901–24

The man who was to become a world-renowned American architect was born into obscurity on March 5 (February 20 by the old Julian calendar), 1901, in Russian-controlled Estonia. His family name was not Kahn, but Schmuilowsky, and although he later came to be known as Louis Isadore, he began life as Leiser-Itze.[1]

According to family research, his father, Leib Schmuilowsky, was originally from Latvia and as a boy worked as an artisan in stained glass, but he was drafted at seventeen into the Russian army. The standard hardships of a military conscript were apparently compounded for Leib by his Jewish origins, which subjected him to the anti-Semitism that was common in that part of the world at the time. But because he could write well, and spoke not only Latvian and Estonian, but also Russian, German, Yiddish, and some Turkish (evidently picked up during his military campaigning), Leib made himself useful to his superiors as a scribe, translator, and sign-painter. Because of his reputation for trustworthiness (if not hard work), he was eventually promoted to the rank of paymaster. Photographs of Leib during his military service show an erect and confident soldier of the Tsar, with a thin mustache primly waxed and curled.

Leib Schmuilowsky (later Leopold Kahn), the future architect's father, while serving in the Russian army about 1900. After his son was accidentally burned by fireplace coals, Leib concluded that the boy would have been better off dead.
© SUE ANN KAHN

On a furlough from the army, Leib met a woman named Beila-Rebecka Mendelowitsch (later Bertha Mendelsohn), a fellow Latvian who was an accomplished harpist. (She claimed a family link to the German composer Felix Mendelssohn.) They fell in love and married in 1900, in Riga. Their first son would insist throughout his life that he was born on an island in the Baltic off the coast of Estonia. Called Ösel at the time (it is now known as Saaremaa), the island was dominated by the town of Kingisepp (now Kuressaare) and its massive fourteenth-century castle. But recently located documents indicate that Leiser-Itze was actually born in Pernau (now Pärnu), a city on the mainland, where his sister Sarah (Schorre) followed him on June 27, 1902, and his brother Oscar (Oscher) on June 29, 1904.

Why the mature Louis Kahn would misstate his birthplace is not clear. Perhaps he was given inaccurate information by his parents, or the Pernau bureaucrats may have consolidated local births to include those outlying areas such as Ösel. He may have preferred to think of himself as having more romantic, "islander," origins. Or he may simply have shared in the factual mix-ups that affected so many émigrés in those years from a part of the world that was a shifting mélange of German, Scandinavian, Slavic, and

The fourteenth-century castle on the island of Saaremaa, off the coast of Estonia, where Kahn claimed he had been born. However, records show that he entered the world in the mainland Estonian city of Pärnu, as Leiser-Itze Schmuilowsky. The image is from a postcard of the castle as it looked during the architect's 1928 visit as Louis I. Kahn. COURTESY OLAVI PESTI, PATRICIA LOUD

Jewish cultures. In any case, Leiser-Itze's family apparently did move for at least a time to Ösel, because Leib later claimed to have worked at the Kingisepp castle, and immigration documents note that Bertha lived on the island with the children.

At the age of three, the boy had an accident that would mark him for the rest of his life. According to family members, he became fascinated by the glowing embers of the coal fire that heated his house. One day, he reached into the grate and scooped some of the coals into his apron, which burst into flame. Parts of his hands and much of his face were scorched before his mother arrived. His intense blue eyes were spared, but the burns were so bad that his parents were not sure the boy would survive. He did, but his face remained permanently scarred. Family accounts record that Leib thought his son would have been better off dead than disfigured, but his mother "insisted that he would become a great man someday."[2]

Many of Leib's relatives had immigrated to the United States some years before and settled in the Philadelphia area. Whether the cause was the takeover by the Russians of his mother's family's farm, anti-Semitism, the threat of a war with Japan (in which Leib would have had to serve), or

Beila-Rebecka Mendelowitsch (later Bertha Kahn) believed firmly that, despite poverty and disfigurement, her son would eventually become a great man. © SUE ANN KAHN

the lure of his kinsmen's New World experience, Leib in 1904 left for America, planning to bring his family later. But after arriving in Philadelphia on June 29 with a mere $4 in his pockets, he discovered that his local contacts, in particular a brother-in-law on whom he had pinned high hopes, would not be of much help. So Leib, although his immigration records listed his work experience as a "waistmaker" in a shirt factory, took a job in construction, and soon suffered a debilitating injury to his back. Bertha arrived with the children in Philadelphia (not through Ellis Island, as the grown Kahn later claimed) on June 25, 1906. She was met at the dock by Leib, only to find that her husband was in serious financial trouble.

Indeed, for a time, the family had barely enough to eat, but Bertha kept things going by doing knitting and crocheting for a local clothing firm. Difficult as her role was, she considered it worth the effort and was determined that her children become full-fledged Americans. Bertha and Leib briefly tried running a candy store, but without success, and money remained an issue. The family lived in a succession of the two- and three-story row houses that characterized the largely Jewish section of northeastern Philadelphia known as the Northern Liberties. (The name dates to

Philadelphia's founding, when the area lay beyond the boundaries of Willliam Penn's original planned city.) Much of the future architect's youthful free time was spent playing with friends on the front steps of the family's lodgings. "The playground," he recalled not long before his death, "was the street."[3] The family moved seventeen times in two years, most often because they could not pay the rent. In the course of this unsettled period, an attack of scarlet fever confined Leiser, by now known by the more American name of Louis, to the hospital, leaving him with a high-pitched voice and weakened legs, and delaying his entry to public school until he was seven. Once there, at the Landberger School, on Fourth and George streets, he at first tended to avoid his schoolmates, who mocked him as "Scarface." He soon showed a talent for drawing, however, and since the teachers valued such skills, Louis, like his father in the Russian army, became useful to his oppressors, who gradually began to overlook his handicap in return for his help on their own work.

When Louis moved on to the General Philip Kearny Grammar School, at Sixth and Fairmount streets, his skill at drawing was quickly recognized.

A 1925 view of the pushcart strip on North Marshall Street in Philadelphia's Northern Liberties section, where Kahn grew up. His youthful enthusiasm for the variety and excitement of city life remained with him and influenced many of his mature designs. PHILADELPHIA CITY ARCHIVES

Although there was sometimes barely enough to eat in their Philadelphia home, the family managed to afford a formal portrait of the children. Kahn is at right with his sister, Sarah (far left), and brother, Oscar, around 1908.
© SUE ANN KAHN

And he was protective of it. Louis recalled in 1971 that his father had "lovingly corrected" a picture he was struggling with, and that "I threw paper and pencil across the room, saying, 'Now it's your drawing, not mine.' "[4] The respect for the value of one's own work would stay with Louis as a professional. Years later, as both a teacher and as a designer, he would almost always place sheets of tracing paper over drawings by others before making any changes.

In time, his unusual ability with a pencil won Louis a rare opportunity to attend Philadelphia's Public Industrial Art School, at Thirteenth and Master streets, an institution that sought out talented youths from the municipal school system. In 1913, he won first prize in the City Art Contest, a competition sponsored by the department-store magnate John Wanamaker. It was at the Public Industrial Art School that Louis met one of the succession of teachers who were to make such a difference in his life. The teacher was James Liberty Tadd, a Quaker and leading educational theorist who had taught at the Pennsylvania Academy of the Fine Arts before becoming head of the public school.

The first of several teachers who recognized Kahn's extraordinary artistic gifts was James Liberty Tadd, who had studied with Thomas Eakins before becoming director of Philadelphia's Public Industrial Art School. To sharpen his students' sense of proportion and scale, Tadd trained them to draw with both hands simultaneously. PORTRAIT BY ANNIE TRAQUAIR LANG, COURTESY OF THE PENNSYLVANIA ACADEMY OF THE FINE ARTS, PHILADELPHIA

As the oldest institution of its kind in America, the Academy was (and remains) one of the pillars of Philadelphia's cultural and social life, offering not only exhibition space, but also instruction in studio art. In 1876, the institution had completed the construction of its new building at the corner of Broad and Cherry streets. The architects were Frank Furness and George Hewitt. Furness, the lead designer, was a Civil War veteran and holder of the Medal of Honor for valor as a cavalry captain. His architecture was no less vigorous than his military exploits. Using a wide range of materials—principally brick, stone, and wrought iron—Furness and his partner drew freely on the romantic traditions of the French Second Empire, Venetian Gothic, Neo-Grec, and the multicolored medieval and Islamic sources, to create a building unprecedented in American architectural history.

The ornamentation of the building is generally considered to be the work of Hewitt, but the massing and the plan owed their impact to Furness. In assembling such a rich combination of forms and spaces, Furness asserted a sort of primitive muscularity that outlasted the critiques of the décor as frivolous and overdone. Despite its excesses, the Academy is widely considered Furness's masterpiece. It even won over the architectural historian and critic Lewis Mumford, who years later colorfully declared the architect's work to be "bold, unabashed, ugly, and yet somehow healthily pregnant."[5] Although Furness may have failed in his quest to create an architecture that was uniquely American, he did leave a powerful legacy, especially in Philadelphia. It is no accident that Louis in later life would cite the Academy's building affectionately for its elemental power.

J. Liberty Tadd was an 1881 graduate of the Academy, where he had trained with Thomas Eakins, the renowned American Realist painter. Eakins urged his students to reject traditional techniques of art education in favor of what Tadd called the student's "self-reliant" thought process.[6] Tadd, an advocate of the romantically oriented Progressive movement, relied heavily on drawing from nature, supplying his students with stuffed animals prepared by taxidermists to augment classroom studies of photographs and plaster casts. The students also were taken on field trips to draw farm animals from life so that their art would be intimately linked to nature, and not merely an intellectual activity in the abstract. One of Tadd's teaching exercises was to draw on a chalkboard with both hands simultaneously. This ambidextrous training sharpened the students' skills at maintaining proportions at different scales and was to become one of his star pupil's own graphic techniques as a teacher. Tadd also emphasized three-dimensional work in wood and clay to develop his students' appreciation of different materials. The goal was to so imbue the students with a facility for visual expression that it would seem as natural as handwriting. And here, too, the early influences were to prove significant for the mature architect. Years later, he was to write of a visit to the fortified French medieval city of Carcassonne that "from the moment I entered the gates, I began to write with drawing."[7] So successful was Tadd's method of "natural education" that it was eventually made part of the Philadelphia public school curriculum.

In addition to his studies with Tadd, Louis was able to take classes on weekends at the Graphic Sketch Club, later renamed the Samuel S. Fleisher Art Memorial in honor of its major patron. The club, at 719 Catharine Street, provided lessons in music as well as in drawing and painting, "for the world to come and learn art." Although he never learned to read music, Louis had an extraordinary ear and became such an accomplished pianist through trial and error that the director of the school gave him an old piano. (There was little room for it in the Kahn household, and Louis remembered sleeping on top of the instrument to save space.) Just as his skills in drawing had helped him in his early school days, his ability at the piano now allowed Louis to help his struggling family by playing the accompaniment to silent films in two local movie theaters. (The job also kept him in top physical condition sprinting the eight blocks between the two theaters after one film ended and before the other began.)

Although his manifest talents had given Louis access to a superior education unusual for a child of his background, he and his family still had to deal with an unhappy social reality in Philadelphia. While the city's reputation for tolerance extended back to Colonial times, that reputation had begun to erode with the construction of Philadelphia's first synagogue, Mikveh Israel, in 1782. The synagogue provided a focus for the growing Jewish community, but also for those Christian Philadelphians who were disturbed by the expansion of what they considered alien traditions in their midst. As time passed, a division also grew between the generally more prosperous Jews of German origin and the poorer Jews who came from Eastern Europe.[8] As members of the second group, Louis and his family helped swell the Jewish population of the city but were consigned to a distinctly lower social class and lived even further apart from the Gentile community. In 1915, Leib became a naturalized American citizen. In the process he officially changed his names from Leib to Leopold and Schmuilowsky to Kahn, a name many of his Americanized relatives had already adopted, perhaps feeling that a more German-American–sounding identity would ease the family's way in their new environment, or just wanting to sound less "foreign." He also denounced "all allegiance to Russia and Tsar Nicholas and Tsarina Alexandra."[9]

But while his musical skills won Louis the offer of a music scholarship from Samuel Fleisher himself, art was the skill that would dictate his next step. As a student at Central High School, at Broad and Green streets, the leading public school in the city, Louis was encouraged by William F. Gray, the head of the art department. Like Tadd, Gray had studied at the Academy of the Fine Arts and had been exposed to the same ideals of artistic romanticism. But Gray was also a student of architecture (he had written architecture criticism for the *Philadelphia Bulletin*) and was a vigorous supporter of Philadelphia's "City Beautiful" movement. His lectures in art history at Central extended to the buildings of medieval Italy, as well as those of the later eighteenth and early nineteenth centuries. As part of his course, Gray required his students to make India ink drawings of famous architectural landmarks representing the major styles: Egyptian, Greek, Roman, Renaissance, and Gothic. Many of Kahn's classmates had difficulty with these assignments, and Louis earned money on the side by helping them with their drawings, deliberately making a few ink blots to conceal his authorship. Gray evidently knew of the ruse but was not about to penalize his star student.

At Central, Kahn regularly won the prizes for watercolors sponsored by the Academy of the Fine Arts, and on May 22, 1919, he was awarded the Academy's first prize for the best "original free-hand drawing" by a high school student in Philadelphia.[10] His record was so impressive that the Academy offered Louis a four-year scholarship. But in his final year at Central, he took a course taught by Gray in architectural history and decided that instead of becoming a painter he would pursue architecture at the University of Pennsylvania. Gray, recalled Kahn in 1973, had "touched the very core of my expressive desires."[11]

The decision was a difficult one for the family. Kahn had been earning a small but steady income playing the piano in the local silent-movie houses, and going to Penn would cut into his working time. (He nevertheless kept playing through his university years, picking up skills at the organ when one of the houses switched instruments. Kahn actually added to his responsibilities by projecting humorous drawings he had done to amuse the audience while the reels were being changed.) To further support his ambitions, Kahn took a summer job as a shipping clerk in a department store. In those days, a first son's future took priority, so Kahn's sister Sarah left school and became a seamstress to augment the finances. Family accounts suggest that Kahn's younger brother, Oscar, resented Louis's opportunity, but there was no question about the final decision to send Louis to Penn. Nevertheless, he had to borrow money to start his studies and would have to take a variety of teaching-assistant positions to see himself through.

The school Kahn entered in the fall of 1920 was self-consciously proud of its status. Although the university as a whole did not rank with Harvard, Yale, or Princeton, its architecture department was arguably the strongest of its day. The 1922–23 edition of the school's catalogue over-reached a bit in describing Penn as "the oldest university in America." (Harvard College was founded in 1636, Penn in 1751, but in 1779 it added professional courses in medicine and law, allowing it to change its name to the University of the State of Pennsylvania.) The catalogue went on to cite some impressive statistics. Referring to the prizes and fellowships offered to the country's architecture students at the time, the authors noted that, "In all of these, from their foundation to 1921," the students of Pennsylvania "have secured a greater number of awards than have those of any other institution." The text went on to explain that "the method of teaching that has brought about these results is an adaptation to American needs of the French system of atelier training as exemplified in the École des Beaux Arts. . . . As in Paris, the students are divided into groups or 'ateliers' and receive individual instruction from practicing architects, all former students of the École des Beaux-Arts."[12]

The image of the Beaux-Arts in America that has survived is one of somber, imposing banks and courthouses embellished with columns and friezes and laid out in often arid regularity. In fact, the tradition on which Penn and all the other leading American architecture schools of Kahn's student days drew was full of life and well suited to conditions in the United States at the time. The Classical origins of the Beaux-Arts approach offered to what was still an extremely young nation a cultural association with the noble virtues of Greek democracy and the Roman Republic. Added to these were the French formal concepts of unity, harmony, balance, and "repose." Beyond that, the Beaux-Arts teachings concentrated on the fundamental issues of city planning, including transportation, recreation, and the design of urban institutions, especially government and cultural monuments. All in all, the lessons of the Beaux-Arts in Paris prepared American architects well for the design of the major buildings that were required of a country that was making its mark as a major world power, yet seeking stability in all aspects of life following the military and social upheavals of World War I.

The search for stability did not necessarily imply architectural sterility, however. Although the country was sprinkled at the turn of the twentieth century with formulaic Neoclassical buildings, the best of the breed were very good indeed. Such works by the firm of McKim, Mead & White as the 1895 Boston Public Library and New York's now demolished 1910 Pennsylvania Station stand out as examples, as do George B. Post's 1904 New York Stock Exchange and John Carrère and Thomas Hastings's 1911 New York Public Library. These buildings acknowledged the new conditions

A charcoal sketch of a male nude made by Kahn while a student at Penn shows his unusual promise as an artist. It also betrays an especially structural appreciation of the human form. COLLECTION OF SUE ANN KAHN

of modern American life (railroads, international commerce, expanded public access to resources once limited to the rich), but accommodated them in ways that anchored growing American cities with respectable municipal monuments.

Kahn's formal introduction to architecture came at the hands of some of the best Beaux-Arts–trained mentors in America. His first design teacher at Penn was John Harbeson, a Beaux-Arts alumnus who had developed a reputation as an especially supportive critic, guiding his students through the basic elements of design before introducing them to more demanding work. Not surprisingly, given his record of past awards, Kahn stood out in the watercolor and freehand drawing exercises that were a fundamental part of the curriculum, so much so that he was made assistant in charge of the life drawing classes. Harbeson at the time practiced architecture professionally in partnership with Paul Philippe Cret, another Beaux-Arts–trained architect on the Penn faculty and widely considered its most distinguished member. Kahn studied with Cret as a teacher in his fourth and final year, and the experience would remain with him throughout his career.

Cret—who was elegantly formal in a European way and favored a large mustache—was not only the leading member of the Penn department, but was also authentically French, giving him an authority in the teaching of the Beaux-Arts–based curriculum that his colleagues could not match. Cret was born in Lyons in 1876 and in 1897 won a prize to study in Paris. He trained at the École in the atelier of Jean-Louis Pascal, a former colleague of Charles Garnier (architect of the Paris Opéra) and Henri Labrouste (designer of the Bibliothèque Ste-Geneviève). While in Paris, a group of Penn graduates learned of Cret's skills as a teacher, and in 1903 they invited him to Philadelphia to become director of design in the architecture program under Warren Powers Laird, who later became the first dean of Penn's School of Fine Arts. Cret had prepared to compete for the Grand Prix de Rome, but rather adventurously decided to accept the Americans' offer instead.

Cret adapted quickly to American architectural ways, concentrating on the design of government buildings and city institutions. In the course of his career, he entered twenty-five competitions, winning six and placing in ten, a remarkable record, especially for a foreigner. In 1938, Cret was awarded the Gold Medal of the American Institute of Architects.

Born in France and trained at the École des Beaux-Arts in Paris, the elegant Paul Philippe Cret became a mainstay of the architecture program at the University of Pennsylvania. He also had a lifelong impact on Kahn's appreciation of architectural order and monumentality.
© PAUL PHILIPPE CRET COLLECTION, THE ARCHITECTURAL ARCHIVES, UNIVERSITY OF PENNSYLVANIA

Cret brought from the Beaux-Arts an emphasis on axial planning, relying on Classical symmetry, but inflecting and simplifying the historical precedents to acknowledge the role of structural steel and modern construction techniques. In a 1923 essay entitled "Modern Architecture," Cret emphasized what he saw as the importance of history to contemporary design. He countered the contemporary criticism that the Classical tradition had lost its appeal, arguing that the best architecture emerged from an understanding of the continuity of the art over the ages. It was a message that Kahn would welcome and make his own.

Cret had returned to France during the First World War, serving first as an infantryman (an experience that left him partially deaf from exploding shells) and then as an interpreter on the staff of General John Pershing, the commander in chief of the American forces. That assignment contributed to his selection after the war to design a number of memorials, which proved to be some of the most moving examples of the genre. Among his most prominent civic buildings were the Pan-American Union in Washington, D.C. (1910), the Detroit Institute of Arts (1927), and the Folger Shakespeare Library (1932), also in Washington. These buildings had an unmistakable similarity to much of the work being done at the same time in Europe, especially in Italy and Germany, and Cret was attacked by some later critics for what they saw as aesthetic links to Fascist and Nazi ideologies. But the comparisons overlooked the refined elegance of Cret's proportions and details, which contrasted with the numbing predictability of the totalitarians. Beneath Cret's version of classicism lay a firm faith in architecture's role as an evolving art, not one frozen for political purposes.

Kahn and Cret became close at Penn, and Kahn retained a deep respect for both Cret's architecture and his example as a teacher. According to Mark Ueland, a Philadelphia architect who studied under him at Penn, Kahn said one night that he had "survived for 20 years" on a brief but positive comment Cret had made during a critique of a project during Kahn's final year at architecture school.[13]

The rigorous dedication to geometric fundamentals taught by Cret would have a lasting impact on Kahn's own work. One aspect of Cret's teaching that Kahn would leave behind, however, was the French architect's aversion to the American tradition of romantic individualism. Cret had no use for the idea that architecture could be substantially changed by people deviating from the continuity of the art over time, and here he was destined to clash with the European Modernists. Moreover, he could never sympathize with that romantic strain of American architecture (embodied most famously by Frank Lloyd Wright) which sought to recognize nature as a source of inspiration. In the French tradition, Cret's architecture was more of the mind than the heart. Nevertheless, Kahn retained warm memories of his student days at Penn for the rest of his life. In a 1971 interview, he recalled that, it "was a nice school then. It was highly religious, not as if it were a certain religion, but religious in the sense that transcendent qualities were considered worthy."[14]

When Kahn graduated from Penn, on June 18, 1924, his transcript showed a respectable record. Although he had been placed briefly on "General Probation" for his academic performance, he was awarded the bronze Brooke Medal for Design. His finances continued to dog him; to earn money on the side, Kahn, who had already established a reputation as one of the best draftsmen in Philadelphia, did renderings for local firms. He was so well regarded that he was admitted to the Architectural Society, a club made up of the best students, a particular honor given the fact that Jews—especially poor ones—had been up to then considered ineligible. But what-

Kahn at his Penn commencement with classmates Hyman Cunin (left) and Norman Rice. The determination expressed in Kahn's face would be severely tested by the Great Depression, World War II, and the collapse of the Beaux-Arts traditions in which the architect had been trained. © SUE ANN KAHN

ever knowledge Kahn had acquired at Penn, the city of Philadelphia had also contributed a major share to his education. In later years, the architect would often describe the city as "a place where a little boy walking through its streets can sense what he would someday like to be."[15]

As a graduate of what was arguably the best architectural school in the United States at the time, Louis I. Kahn was eminently well prepared to enter the profession. Unfortunately, the profession at the time was not as well prepared to receive him.

CHAPTER TWO

TO CHANGE THE WORLD

THE LEAN YEARS

1924–47

The University of Pennsylvania may have been widely considered one of the leading American schools of architecture in 1924, but it was destined to tumble in stature as the architectural world expanded. And the expansion was taking place at an explosive rate.

In the United States, the changes had been set in motion most dramatically by the work of Frank Lloyd Wright, the egotistical, cantankerous, but brilliant Wisconsin native whose 1910 Robie House in Chicago had become an instant landmark. Its low profile, sweeping horizontal lines, and free-flowing interior spaces had stunned the American architectural community, which was mired in an increasingly stale eclecticism that accepted Classical, Colonial, and Gothic imitation almost indiscriminately. But the impact of the Robie House, along with that of Wright's other revolutionary designs, was felt even more strongly in Europe, where a collection of the architect's built works and projects was published in 1910 by a German company and came to be known as the Wasmuth Portfolio. It was required reading for the avant-garde on both sides of the Atlantic.

Wright's rejection of conventional American architecture came at a time when such European radicals as Adolf Loos were already exploring new forms intended to replace an architectural tradition of Neoclassicism that had lost its aesthetic energy. And following the First World War, Dutch, French, and German progressives were linking the formal opportunities provided by such synthetic industrial materials as glass, steel, and concrete to the widespread need for housing, especially for the masses of industrial workers swelling the labor force. In 1919, the German architect Walter Gropius established a revolutionary school in Weimar that combined instruction in architecture with courses in the applied arts. Recalling his original goals for the Bauhaus years later, Gropius wrote: "I became obsessed by the conviction that modern constructional technique could not be denied expression in architecture, and that that expression demanded the use of unprecedented forms."[1]

These developments were destined to affect American architecture, and there was no better preview of the turmoil ahead than the competition

A touseled, pipe-smoking Kahn in about 1930 with (from left) his sister-in-law Rosella, his mother, and Joe Rovner, a family friend. The young boy is Rosella's son, Alan Kahn.
COURTESY ALEXANDRA TYNG

organized in 1922 by the *Chicago Tribune* newspaper company for its new headquarters. The competition drew 204 entries from 23 countries, including submissions by such leading European architects as Loos, Gropius, and Eliel Saarinen. (An additional 59 entries arrived after the deadline.) The American entries were without exception conservative, most of them dropping vaguely Roman or Venetian "hats" on stacks of Neoclassical office floors. The winning entry, by Raymond Hood and his partner John Mead Howells, was a no-less-shamelessly traditional tower draped in Gothic detail and topped off with flying buttresses.

Hood made no apologies for clinging to the past. In an essay in *Architectural Forum* two years after winning the competition—and three months after Kahn's graduation from Penn—Hood declared in discussing "Exterior Architecture of Office Buildings" that the architect should "take the exterior of your building, divide it into the proper number of stories, make an arrangement of windows that is dictated by the renting and lighting conditions, and then proceed to make the resulting mass attractive, by one means or another. This is the only way to go about it."[2]

Such practical but ultimately banal observations were soon to be swept aside by the rhetoric of the Europeans. A year before Kahn graduated from Penn, the Swiss-French architect Charles-Édouard Jeanneret-Gris, better known as Le Corbusier, had published a slim volume entitled *Vers une architecture*. Although it was not translated into English, as *Towards a New Architecture*, until 1927, it had already made an enormous impact on American architectural thinking. Le Corbusier wanted to do away with the architecture of the past and create a new one based on industry and the machine. He was entranced by such symbols of modern life as the automobile, the airplane, and the ocean liner. "The Engineer's Aesthetic, and Architecture, are two things that march together," Le Corbusier declared on his opening page.[3] Liberally illustrated with photographs of American and Canadian grain storage elevators, engine parts, and factories, the book pulsated with polemical rhetoric that might be seen as a model for Kahn's own flowery pronouncements in later years. "A great epoch has begun," declared Le Corbusier. "There exists a new spirit;" "The 'styles' are a lie."[4] Linking the new industrial aesthetic of mechanical efficiency with the fundamental architectural principles expressed by the ancients in the Parthenon and the Pantheon, the author called simultaneously for a return to basics and a charge forward into a new age. His most notorious statement was that a house was "a machine for living in."[5]

Although the leading American architecture magazines of the day—*Architectural Forum* and *Architectural Record*—contented themselves largely with appreciative articles on traditional country houses and city mansions, the European rumblings were beginning to be heard in the editorial offices of New York and Chicago. While the precise shape of what was to come may have remained murky, the editors at *Architectural Record* seemed to sense the magnitude of the changes underway and that they had emerged at least partly from the work of America's own. In the issue published in June of 1924, the magazine included an obituary for Louis Sullivan. More than any other architect, Sullivan had appreciated the opportunities created by structural steel and the elevator for the tall building, and had said so most eloquently in his essay "The Tall Office Building Artistically Considered" in 1896. Referring to an article Sullivan had written attacking the timid American showing in the *Tribune* competition, the obituary's author, A. N. Rebori, recalled the architect's prophecy of "a time to come, and not so far away, when the wretched and the yearning, the sordid and the fierce, shall escape the bondage and the mania of fixed ideas."[6]

Kahn's first job upon graduation from Penn could not have offered a greater contrast with Sullivan's hopes, or what was happening in the European avant-garde. The position was with John Molitor, the city architect of Philadelphia, whose usual commissions were for police stations, firehouses, and hospitals. Like so many of Kahn's teachers at Penn, Molitor had trained in Paris, and his work was comfortably traditional. Kahn spent a year in Molitor's office working as a common draftsman, but in 1925 he enjoyed a professional windfall. To celebrate the 150th anniversary of the signing of the Declaration of Independence, Philadelphia was planning in 1926 to host the Sesquicentennial International Exposition. Molitor was put in charge of the major buildings, and he set up a special office for the purpose, making Kahn a member of the design team. Kahn later recalled having been chief of design, but his citation on the publication of the work in *Architectural Record* listed him as "architectural designer," third in line behind two "assistant architects."[7] Whatever his level of responsibility, Kahn was dealing with six buildings encompassing more than 1.5 million square feet on a site that covered roughly 1,500 acres. And although the buildings were temporary—made of wood and stucco on steel frames—they provided an oppor-

tunity to think and design at a scale the twenty-four-year-old Kahn had
never known.

Even though the Sesquicentennial buildings were demolished and the
site converted to a park after the exposition closed in 1927, Kahn's work on
the project must have provided a thrilling experience for such a young
architect. Indeed, he seems to have invested more in the project than his
employer was prepared to accept. Having noticed in the local papers that
Kahn was putting in additional time with a local builder beyond his assignment for Molitor on the Palace of Fashion, the city architect wrote Kahn that
"I had no idea it would involve anything like the amount evidently that you
have put on it. I, therefore, notify you that you cannot do work of this kind
and stay in this office . . . otherwise it will be necessary for us to make
another arrangement."[8]

Kahn evidently made amends with Molitor, and with the end of the
Sesquicentennial, he returned to designing playground buildings and other
municipal facilities. But he was eager for more demanding work. His next

step was a year with the office of William H. Lee, whose specialty was movie theaters, but who was at the time working on several commissions for Philadelphia's Temple University. Comfortable as Kahn's position was, it evidently did not satisfy his creative ambitions, and he began to look beyond Philadelphia for inspiration.

At the time, Modernist European émigrés were already making their mark in the United States. One of the most prominent was Rudolph Schindler, a Viennese who had come to America and worked for Wright before establishing his own practice in California. Schindler's Lovell Beach House, built in 1926 for a wealthy family in Newport Beach, displayed all the emerging traces of the European innovators: spare geometric forms in concrete and stucco, wide expanses of glass, and a total absence of ornament. Schindler's fellow Austrian, Richard Neutra, a follower of Adolf Loos, also worked for the Lovell family, designing a "health house" in Hollywood in 1929 that was built on a prefabricated steel skeleton.

How much Kahn knew of the California work is not clear, but in any case architecture was by no means the only subject of interest to him at this stage of his life. At a party in 1927, Kahn met a lissome, dark-haired beauty named Esther Virginia Israeli. Although Esther had studied dramatic arts before entering the University of Pennsylvania, she was planning to pursue a doctorate in experimental psychology. Esther's family was of Russian-Jewish origin but had become so assimilated into American culture that the main holidays her parents celebrated in their home at 5243 Chester Avenue were Thanksgiving, Christmas, and Washington's Birthday; they observed few Jewish holidays and at Passover attended seders at friends' houses instead of having them at home. The Israelis had made substantial strides both socially and professionally. Esther's father, Samuel, had attended Yale and the University of Pennsylvania Law School, and was an enthusiastic Republican member of the Philadelphia City Council. His sister was a doctor, and one brother was an architect. Most of the family's friends were involved in law, medicine, or the arts. But the social integration was not total. Esther was a serious and ambitious student. A relative remembered that "she liked to be at the head of the class."[9] Despite her accomplishments and her family's all-American profile, Esther, like virtually all daughters of East European Jews, was excluded not just from the Christian social clubs at Penn, but also from the German-Jewish sorority, and had to join the less prestigious sorority made up of the daughters of Russian ancestry.

At the party where Esther met Kahn, she was with another man. Kahn rode home with her and her escort, who lived near Kahn. During the trip, Louis mentioned a book he had recently bought, about the French sculptor Auguste Rodin. Kahn was smitten with the elegant Penn student, and later sent her a copy of the Rodin book as a graduation present. Although Esther was still involved with her original beau, she and Kahn began to see each other on the side. On one outing they passed a flower shop, and Esther marveled at the dahlias in the window. The following Friday, Esther came home to find a huge delivery of flowers—dahlias included. Kahn had not known what dahlias were, so he bought all the flowers in the store window just to be safe. Impressed as she was by the gesture, Esther was puzzled by her new acquaintance. Reminiscing in 1982, she said, "I knew nothing about architecture, and I was very accustomed to the 9-to-5 working schedule, thus for me it was very difficult to understand Lou, who never quit working at 5 o'clock."[10]

Having lived with his parents and saved as much of his salary from Lee's office as he could, Kahn was now ready to embark on his version of the Grand Tour of Europe that had long been considered essential to the early career of any American architect who planned to rise in his profession. Telling Esther that "not even you are to keep me back," Kahn set off in the spring of 1928.[11] But as someone who was as gifted in the graphic arts as he was in architectural design, Kahn had more than the usual professional motivation for the trip.

Kahn arrived in England on May 3, and spent two weeks sketching before continuing on to the Netherlands and northern Germany. From there, he proceeded to Denmark, Sweden, Finland, Latvia, and Estonia, where he visited his childhood home. He spent nearly a month there, sleeping on the floor in his maternal grandmother's one-room house.[12] On Saaremaa, he again saw the brooding medieval castle that still dominated the city and which may well have seeded his lifelong affinity for monumental structures that had survived the centuries. Kahn went on from Estonia to Germany, where Walter Gropius's designs for low-income housing were under construction in Berlin as part of the Siemensstadt Siedlung, a housing complex for the Siemens electric company workers. From Germany, Kahn traveled to Austria and Hungary, and, on October 4, to Italy.

Kahn spent five months in Italy, traveling to Assisi, Florence, Milan, and San Gimignano, whose towers would later be cited by some scholars as

Kahn's graphite sketch of the Monastery of St. Francis at Assisi shows a growing interest in the way buildings interacted with each other. His visit to Assisi would pay dividends some thirty years later in his collaboration with Jonas Salk on the Salk Institute for Biological Studies in California.

the formal inspiration for his 1965 Richards Medical Research Laboratories at Penn. He proceeded to Rome, and down the Amalfi Coast to Paestum, where he would have seen the sixth- and fifth-century B.C. Greek temples.

The drawings and paintings Kahn made on his trip document an intriguing transition from the formal exercises required of his generation of architecture students at Penn. In the Italian sketches, he shows a muscular ability to simplify the complex forms before him and render them with powerful impact in only a few strokes of graphite stick or watercolor—rather crude media for someone trained in the precise demands of ink and graded wash. The difference of Kahn's approach is clear in a comparison of his work with that of other American architects taking the Grand Tour at the same time, whose drawings concentrated on outline and detail, while Kahn's was much more about form and volume. When he wanted to, he could draw a building with almost photographic precision. (He did not, and never would, own a camera.) But his more interesting, and more numerous, drawings reduced the subjects to their formal essence. A 1929 graphite image of the Monastery of St. Francis at Assisi shows a simple composition of masses verging on the abstract. The drawings rarely include human figures, and those few are surprisingly lifeless.

In March, Kahn moved north to Paris, where he visited Norman Rice, a classmate and friend from the Industrial Art School and Penn, and one of the first Americans to work with Le Corbusier. By this time, Le Corbusier had already designed his visionary "City of Towers," an unbuilt project for sixty-story apartment buildings rising 700 feet amid acres of gardens and multilane highways. And his stuccoed-concrete houses raised on pilotis, or narrow steel columns, had become icons of the modern movement in France and beyond.

Although Rice later reported that his friend showed little interest in Le Corbusier's work, it is hard to imagine that an ambitious young American architect touring Europe could have totally ignored the revolution that Le Corbusier was helping to foment, and about which Rice was so enthusiastic. In a reminiscence published after his return home, Rice described his stay in Le Corbusier's studio at 35 Rue de Sèvres in nearly ecstatic terms as "a wonderful time—working, discussing, working, arguing, always about architecture. With him, between ourselves. First it was purgative—then stimulant, manna—then nutrient—often ambrosia. And we were in Paris! . . . It is exhilirating [sic] to be with a great genius."[13] Whatever the level of Kahn's curiosity about the work of Rice's employer, the experience of talking with his friend about contemporary French architecture within months of seeing the temples of Paestum must have significantly stretched the traveler's creative imagination. In April of 1929, Kahn returned to an American architectural community that was increasingly receptive to such concerns, but to a nation that was on the verge of economic collapse.

Before he got back to Philadelphia, Kahn had expected to establish a practice with a Penn classmate and fellow alumnus of the Molitor office, Sydney Carter Jelinek. But Jelinek had died by the time Kahn arrived home. Undeterred, Kahn managed to secure a position with his former teacher, Paul Cret, as a designer. At the time, Cret was working on the Folger Shakespeare Library in Washington, and Kahn was put to work studying the building's circulation pattern. Meanwhile, he also began to exhibit the sketches and paintings he had made on his European tour, entering the annual watercolor shows at the Pennsylvania Academy of the Fine Arts. Significantly, the entries showed little interest in the radical

abstraction of the emerging Modernist trend, remaining largely represen-
tational.

Aside from the world of architecture, Kahn rekindled his relationship
with Esther Israeli. Although they had become close before Louis's trip,
Esther was still involved with another man. With Kahn away for nearly a
year, Esther had become engaged. When Kahn discovered this on his
return, he was, according to Esther, "furious." Having brought back a ship-
ment of presents for her, Louis promptly gave them all away. But Esther
eventually broke off her engagement, complaining to her mother that her
fiancé was boring. Her mother opposed renewing the relationship with
Kahn, who was hardly her daughter's social equal, but Esther was not to be
put off. After she spotted him at a Philadelphia Orchestra concert she was
attending with her father (the program included Beethoven's *Pastoral*
Symphony), she wrote to him. Louis called her immediately, and they were
married three months later, on August 14, 1930. Esther would have been
happy to dispense with a religious ceremony but gave in when her fiancé,
probably following his parent's wishes, insisted on having a rabbi. They
began their honeymoon in the Adirondacks, traveling north to Montreal and
Quebec, and then back through Boston to Atlantic City.

But just as things were looking so promising both professionally and
personally, the Great Depression, which had begun with the stock market
crash in October of 1929, was beginning to take hold. Esther kept on with
her studies, earning a master's degree in experimental psychology from
Penn in 1933, but took a job as a research assistant in the university's
Department of Neurology. Kahn moved in with his new spouse at the
Isrealis' house at 5243 Chester Avenue. The newlyweds contributed $25 a
week to help out with expenses.

The economic situation was growing steadily worse, and soon reached
even Cret's office. In September, Kahn's former teacher let him go, leaving
Esther as the family breadwinner. It was a role she would continue to play
for the next twenty years. Kahn was reduced to seeking work designing gas
stations, and even those efforts brought disappointment. A letter from Shell
Eastern Petroleum Products responding to an inquiry from Kahn informed
him that his interest in working with the company was appreciated and that
"there are, undoubtedly, improvements to be made in our station design."
But the writer added that "it would not be worth your time to develop the
matter further with us."[15]

When she met Kahn, Esther Israeli was a scholar with a promising future. Here she poses in academic robes upon the award of her master's degree in psychology from the University of Pennsylvania in 1933. COURTESY SUE ANN KAHN

Although the professional horizon was bleak, life at home was remarkably happy. In July of 1931, Esther had written in her journal: "Our life together has been really beautiful. Fortunately, our likes and dislikes, and, more strongly, our interests and ideals, coincide. We find our pleasure in music and theater and friends. Our days are filled with work we like, and our evenings with work of our own at home. We love each other dearly and respect each other's wishes and desires. Lou is a perfect darling—considerate, sweet, quiet, gentle—and extremely brilliant." But life was not perfect. As Esther went on, "Lou says I mope—I do, but only about money. This problem is quite a large one."[16]

Kahn had hoped to make some money selling his European drawings at exhibitions, but he had no more success at that. Nevertheless, his interest in two-dimensional art endured. In 1931, he published several of his works accompanied by an essay entitled "The Value and Aim in Sketching" in the *T-Square Club Journal*, the publication of a local architectural organization. In the essay, Kahn provided a glimpse of the rather cavalier approach he would take to the wishes of his clients in later years: "I try in my sketching not to be entirely subservient to my subject, but I have respect for it, and regard it as something tangible—alive—from which to extract my feelings."[17]

Cret, meanwhile, had been able to find Kahn a position with the respected Philadelphia firm of Zantzinger, Borie & Medary, which had designed the Philadelphia Museum of Art and was then at work on the Justice Department Building in Washington. This, too, was a short-lived assignment, and in January of 1932, Kahn was informed by letter that his job had been eliminated. Although praising "the character of work that you have so well performed for us during your term in this office," it made clear that "we shall not require your further assistance."[18]

As Kahn struggled to make his professional ends meet, the architectural environment was becoming almost chaotically mixed. While progressive architects and students feverishly debated the developments in Europe, they did so in an environment of architectural nostalgia. On Penn's own campus, the distinguished Philadelphia firm of Cope & Stewardson had as far back as 1895 created a complex of Tudor and Jacobean dormitories to demonstrate the university's affection for English scholarly traditions. At Harvard, the Philadelphia architect Horace Trumbauer in 1913 had completed the majestically conservative Widener Library, which combined the Neoclassical and Neo-Georgian. The Princeton campus was dominated by the work of the dedicated Gothicist Ralph Adams Cram. And at Yale the university was being transformed by James Gamble Rogers and other masters of eclecticism into a visually charming but stylistically retrograde complex based on the medieval buildings of Oxford and Cambridge.

The American architect who made the most dramatic stand against this trend was one who knew it intimately, George Howe. Well born (he was a descendant of William Bradford, the second attorney general of the United States), and educated at Groton, Harvard, and the École des Beaux-Arts, Howe began his career as an architect designing romantic *faux châteaux* for the Philadelphia upper crust, but his association in 1929 with the Swiss-born Modernist architect William Lescaze led to a violent change of aesthetic heart. Together, Howe and Lescaze designed for the Philadelphia Savings Fund Society (PSFS) what would come to be considered the world's first truly Modernist skyscraper. Rising thirty-two stories in the center of the city, the building was an elegant shaft of glass, steel, and stone divided into separate areas for banking, offices, and building services. Gone were the

Despite the effects of the Depression and Kahn's chronic lack of work, the early years of marriage were happy ones, allowing Kahn and Esther time away from Philadelphia, including a holiday trip in 1933.
© SUE ANN KAHN

trimmings that Raymond Hood had recommended to make tall buildings "attractive." In their place was an unflinching statement of the architectural potential of modern materials and clarity of function.

In an article written in 1932, a year after the completion of PSFS, Howe—in a sort of *mea culpa* for his former "sins"—declared: "The broker who motors to town everyday from an imitation thatched cottage is in fact playing at doll's house. The architect who builds it for him is doomed to produce a work without mature significance. There is more real beauty in one straight line of a well-designed country house, standing in bold relief against the irregularities of nature, than in all the soft contours recreated by the romantic in painful imitation of the peasant's handiwork."[19]

Howe not only practiced Modernism; he also vigorously promoted it through his role as president of the T-Square Club and his funding of the influential *T-Square Club Journal*. As a result, he was one of only a handful of American architects to be included in the landmark architecture show that opened in February of 1932 at New York's Museum of Modern Art. Organized by Alfred Barr, the museum's director, the art historian Henry-Russell Hitchcock, and Philip Johnson, then a young curator, the show was the introduction for most Americans to the breadth of Modernism, which the organizers dubbed "The International Style." The show, and the book that followed it, concentrated on the work of Le Corbusier, Mies van der Rohe, and other leading Europeans, but conceded that Howe, and even Hood (who had shed his Gothic details in the design of the 1931 McGraw-Hill Building in New York City) had a place in the future of architecture. After opening in New York, the show traveled to the Philadelphia Museum of Art.

Although the MoMA show made a major contribution to America's awareness of European developments, it concentrated much more on the stylistic aspects of Modernism than it did on the powerful impulse for social betterment that had motivated most of the architects whose work it exhibited. As Barr, Hitchcock, and Johnson saw Modernism, the movement offered a stylistic alternative to the tired "neo" phenomenon that still dominated most of the American architecture scene. The domesticated Modernism of the MoMA show soon recommended itself to the corporate world, largely because it was relatively easy to imitate and cheap to produce.

Kahn, however, remained attached to the social agenda of Modernism, convinced that architecture could help change the world for the better. Some of his persistent idealism came through in a speech he gave at Penn in January of 1933, extolling the value of architecture as an instrument of social progress, while damning a building that would come to symbolize urbanism at its best. "It is, I think, clear," Kahn told the students, "that the good life, both for the individual and the community as a whole, should be the object of any effort," and that "architecture should be regarded as one phase of the effort for the good life." Architects, he declared, "can contribute to the good life not only in the ordinary sense of providing beauty for people to see, but also by promoting projects which they believe tend to advance the common good . . . rather than socially destructive projects like Radio City, which, even if successful to its financial backers, will probably hurt the rest of the community."[20] Kahn's dismissal of Radio City, better known as Rockefeller Center, which became a landmark of successful urban design, would be overtaken by time, but his impulse was clearly heartfelt.

Despite the grim employment situation, Kahn was not idle. He and a number of other out-of-work designers, including some veterans of the

Philadelphia Sesquicentennial, had come together in 1931 to form the Society for the Advancement of Architecture, or SAA, soon renamed the Architectural Research Group, or ARG. Primary among its objectives was "to gather and correlate the most advanced ideas of architecture based upon the needs of man and his activities."[21] The group, which met weekly at an eatery called Ethel's Restaurant, discussed all the current developments in architecture, including the work of the quirkily innovative engineer and theorist Buckminster Fuller, whom Kahn came to know during this period.

The ARG's primary focus was on mass housing. The spreading effects of the Depression had made accommodations for the poor and the out-of-work a national priority, and Kahn and his unemployed colleagues were acutely aware of the need themselves. A month after its founding, the group submitted a proposal for the rehabilitation of Philadelphia's slums to an exhibit sponsored by a group called the Better Homes Committee. Kahn was credited as chief designer of the project, which was almost achingly ambitious. Its concept of "Garden Courts" containing modest residential units would, according to the draft of the proposal, result in "a better city," a "more contented population," and "a check to crime and disease." Further, the ARG declared, "Every dollar invested now in low-cost housing will: Give work to some desperate father; provide milk for some under-nourished child; Boost trade wherever it goes on its journey; Up-build liveable shelter for present and future generations; Help make our city better and more humane."[22]

If such manifestolike prose had a socialist ring to it, there was a reason. The Soviet Union was only slightly more than a decade old, and it had not yet acquired its sinister reputation in the United States. Indeed, it was seen by many Americans, especially artists and intellectuals, as the main hope for solving humanity's problems through government intervention. Not surprisingly, the eager idealists of the ARG in 1933 took part in a competition to design a monument for the Russian port city of what had been St. Petersburg but was by then Leningrad.

Kahn was the designer of the project, and the prose of the competition document soars beyond even that of the Philadelphia housing scheme. "The primary concept of the monument," read the ARG proposal, "is that of an open meeting place for the masses of workers." But its form was to be propagandistic almost to the point of caricature. "Through the portals of two great towers of red glass," the architects enthused, "one descends into the large circular plaza, enclosed by two sculptural arms of stone whereon is depicted the epochal emergence of the Proletariat and the Peasant—from Exploitation, through Struggle, to Victory and Achievement." The proposal concludes: "Seen from afar, on land and sea, the two great red towers, beacons of Lenin triumphant, dominate the horizon."[23]

Although Kahn's professional efforts had not yet produced much built work, and the ARG disbanded in May of 1934, the architect had enough experience to apply for his architectural registration and did so in July. In his covering letter, he plumped up his stay in the Molitor office, claiming that he had held the title of "Chief of Design for the Sesqui-Centennial Exposition."[24] He enclosed a check for $25 to cover the examination fee, and it is perhaps a reflection on how strapped Kahn was at the time that the check was returned for insufficient funds. Worse, his interview, according to the examiners, betrayed "a general lack of clear understanding of most of the questions asked."[25] But by the spring of 1935, Kahn had reassured the examiners and sent them a new check. A letter from the managing director of the Philadelphia Housing Authority to Kahn congratulated him on the results. "If you will keep on being as practical and yet as ingenious as you have already shown yourself to be," wrote the director, "we shall see big things come from you."[26] For the moment, however, the biggest commission Kahn was able to secure was for the congregation of Ahavath Israel, for whom he designed an unexceptional brick synagogue tucked into a row of two-story houses in North Philadelphia.

Among the unsuccessful contenders in the Lenin competition had been two other immigrant architects, Alfred Kastner and Oscar Stonorov. Born in Germany, Kastner had trained in Hamburg before coming to the United States in 1924, and had worked briefly for Raymond Hood, the winner of the *Tribune* competition. Stonorov, who had been born in Frankfurt and studied in Italy and Switzerland, had lived in Paris, where he was one of the editors of the first volume of Le Corbusier's *Oeuvre complète*, before coming to America in 1929. Together, Kastner and Stonorov had designed a complex of workers' housing in Philadelphia called the Mackley Houses. The buildings were the first to appear in America on the European *Siedlung* model, and they were widely admired. Kastner had since moved to Washington to work for the Division of Subsistence Homesteads, and in December of 1935 he called on Kahn, whose work with the ARG had made him a recognized authority on the subject, to help with a project called

Jersey Homesteads that was intended to house garment workers being relocated from New York City to a site near Hightstown, New Jersey. Although Kahn was then overseeing the construction of the Ahavath Israel building, he took up the new assignment. The Jersey Homestead designs were humble in every way, but they allowed Kahn to put his concern for community improvement to practical use by working out the small-scale problems of space allocation and construction on a tight budget.

In early 1937, Esther's father died of a heart attack while shoveling snow, further reducing the family's finances. Esther, reviewing in her journal her husband's struggle to find consistent work, wrote that "Lou is not discouraged. I feel that he may soon begin to be recognized. He has such talent and ability, plus the enthusiasm and desire for his profession, that he will get ahead. But I hope it will be soon."[27]

The hope would have to be postponed. Kahn was again let go, but not before the Jersey Homesteads had been exhibited at the Museum of Modern Art in New York as part of a show entitled "Architecture in Government Housing." Among the critics who praised the work of Stonorov and Kahn was Lewis Mumford, whose "Sky Line" column in the *New Yorker* magazine and whose books on aesthetics and architectural history had made him one of the most influential commentators in the country. Mumford was deeply concerned about the condition of America's cities and pushed forcefully for a comprehensive approach to their renewal that would promote an increased sense of community in their design. One of Mumford's most ardent followers (and eventual lover) was Catherine Bauer, a friend of Stonorov's who had studied contemporary housing developments in Berlin and whose book *Modern Housing* was published in 1934. In it, she took aim at the self-absorption of the architectural profession and chastised it for ignoring the larger social context. "Rampant individualism in architecture," she declared, "creates, not a sum of individual expressions which one may accept or discard according to one's individual taste, but a single amorphous chaos. . . . If buildings do not express an integrated society (or at least a desire for such a society) they merely state the fact that society is discordant—and little more."[28] Such pronouncements only confirmed Kahn's own emerging views on maintaining a sense of community within the Modernist idiom.

In the eyes of many, however, *any* version of Modernism was suspect. In his autobiography, written in 1936, the unrepentant Gothicist Ralph

Adams Cram declared that Modernism "has its own place and it may and should go to it. Its boundaries are definite and fixed, and beyond them it cannot go, for the Angel of Decency, Propriety, and Reason stands there with a flaming sword."[29] It was a lost crusade. As if responding to Cram, Walter Gropius wrote in the same year: "The ethical necessity of the New Architecture can no longer be called in doubt. And the proof of this—if proof were still needed—is that in all countries Youth has been fired with its inspiration."[30] The following year, Gropius was made head of the architecture program at Harvard's Graduate School of Design, casting every other school in the country into the pedagogical shadows. One of his administration's early decisions was to remove the study of architectural history from the GSD curriculum, forcing Harvard's architecture students to get their history with the undergraduates of Harvard College.[31] Gropius explained the move by saying that he feared his students would be intimidated by exposure to great works of the past and would be unable to do original work of their own. Even the plaster casts of the Classical orders were removed from Robinson Hall, where the school was housed.[32]

Kahn's own path to original work took a crucial turn in 1938, when the Philadelphia Housing Authority sponsored a competition for the rehabilitation of a blighted section of South Philadelphia. Among the contenders was George Howe, who had become a leading figure of American Modernism as a result of his PSFS tower in Philadelphia and asked Kahn to work with him as part of a team on a submission to the PHA. The collaboration made complete sense professionally. Howe was an established figure with powerful professional contacts, and Kahn had experience with the sort of community work the competition required. But socially, Howe and Kahn made a decidedly odd pair: a Brahmin Episcopalian and an immigrant Jew. Whether despite, or because of, their radically different backgrounds, Howe and Kahn forged a professional and personal bond that was to outstrip Kahn's commitment to Cret and would endure to the end of their lives.

The PHA project was eventually abandoned by the city after a bitter debate over whether poor people "deserved" their fate.[33] Kahn reacted by throwing himself into other efforts to promote low-income housing. In 1941, a year after the birth of his daughter Sue Ann, an event that could only have intensified his concern for the state of families with limited means, he embarked on the design of a series of workers' communities that produced 2,200 units. Although the Howe-Kahn team had disbanded with the death

Even though he devoted the majority of his time to his work, Kahn found time for an annual vacation, here with Esther and their daughter, Sue Ann, on the beach at Atlantic City in 1947.

of the PHA project, the architects reconnected when Howe suggested that they become partners to pursue the government work that was bound to grow with the demands of wartime expansion. They, in turn, brought in Oscar Stonorov. Their first important work was Carver Court, a housing complex for steelworkers outside Coatesville, Pennsylvania. (In a reflection of the lingering racism of the time, the workers to be housed were all black.) The 100-unit project, which was made up of simple boxy structures raised off the ground to provide for carports below, was included in an exhibition at the Museum of Modern Art in 1944 entitled "Built in USA, 1932–1944." Showing a debt to Le Corbusier's houses raised on pilotis, the Carver Court buildings drew favorable attention and gave Kahn his first major public exposure.

The growing pace of Kahn's professional activities was beginning to take a toll on his relations with his own family. His parents had moved to California in the late 1930s in hopes of improving Leopold's fragile health, but his mother had since developed pains in her legs, and in 1942, Kahn received a typical letter from his father chastising him for his lack of attention. In prose that still showed traces of his European origin, Leopold wrote, "We are very much satisfied with Esther's attention to writing to us in which

Carver Court, a 100-unit housing complex for Pennsylvania steelworkers designed in collaboration with George Howe and Oscar Stonorov, was included in a 1944 exhibition at New York's Museum of Modern Art and gave Kahn his first important public exposure.
© LOUIS I. KAHN COLLECTION, UNIVERSITY OF PENNSYLVANIA AND THE PENNSYLVANIA HISTORICAL AND MUSEUM COMMISSION

we are very thankful, but *you* dear Son, leave it be a few lines, but for Mother's sake please do it."[34]

By this time, Howe had moved on to Washington as supervising architect of the Public Buildings Administration, but Kahn and Stonorov continued to design low-income housing projects, experimenting with a variety of room arrangements and construction materials to provide some individuality to what were necessarily ordinary buildings. The most influential work produced by Kahn and Stonorov during this period was not, however, in construction, but in publishing. At the request of the Revere Copper & Brass Company, the architects created two booklets on neighborhood planning, using Philadelphia as the model. The first, *Why City Planning Is Your Responsibility*, was published in 1943. The second, *You and Your Neighborhood*, came out a year later. Calling for preservation and renovation of existing buildings as well as new construction, the booklets opposed the "clean-slate" approach of what was then called slum clearance, and working on them helped Kahn to clarify his thinking about the role of historical and cultural continuity in the success of urban communities.

Kahn's emerging role as a propagandist expanded in 1944 when he wrote an essay entitled "Monumentality" for a symposium on city planning. The text provided a taste of the epigrammatic prose style that would become all too familiar to Kahn's students and clients, declaring, for instance, "Still untried but pledged stand the noble principles of the Atlantic Charter," and "Sculpture shows the tendency to define form and construction."[35] The staccato rhetoric appealed to many who were persuaded of Kahn's wisdom, but it was in fact closer to an emerging system of notation by which he would cite a topic and rush on without much in the way of development. Sue Ann Kahn summed up her father's habit this way: "People took it as poetic, mystical. But it was Lou working his ideas out."[36]

The major idea that Kahn was beginning to work out had to do with what architecture could provide beyond the basic needs of shelter, which had been his main focus up to that time, and the exploitation of technology and materials, which was a focus of Modernism. "Monumentality in architecture," Kahn declared in his opening paragraph, "may be defined as a quality, a spiritual quality inherent in a structure which conveys the feeling of its eternity, that it cannot be added to or changed."[37] Kahn was not merely talking about monumentality as bigness. Invoking the great buildings of the past, he reminded his readers that "their faithful duplication is unreconcil-

Although Kahn eventually became something of an absentee father, he always had a special facility for relating to children. Here he takes time with Sue Ann at Lake Placid in 1949 or 1950. © SUE ANN KAHN

able. But we dare not discard the lessons these buildings teach for they have the common characteristics of greatness upon which the buildings of our future must, in one sense or another, rely." With these words, Kahn was beginning to express a growing frustration with the limitations of Modernist orthodoxy, in both its reliance on technologically based forms and light-weight materials, and in its rejection of architectural history.

But for the moment, such issues remained largely unformed. Kahn's more immediate concerns were in community activism and led him to membership in the American Society of Planners and Architects, an organization intended to bridge the work of city planners and architects. The membership included Harvard's Walter Gropius, G. Holmes Perkins, who would become head of the Penn architecture program, and Howe, who gave the keynote speech at the first general meeting, on January 27, 1945.

Although Kahn in his ASPA role became a recognized figure in the architecture and planning community, his commissions did not reflect his growing prominence. The main fare of the Kahn and Stonorov office was row houses, renovations, and camp dormitories, as well as speculative work that included a design for a 200-room hotel. In August of 1945, the architects were invited to design a solar house as part of a program backed by the Libbey-Owens-Ford Glass Company. At the time, a young woman named

Anne Griswold Tyng had joined the office following her graduation from Harvard's Graduate School of Design, and she and Kahn took charge of the project. Kahn had begun to feel that he was doing more for the office than Stonorov was, and when a disagreement flared over credit for the final design of the solar house, the two parted ways. Tyng, however, would remain with Kahn, becoming increasingly important to his development as an architect, and eventually establishing a long-lasting romantic relationship.

Kahn set up his own office in a second-floor room at 1728 Spruce Street, sharing the space with an engineer. (George Howe had space on the first floor.) He already had a commission for a psychiatric hospital, but also began to design a number of private houses. For these buildings, Tyng's interest in rigorous geometry was important, as was the freedom to experiment with materials made possible by private clients with money. But Kahn's political commitment lingered, and in 1947 he joined the Progressive Citizens of America, an organization dedicated to international cooperation. In the same year, Kahn took part with 170 other architects in the competition for the Jefferson National Expansion Memorial in St. Louis. His proposal—for a complex of buildings that included a memorial, a park, and a cultural center—failed to impress the judges, even though Howe was in charge of the competition, and Kahn did not make the second round. (The competition was won by Eero Saarinen with his majestically simple Gateway Arch.)

Although Kahn was disappointed by the failure of his design for St. Louis, the impact was mitigated by an invitation to teach at the Yale School of the Fine Arts. The timing was providential, for it gave Kahn an opportunity to consolidate the practical design and construction experience he had accumulated up until then with the intellectual and artistic issues that were beginning to preoccupy him. And he was ideally prepared. The training in architectural history that began at Central High School and continued through Penn with Cret had given Kahn an advantage over those of his colleagues who had either missed such exposure or later chose to reject it. Kahn understood to his core that architecture was a continuum over time. So he did not make the mistake so common to those younger members of his generation of embracing Modernism to the exclusion of the rest of architectural history.

In 1959, Lewis Mumford was to inveigh against those who had "naively" followed the cause of Modernism. Writing in the preface to the second edition of his collection of essays *Roots of Contemporary American Architecture*, Mumford said sharply—and a bit prematurely—"The International Style" was only an eddy, in some ways a regressive backwater, in the development of contemporary form; for . . . it turned more and more into an external imitation of the outward forms of a mechanically functional architecture, with a sedulous disregard of human needs, functions, and purposes."[38]

As if he had already heard Mumford's warning, Louis Kahn, as he was to do from other sources so often in the future, was taking from Modernism a great deal, but he was incorporating it into the understanding of time that he had absorbed from his earliest school days. Yale represented a symbolic transfer of Kahn's loyalty from the Beaux-Arts, under whose principles he had trained at Penn, to the era of Modernism, but it would give him a chance to challenge that ideology as well.

CHAPTER THREE

ACADEMIA AND EMERGENCE

THE YALE UNIVERSITY ART GALLERY
1947–53

Nowhere was the turbulent evolution of postwar architecture in America more evident than at Yale University's School of the Fine Arts. While Harvard's Graduate School of Design had surged under Walter Gropius and Marcel Breuer in the 1930s and 1940s, its allegiance to orthodox Modernism had left it rather isolated by the 1950s. The style had become stuck in an ideology that was being gradually annexed by corporate imitators and in which there was no natural stylistic or theoretical room for growth. "Glass boxes" were no longer novel, and their deadening effect on American cities was becoming all too apparent. Kahn had never been entirely seduced by the Modernist creed, and although he was as yet, even in middle age, not fully formed as an artist, his direction was becoming steadily more clear. In New Haven, Kahn was to play a major role in Yale's own artistic development. And Yale in turn would give Kahn the commission that transformed his career as an architect.

Yale's architecture department, at the time a division of the School of the Fine Arts, had always looked anxiously over its shoulder at Harvard, but in the late 1940s the artistic climate in New Haven was in some ways

Yale University Art Gallery.
ARCHIVES, YALE UNIVERSITY ART
GALLERY

more conducive to creativity than that in Cambridge. Like Penn, Yale had in the early years of the century been devoted to the Beaux-Arts tradition, but partly in response to Harvard's Modernist boldness it had begun a cautious transition into uncharted areas. Located in a small Connecticut city some 80 miles northeast of New York, Yale was hardly a magnet for the most talented and ambitious architects, who could not expect to establish a major practice in the area. On the other hand, New York was close enough to provide easy access to the country's leading practitioners. In any case, dissension among the resident faculty over the years had culminated in a near revolt against the administration, and a number of teachers had resigned. To compensate for those drawbacks, the dean of the School of the Fine Arts, Everett V. Meeks, began to import visiting faculty. Meeks, an architect who had worked in the distinguished New York firm of Carrère & Hastings (architects of the 1911 New York Public Library at Forty-second Street), had begun his term as dean in 1922. He had little sympathy with Modernism and was rarely seen in the design studios, where he was known behind his back as "Mr. Pooh-bah" and "The Little King," in reference to his short stature and portly shape. But what Meeks had put in place with his system of visiting critics as a stopgap measure, he gradually began to recognize was a way to enrich the Yale academic environment with prominent professionals.

However, it was not until after Meeks retired, in 1947, that the school began to change in more than superficial ways. In January 1948, Yale's president, Charles Seymour, established the Division of the Arts to better coordinate the university's professional offerings in all its artistic disciplines, including architecture, painting, sculpture, drama and music. Meeks's successor as dean of the School of the Fine Arts was Charles Henry Sawyer, a Yale College alumnus (1929) and art historian who had run the Addison Gallery of Art at Phillips Academy in Andover, Massachusetts, as well as the Worcester Art Museum. But Sawyer also became director of the new division. He had been attracted to Yale by Seymour's plans for reorganization, feeling that he could be "a kind of catalyst" in bringing the artistic disciplines together for common benefit. "I had an almost religious conviction about the importance of the spirit of interaction between the arts," he said.[1]

Partly because Sawyer was not an architect, the position of chairman of the architecture department was created to assure professional experience in the oversight of the architectural curriculum. The position went to Harold Hauf, a professor of architectural engineering. Hauf's administrative role was augmented by such leading members of the profession as Edward Durell Stone, architect with Philip L. Goodwin of the 1939 Museum of Modern Art in New York, who was made senior critic responsible for student design work in the studio.

One of the visiting critics in 1947 was to have been the distinguished Brazilian architect Oscar Niemeyer, but Niemeyer was denied entry to the United States because of his Communist sympathies. Sawyer appealed to Secretary of State Dean Acheson, yet another Yale man, but to no avail.[2] Faced with a gap in his faculty, Hauf invited Kahn to take Niemeyer's place. Although Kahn was not widely known as a builder, he had come to Hauf's attention through publication of the low-income-housing work he had done during the war, and through his service to the American Society of Planners and Architects.

Kahn was instantly popular as a teacher and soon began to make a mark on the school at large. Students remember that he almost always had

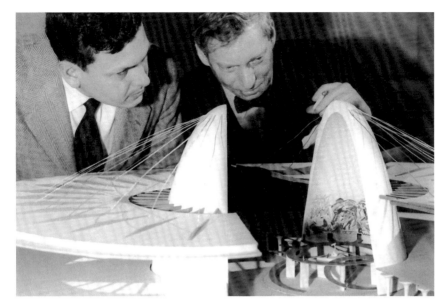

As a member of the faculty of the Yale architecture department, Kahn was known as an inspiring teacher with little patience for students who were content with established ways of doing things. Here he studies a model of a headquarters for UNESCO developed as a collaborative problem by students of architecture, painting, and sculpture in the School of the Fine Arts. YALE UNIVERSITY NEWS BUREAU, ARCHIVES, YALE UNIVERSITY ART GALLERY

a piece of charcoal in one hand. In the other, he was likely to have a small cigar, which dropped ashes on the students' drawings as he bent over them. Kahn seemed oblivious to the mess, working the ashes into the charcoal with a kneaded eraser and ignoring the stains on his hands. One of Kahn's teaching techniques was to have his students make what he called "energy drawings," quick sketches intended to capture the fundamental idea of a project before moving on to a more formal version.[3]

Kahn was a demanding critic but not a harsh one. Wilder Green, a 1952 graduate of the program, remembered a day when he presented a scheme to his teacher. "That's fine," Kahn observed. But then he added, "Tear it up and do it again." Green recalled that Kahn used "lots of paper, throwing sketches away," and was "always digging, always questioning. But if you had a good idea, Lou was the first to accept it. There were some students who were very slick, and he didn't cotton to that. He preferred the students who were struggling with ideas, rethinking problems, coming up with new ways to do things."[4]

But while Kahn was intensely focused on his students' work—and most of them were totally focused on Kahn's often rambling critiques—there was, as Green recalled, "a remoteness about him. He held his own territory."[5] Duncan Buell, an architecture student who later went to work in Kahn's office, remembered that Kahn "hung out with nobody as a buddy. Lou marched to his own drummer."[6] Nevertheless, Kahn was so successful

George Howe was an urbane architect who had converted from traditionalist design to Modernism but retained an appreciation of history. He and Kahn forged a deep bond that was as much personal as it was professional, and which led to Kahn's commission for the addition to the Yale University Art Gallery. MANUSCRIPTS AND ARCHIVES, YALE UNIVERSITY LIBRARY

as a teacher that within a year he was appointed chief critic, coordinating the other visiting critics, who included such influential figures as Pietro Belluschi and Hugh Stubbins.

When Hauf resigned, in September of 1949, to become editor of *Architectural Record*, Kahn, who had just returned from a brief trip to Israel to study housing development, began lobbying the school to appoint his former colleague from Philadelphia, George Howe, to the chairmanship. Sawyer consulted Saarinen, Stone, and Hauf, then endorsed Howe's appointment. It was an auspicious selection. Howe was then sixty-three, semiretired from his practice and living at the American Academy in Rome, where he was architect in residence. But as a once traditional architect who had become a celebrated convert to Modernism—and was not a European like Gropius at Harvard or Mies van der Rohe at the Illinois Institute of Technology—Howe was a worthy representative of the American architectural experience of the day. Indeed, even though his best design work was behind him, he seemed uniquely qualified to help Yale set a course of its own. Howe was delighted by Yale's offer and took up his duties on January 1, 1950.

If Howe seemed to be Yale's ideal chairman, he also represented an ideal for Kahn. William Huff, a former student and employee of Kahn's, suggested that, up to that time, "there was always the suspicion that Lou had never got very far because of his Jewish background; he wasn't in the elite."[7] Howe was very much in the elite, and—apart from the professional bond they had established by working together in Washington and Philadelphia—he was someone whose support now validated Kahn socially as well. According to Wilder Green, Howe "recognized Kahn as a man of exceptional talent, even genius."[8]

While Howe was a professional above reproach, he had a conspicuously naughty side. He liked to dress in donnish tweeds and gray flannels but would occasionally top them off with a touristy Tyrolean hat. His students remember him making such risqué remarks as, "Do you know, statistics show that eighty-five percent of New York businessmen like to fornicate by north light?"[9] And, during his years as a residential architect in Philadelphia, he was extravagant with his clients' money. He once told Earl Carlin, a student who had fought on Okinawa with the Marine Corps, that when building a house "it was no fun if you didn't open up a new quarry" to supply the stone.[10] One student remembered that Howe always had alcohol close at hand. "George was a martini man," said his biographer Robert A. M. Stern. "He always carried a flask, especially to student parties, because he was afraid they would only be serving rotgut whiskey or cheap wine."[11] Howe may have become a model to Kahn in yet another way. "I have been unfaithful to the same woman for 25 years," he once quipped to Carlin, leaving the battlefield veteran unsure whether Howe was joking or not.[12]

The creative climate at Yale was enriched by its other professional departments, including drama, music, and art. More than perhaps any other institution of its stature, Yale—despite the reputation of its undergraduate college at the time as a feeder of the Republican establishment—was receptive to the lively arts. Nevertheless, Sawyer recalled that "there was very little interaction between the different departments in the visual arts at Yale at this time, and I thought it important to break these walls down."[13]

One way to do that, Sawyer realized, was to shake up the faculty. Accordingly, he turned to Josef Albers, a leading German designer who had been at the Bauhaus with Walter Gropius but had left Germany in 1933 for the famously Bohemian Black Mountain College in western North Carolina. Sawyer had heard Albers lecture at Harvard in the late 1930s and invited him to be a visiting critic in 1949. He was appointed chairman of Yale's newly established Department of Design in June of 1950, overseeing the annual "Collaborative Problem" assigned to students of architecture, sculpture, and painting. The appointment caused several faculty members to

Anne Tyng, a Harvard-trained architect who became fascinated by geometry, joined Kahn's office while he was still working with Oscar Stonorov. When they separated, Tyng followed Kahn as he set up his own practice at 1728 Spruce Street. They soon became lovers as well as colleagues. ANNE G. TYNG COLLECTION, THE ARCHITECTURAL ARCHIVES, UNIVERSITY OF PENNSYLVANIA

resign over what they felt was an abandonment of Yale's traditional ways in favor of a Bauhaus program of interdisciplinary studies—which it was. With his mane of white hair, thick glasses, heavy German accent, and sober demeanor, Albers came to dominate a generation of artists who dutifully pursued his rigorous investigations of color and form. One of Albers's first acts was to establish a new program in graphic design. Duncan Buell recalled that his wife, who was studying painting, reported that "when Albers arrived, the school just flipped."[14]

While Albers was busy remaking the art department, Howe was turning to what he saw as the shortcomings of his own program. Primary among them was the lack of attention paid to the students in their first year, when he felt the new arrivals should be imprinted with the creative potential of their profession. "We must not lose sight of the fact that the primary purpose of architectural schools is to create architects," Howe declared, "not to prepare draftsmen for office work."[15]

To improve the situation, Howe called on Eugene Nalle, someone who, like Kahn, was a stranger to Howe's own world. A Texan from Highland Park, who had been forced to pass up college because of the Depression,

Nalle had been badly injured when the airplane he was copiloting crashed during a wartime night flight in California. He had come to New Haven in 1944 to be close to family members living in New York City and for medical treatment at the Yale Medical School. With a background in woodworking and general contracting, however, he was soon drawn to the architecture program, and applied. Like many professional schools at the time, Yale did not require an undergraduate degree, and admitted him on the strength of his work experience. As Nalle remembered it, Everett Meeks came up to him one day not long after he had begun his studies and said, "You look as if you've had a little experience. Could you help us?"[16] Nalle agreed, seeing his role as "helping my fellow students get going."[17]

According to Nalle, the architecture department was in disarray at the end of the war, and no one seemed to be entirely in charge. Despite his lack of academic credentials, Nalle was assigned oversight of the first-year program. He quickly seized the opportunity in an unorthodox way, steeping his students in the fundamentals of construction and the use of materials, especially wood and stone. As Estelle Thompson Margolis, one of Nalle's students (and one of only three women in her class), later remembered: "We were the people who were going to rebuild the world after the war. We forged ahead with great enthusiasm, but little knowledge." According to Margolis, Nalle was determined to help them: "He was the heart and soul of the transition. He was preparing us to think in a creative way."[18] Another member of the same class, James Stewart Polshek, recalled Nalle as "an architectural maverick" who "synthesized the teaching of design, drawing, and technical subject matter in a progressively complicated series of problems, all supported by an eclectic range of readings from Giedion to Spengler and Ortega y Gasset." The atmosphere, said Polshek, was "sometimes mystical, insular, and intensely intellectual."[19] So determined was Nalle that his students focus on the basics that he banned current architectural magazines from the studio. One of the results was that he was considered an "anti-intellectual" by some members of the art history department who taught in the architecture school. Vincent Scully, then a junior member of the art history faculty, recalled that Nalle "was running the department, but he hated books. He was just interested in Fiji huts."[20]

Not the least of Nalle's appeal to Howe was that, although he had not had Howe's broad cultural exposure, he believed that architecture students should learn more than the technical aspects of their profession. Nalle remembered Howe telling him that Yale had been content for too long with a lesser product. "This is not educational," Howe would say to him when reviewing students' work, "this is strictly trade school."[21] Howe also respected Nalle's concern for history, a concern Howe himself had acquired through his family and in his Beaux-Arts years but had augmented during his stay in Rome. Nalle complemented Howe's European-based knowledge with a self-taught but extensive knowledge of Japanese architecture, which he admired for its focus on materials and how they were put together. At the time, wood was an almost quaint material; students were more interested in steel, concrete, and glass. But together, Howe and Nalle developed a rigorous series of exercises to teach the students to see design from the roots. Some saw it as excessive—"almost copy-book stuff," as one student remembered it.[22] Nevertheless, Nalle's approach provided Yale students with a unique appreciation of architecture at its most basic.

Kahn and Nalle were never particularly close personally, and Kahn reportedly thought that Nalle's step-by-step approach to design was lacking in "pizzazz."[23] But their shared interest in the fundamentals of architecture, its materials, and how they were assembled created a strong professional bond.[24] So did their status as outsiders—Nalle because of his lack of credentials, Kahn because of his origins. The fact that they had both suffered grievous burns on their faces may also have drawn them together. "They were both anomalous characters, lone wolves, philosopher kings on the edge of society," recalled James Polshek.[25] Nalle remembered occasionally repairing with Kahn to the top floor of Weir Hall, located to the north of the old art gallery, where they would "just shoot the bull. Kahn was a fairly altruistic guy, but he had gotten very disappointed in the idea that you could help people by architectural means. And he was beginning to question the idea of applying a style to a building. He and I were both interested in whether you could start with construction, and let the joints be a point of expression."[26] Soon enough, Kahn would be putting those musings into practice.

When he was not probing the depths of his art and profession, Kahn enjoyed taking his Texas colleague to buy kosher food on Legion Avenue, a now vanished part of New Haven that was then the Jewish section of the city. "It was like the Lower East Side of Manhattan, complete with pushcarts," recalled Leona Annenberg, one of Nalle's students, who later married her teacher.[27]

Having restructured the resident faculty, Howe nevertheless continued Meeks's practice of bringing in talented outsiders as visiting critics. Among them was Eero Saarinen, a 1934 graduate of Yale who had gone on to work with his distinguished father Eliel. After Eliel's death, in 1950, Eero emerged as an outstanding architect in his own right. Another member of Howe's new team was Philip Johnson, the brilliantly articulate Mid-westerner who had come to the profession after serving as the first curator of architecture at the Museum of Modern Art, where he helped Henry-Russell Hitchcock organize the International Style show. Educated at both Harvard College and Harvard's Graduate School of Design under Gropius and Breuer, Johnson had been one of the earliest American advocates of Mies van der Rohe. Drawing on Mies's examples, Johnson designed a house for himself in 1949 in New Canann, Connecticut, that catapulted him to international fame. The "Glass House" was a rectangular solid glazed on all four sides and pierced by a brick cylinder containing the bathroom. The form's simple elegance owed almost everything to Mies, but its placement in the landscape made it an instant icon of American Modernism.

As a teacher at Yale, beginning in 1950, Johnson pursued his interest in architectural history, but rejected the materials-based teaching of Nalle by assigning design projects based on the more form-oriented work of Mies and Le Corbusier. But his impact was mixed. Sawyer described Johnson as "something of a gadfly with the students, and there was considerable disagreement among them as to his effectiveness as a teacher."[28] Whatever the judgment on Johnson as a teacher, he was always an acute spotter of artistic talent, and, having met Kahn before he came to Yale, Johnson became an enthusiastic supporter. No less provocative than Johnson in an entirely different field was Buckminster Fuller, the engineer who had raised the study of his discipline to an almost mystical dimension. Kahn and Fuller had known each other during the Depression, and Kahn used to joke about how they had bought each other lunch: "One day I paid for the apple, the next day Bucky did."[29]

Yale under Howe was by no means all business. He and a number of faculty members and a few students came together in the evening as the "Digressionist Club." The group met for drinks in Weir Hall, and went on to dinner at Mory's, the traditional Yale watering hole for students, faculty, and returning Old Blues. "It was all for George's entertainment," Wilder Green recalled. "It was George's intellectual cocktail hour."[30] No less intellectual, but nonalcoholic, gatherings with students went on late into the night over coffee at the bleak, neon-lit Waldorf Cafeteria on Chapel Street.

In February of 1950, Kahn received a letter that would have a lasting impact on his career both as a teacher and as a designer. The letter was from Laurance P. Roberts, the director of the American Academy in Rome, inviting him to the Academy as architect in residence. It read in part: "The duties will be to act as advisor to the Fellows in architecture, to accompany them on occasional trips, and perhaps to supervise the collaborative exercise between architects, painters and sculptors. These duties will not be at all time-consuming and should leave you ample time for your own sightseeing, work and recreation."[31]

Since its founding by the distinguished Renaissance Revival architect Charles Follen McKim (a partner in the firm of McKim, Mead & White) in 1894, the Academy had become a haven for American artists and scholars eager to steep themselves in the Classical tradition. Following World War II, during which the Academy was closed, Roberts had brought the institution back to life by encouraging visits from artists with a more modern direction. Kahn's interest in the Academy went back to 1947, when Philip Johnson had suggested him for a fellowship, but the process stalled, partly because Kahn was considered too mature a practitioner for a position that normally went to younger men. (There were no women at the Academy then.) Once again, George Howe intervened, writing to the Academy and urging it to accept Kahn, but as Howe's successor in the role of architect in residence. As the first Modernist architect to have held the position at the Academy, Howe had influence beyond that of his professional reputation. In December, Kahn arrived in Rome.

During his time there, Kahn came to know Frank E. Brown, a distinguished classicist and art historian from Yale, and the Academy's resident archeologist, as well as a cluster of stimulating people in architecture and the other arts who gathered regularly for dinner and conversation around a common table. Kahn not only immersed himself in the treasures of the city and such other monuments as the ancient Greek temples at Paestum that he had seen in 1929, but also took advantage of the Academy's invitation to do some more distant sightseeing. In January and February of 1951, his side trips took him to Greece and as far as Egypt, where he visited Karnak, Aswan, and the pyramids at Giza. In France, he saw Le Corbusier's revolutionary housing block the Unité d'Habitation, then under construction in

Marseilles, now taking more interest in the Swiss-French architect's work than he had on his earlier trip.

Although Kahn's stay under the Academy's auspices was brief—only three months—it evidently had a significant impact. Many of his youthful sketches and paintings from his first journey had been highly skilled, but often minutely detailed and ultimately picturesque, betraying an understandable debt to the graphic training he had received at Penn. Kahn now showed an almost fevered interest in the elemental shapes of the ancient monuments and the brilliant colors of the Mediterranean landscape. In 1928–29, he had been looking at the monuments for the first time—and through the eyes of a twenty-seven-year-old. He was now nearly fifty and had seen the limitations of many of his youthful ideals about social change through architecture. World War II had been over for only five years, and the

Kahn's stay at the American Academy in Rome allowed him to travel to Greece and Egypt. His 1951 view of the Acropolis in Athens, drawn in pastel and charcoal pencil, conveys an affection for the power of a "citadel," an architectural type that would assert itself years later in his work on the Indian subcontinent.
PRIVATE COLLECTION

places Kahn visited still showed the scars of that conflict. From the images he made on the trip, Kahn now seemed to be admiring the monuments that had survived the war as much for their durability over time as for their inherent beauty. If many of Kahn's sketches of the ancient sites in 1928–29 were largely illustrative, his comparable drawings done in Greece nearly two decades later had become deeply conceptual, exploring universal themes of form and materials.

Moving from the literal to the abstract is a frequent trajectory for an artist over time, but in this case Kahn seemed to be extracting a different message from his sources—one of persistent architectural values. When Kahn returned to New Haven, he was prepared to embark on a new path.

The New Haven of 1951 was a lively place, especially if one was involved with Yale. As a commuter from Philadelphia, Kahn was occasionally assigned to the guest suite of Timothy Dwight College, one of the undergraduate residences, of which Charles Sawyer was master. That spring, the famously contrarian Frank Lloyd Wright came to Yale to deliver a public lecture on his own architecture, and after the event the visitor was invited back to the college for cocktails and conversation. The other guests included Howe and Kahn, along with Edward Stone and Eero Saarinen. As the evening wore on, the conversation grew heated. Just as it was reaching the boiling point, Kahn suddenly strode to the piano in the corner of the room and began improvising a medley of Bach and boogie-woogie. Civility promptly returned.[32] Music was no help, however, on another night. The painter Willem de Kooning, who was teaching in the school's art department, had been assigned the same room at Timothy Dwight as Kahn, but on different nights. After a long day, Kahn unexpectedly decided to extend his stay, and, according to his usual practice, went to bed naked. Needless to say, he was surprised when de Kooning stumbled in some time later and climbed into bed with him. The resulting uproar became known in local lore as "The Battle of the Naked Men."[33]

Swelled by the likes of Kahn and de Kooning, the Division of the Arts desperately needed more space, as did the art gallery. When the School of the Fine Arts opened to students (who included women) in 1869, Yale became the first institution of higher learning in the country to recognize the visual arts as an important part of a university curriculum. The gallery designed by Evarts Tracy and Egerton Swartwout and finished in 1928 had accommodated Yale's collection in a Romanesque-inspired palace of stately rooms and ornamented staircases. But by the late 1940s, the arts in general were exploding in America. Indeed, the country had overtaken France as the world leader in artistic innovation. And the impact on Yale was immediate. Katherine S. Dreier and the artist Marcel Duchamp had made a gift in 1941 of the so-called Société Anonyme Collection, a trove of more than 600 American and European works by early-twentieth-century artists, which catapulted Yale to the forefront of modern developments. But potential donors with other valuable collections could not be sure that their works would ever be displayed for lack of space in the existing gallery. The school's new academic offerings—including a program in city planning and a course cotaught by Kahn in the design uses of plastics—demanded new facilities. Meanwhile, returning World War II veterans had increased enrollment by a third, and there had been no corresponding increase in the teaching space in Weir Hall. "Our present building with its thick walls and inflexible interior," wrote Sawyer in a letter to one supporter, "is the greatest single handicap we face in the development of a full University program in the Arts."[34]

Plans for an addition to the Swartwout building had been drawn up as far back as 1941 by Philip Goodwin, a Yale College graduate (1907). The plan was shelved because of the war, but Goodwin revised it repeatedly from 1946 through 1950. By then, however, the university was beginning to lose confidence in his ability to come up with what they wanted.[35] Goodwin, for his part, was growing frustrated by the university's changing requirements, and when eye trouble forced him to schedule an operation, he chose the occasion to withdraw from the commission.

At this point, Sawyer was head of the building committee for the gallery addition, and he quickly began to search for a replacement for Goodwin. An obvious candidate was Eero Saarinen, who was a member of the advisory council. Saarinen was approached, but turned the offer down, explaining that his design work on the vast General Motors Technical Center in Warren, Michigan, left him no time for the Yale job. (He may also have felt that, because so many of the fundamental decisions about the building had already been made, there was not much left in the way of architectural opportunity.) Saarinen, with Sawyer and Howe, suggested Kahn. Philip Johnson was a more conspicuous candidate, but Howe evidently decided that this was Kahn's moment. The final decision, however, rested with the president of Yale, A. Whitney Griswold, a classmate of

Sawyer's at Yale College who had taken office in 1950. Griswold was reported years later as saying to an undergraduate that "we don't want one teacher or one architect at Yale. A great university should look at architecture as a way of expressing itself. It can do this only by choosing to use the very best architects of its generation, men who see history as a continuing stream, not a stagnant pool."[36] (The selection of Kahn was the first of several bold architectural choices that Griswold would make during his presidency, assuring him a legacy as Yale's greatest patron of innovative architectural design.) At the time, Kahn was still in Rome, so Sawyer and Howe telephoned the Academy and made the offer, which Kahn accepted.

Kahn's credentials as a builder were so thin that, according to William Huff, he and his fellow students were stunned when word got out that Kahn had received the commission: "We knew all the people who were important! So, what about him? It seemed logical and obvious to us that the architect would be Eero Saarinen." When Kahn was chosen, "we just resigned ourselves that we'd get another second-rate building by a second-rate architect."[37]

But the students, along with the other skeptics, soon came around, and on reflection years later, Huff suggested that there may have been more than mere professional promise involved in the selection of Kahn. Huff sensed that the architect had a special appreciation of Yale, which was a university centered on its undergraduate college and the richly appointed faux-Gothic and faux-Georgian buildings that served them. "Instead of society, he saw institutions as the important entities of man's cooperative interactions," wrote Huff. "It was the school, the church, the dormitory, the gallery, the parliament that he wanted to service." As Huff saw it, Kahn "loved Yale, where he found greatness as an institutional awareness—more so than his own alma mater. He recognized the facilities of Yale as its gesture to the all-important student-teacher relationship. He said that students recognized this, and that is why they became such faithful alumni. He saw the dining halls as a glorious gesture to the student."[38] Marshall Meyers, a student under Kahn in the architecture program who would later go to work for him, felt that "there was something he loved about Yale. He would say that it was the 'traffic' at Yale; that it was the people who passed through; those whom he came in contact with. Not just through the architecture or art department, but also through the University at large."[39] In light of Kahn's evident disillusionment with public housing, these reminiscences suggest that he was beginning to see that his chances of improving the world lay not only in the conventional socialist thinking he had embraced in Philadelphia, but also in the institutions that could have an impact beyond their immediate precincts.

Assured of Kahn's artistic potential, Yale was nevertheless concerned about his limited construction record. To be safe, Griswold asked that Kahn work with the New Haven-based office of Douglas Orr, a 1919 graduate of Yale College, a past president of the American Institute of Architects, and a proven professional. Orr would be responsible for keeping Kahn out of trouble.

When Kahn returned from Rome, he set to work in earnest on the design of the gallery addition. And for the first time in his professional life, he began to appreciate the importance of having a client with whom he was sympathetic. Although Yale University and its various committees were the client of record, Howe was the client in fact. Indeed, the program for what was now called the New Art Gallery and Design Center had been largely written by Howe, who specified the length and width of the building, and even the number of structural bays. In response to Sawyer's insistence on "maximum flexibility," half the space was to be devoted to loftlike areas for educational purposes—including the architecture program—half to collections and exhibitions. The hope was that the entire building could be turned over to the gallery if additional teaching space became available. (This happened in 1963, with the opening of Paul Rudolph's Art and Architecture Building, immediately across York Street.)

So much of the building's program had been worked through before Kahn received the commission that he was understandably eager to find some way to mark it as his own. His first departure from the schemes developed by Goodwin was to abandon windows on the Chapel Street side, thereby shielding the interior from both traffic noise and the damaging south light; the unembellished brick plane was interrupted only by four horizontal strips of stone marking the floors within. The north and west walls, by contrast, were clad entirely in glass, the steel mullions making a vigorously Modernist composition that provided views into the exhibition areas from a sculpture garden and compensated for the anonymous street façade. More important was Kahn's decision to concentrate the services—bathrooms, stairs, the elevator—in a discrete rectangular zone at the core of the building. This was a commonsense move, liberating the maximum amount of space for exhibitions and classrooms, but it had a compelling geometrical logic that recalled the orderly Beaux-Arts plans Kahn had studied at Penn.

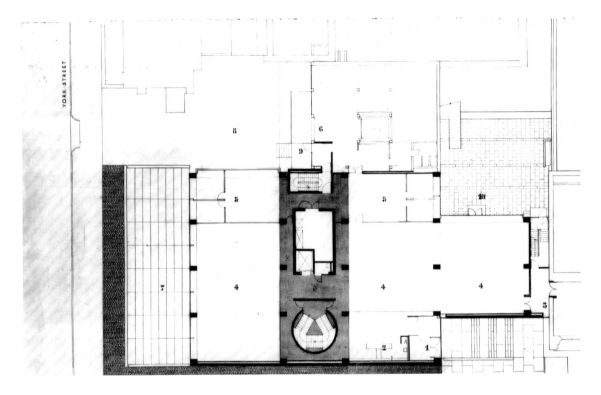

Many of the decisions about the design of the Yale Art Gallery addition had been made before Kahn won the commission. His main contributions were the cylindrical concrete stair tower and the clustering of the mechanical equipment in a separate zone. It was the beginning of the distinction he later came to make between "served" and "servant" spaces. © LOUIS I. KAHN COLLECTION, UNIVERSITY OF PENNSYLVANIA AND THE PENNSYLVANIA HISTORICAL AND MUSEUM COMMISSION

Kahn would begin to characterize this separation in his later work as the distinction between what he called "served" and "servant" spaces.

Even bolder than the clustering of the services was the circular concrete drum that enclosed the main stair in the service bay. Several versions for the stair had been proposed, but Kahn—possibly drawing on Philip Johnson's recently completed "Glass House"—settled on a cylinder. Kahn used it as a unifying element that penetrated the full height of his four-story building, pinning the floors together. More important, it enclosed a triangular staircase that itself was a stunning work of sculpture. The stair treads and railings received equally close attention, rendering the act of ascending or descending a dramatic experience in itself. The stairwell was lit from above by a clerestory partially blocked by an enormous triangle of concrete that declared the role of elemental geometry in the space while admitting the indirect natural light that would become an increasingly powerful element in Kahn's work.

Kahn's attention to detail extended to the smallest elements of the design. Rather than use the 8-by-16-inch concrete blocks that were standard in the construction industry, Kahn commissioned blocks that measured

4 by 6 inches, making the scale of the interior surfaces more appropriate to the works of art that would be displayed.[40] He insisted that the marks of the wooden forms used to shape the concrete of the walls be left untouched, expressing the process by which the walls were made. The joints between columns and walls were accentuated, creating visual elements that began to fulfill the ambition Kahn had expressed to Nalle of letting the intersections of his architectural elements play the role of ornamentation.

Goodwin's discarded plan had called for a steel-frame building, but a shortage of structural steel caused by the Korean War moved the Truman administration to ration the material for "essential uses," which in the case of universities included classrooms but not galleries. To get around the restrictions, Yale relabeled some of the original gallery spaces as teaching areas.[41] But the limitation on steel had evidently prompted Kahn to think about reinforced concrete, which used less metal than steel-frame construction. In any case, what emerged was a design in concrete, but a most unusual one. Kahn devised a slab that was to be poured on metal forms in the shape of three-sided pyramids. When the forms were removed, they left a thick mass of concrete imprinted with tetrahedral openings. The slab idea struck all who saw it as an innovative way to create a long span that would provide the flexible loft space demanded by the program. Even better, the three-dimensional elements were separated by channels of open space through which could be threaded conduits for electricity and air-handling. At a stroke, Kahn had apparently found a way of combining structural and mechanical needs in a single element.

This innovative solution was not Kahn's alone. He was assisted to an important degree in the design of the slab by Anne Tyng, the young architect who had joined the Stonorov-Kahn partnership in 1945 and had since become Kahn's lover. Born in 1920 in China to Episcopal missionary parents, Tyng had studied at Radcliffe and then at Harvard's Graduate School of Design under Walter Gropius and Marcel Breuer. There, she recalled, "the missionary zeal of the Bauhaus-influenced faculty" matched "my own newly awakened fervor."[42] In addition to Gropius and Breuer, Tyng met such other creative thinkers as the housing specialist Catherine Bauer, whom Kahn had known in Philadelphia. After graduation, Tyng herself moved to Philadelphia. A strikingly attractive woman with gleaming blond hair and a sharply determined look in her eyes, she was the only female in the office and later insisted that she was shocked to be told that she could "think like

The austere treatment of the south façade of the gallery reflected the need to protect the interior from sunlight and traffic noise and was only partly relieved by the stone strips marking the floor levels. The composition of the glass above the entrance shows Kahn's lingering debt to orthodox Modernism, with which he was still negotiating. LIONEL FREEDMAN, ACHIVES, YALE UNIVERSITY ART GALLERY

a man."[43] Like so many creative women who would follow her into Kahn's office and life, Tyng was instantly fascinated by the architect, whose blue eyes she described as "on fire from within, compelling me to look beyond the scars." He had, she wrote, "an aura of primacy like a king without a kingdom. If he wanted a kingdom, I would help him."[44]

But theirs was hardly a conventional office romance. From her days at Harvard, Tyng had been drawn to the symbolic—even mystical—potential of geometry, and she brought Kahn into her enthusiasms, at least temporarily. "We were able to bring out each other's creativity, building on each other's ideas," she wrote. "My giving structural body to his visions became an energizing connective force between us."[45] From 1951 to 1953 she worked on the Art Gallery, and although many of Kahn's students knew he was having an affair, Tyng was rarely seen in New Haven. Nevertheless, Earl Carlin, who worked on the Gallery project for two and a half years after graduation from Yale and served as the liaison between Kahn's office and the university, supported the idea that Tyng contributed to the slab design.

"Lou didn't just snap his fingers and have an idea come up," he said. "He sweated bullets, and Anne was very helpful."[46] Tyng felt that she was more than helpful. In 1984, she told her college alumnae magazine, "I persuaded Kahn to use a triangulated space-frame order for the ceiling/floor structure of the Yale Art Gallery."[47]

A more distant source for the shape of Kahn's striking slab was Buckminster Fuller, the visionary engineer who had invented the geodesic dome. Having known Fuller since the Depression, Kahn could not have ignored his colleague's investigations of structural geometry, especially his development of space-frame technology. And after the gallery design was complete, in 1952, Fuller was invited to Yale to teach. (His students remember building a cardboard geodesic dome on the roof of Weir Hall, only to see it disintegrate and blow away in a rainstorm.) But strong as the influence appears in retrospect, it was indirect. Fuller did not participate in the slab's design.

As the gallery project was moving forward, Kahn's relationship with Tyng suddenly took on a grave dimension when she became pregnant. Kahn

The north façade created a more inviting and intimate experience of the gallery, allowing visitors to see into the building as they explored the works of sculpture in the sheltered courtyard formed by the adjacent structures. The most interesting feature is the artful composition of the mullions. ARCHIVES, YALE UNIVERSITY ART GALLERY did not respond well. "I tried discussing the problem with Lou, who offered no suggestions," recalled Tyng. "If he didn't want to deal with something, he simply clammed up."[48] Having children out of wedlock was still considered shameful by many, and Kahn and Tyng decided that she would go to Rome to have the baby, whom they named Alexandra.

It was at this point that Kahn began to create a parallel life outside his own family. According to Kahn's first daughter, Sue Ann, her mother, Esther, knew about the affair with Tyng but chose to overlook it. "That way it didn't exist," said Sue Ann, who as a young child used to work on tetrahedral structures with Tyng in the office. "And you didn't get divorced in those days. My father never talked about it, either. That would have been hurtful, and his last wish on earth was to hurt anybody. He was probably ashamed of his behavior. He aspired to moral rectitude." Indeed, Kahn could even be prissy at home, chiding Sue Ann as a teenager for using lipstick. But he, too, may have missed or chosen to ignore some of what was happening around him. Sue Ann recalled that her mother, for her part, later "had a steady gentleman, and I don't know if my father knew about it."[49]

While Tyng was in Rome, she and Kahn corresponded frequently, Kahn waxing poetic about their relationship (although, according to coworkers, he had already struck up a new office romance) but also promising to send more money, and more often reporting on the situation at Yale. At one point, with his characteristic disregard for punctuation, he noted that "the collaboration amongst the graphic art's section the painters and the architects is somewhat cloudy. However that is Yale—no system—all freedom."[50]

Like others involved in the gallery, Henry Pfisterer, an associate professor of architectural engineering on the Yale faculty who was assigned to the project as an adviser, was concerned about the slab's strength. "Pfisterer thought that Lou was charming and talented," recalled Peter Millard, a 1951 graduate of the school, "but he also felt he didn't know his ass about structure."[51] Accordingly, several modifications were made, transforming what had been something close to a truly self-supporting space frame into a more conventional system of beams resting on columns. On Howe's suggestion, Pfisterer scheduled a stress test, not unlike the one Frank Lloyd Wright had famously used to demonstrate the load-bearing capacity of his "lily pad" columns for his 1939 Johnson Wax Building in Racine, Wisconsin. The test was conducted by the G. B. Macomber

Company, contractors for the gallery addition. The purpose, according to the Yale University news release, was to "determine if the new floor span meets minimal safety requirements. Bags weighted with crushed stone giving a load of 215 pounds per square foot will be placed on the model span." Kahn enjoyed the replay of Wright's drama, and was so sure of his own structure that he said he would be happy to "sit under the span during the tests and drink tea."[52]

Not surprisingly, the slab passed the test, but those involved in its design and manufacture knew that it was now less a triumph of engineering than one of sculptural bravura. The people in Kahn's office who were working on the project were skeptical of all the attention paid to the slab's design. "It had one strong beam, and the rest were pretty much decoration," said Earl Carlin.[53] Kahn deftly skirted the space-frame issue by calling the slab "three-dimensional construction."[54] "I don't think Lou gave a hoot what it was called," remembered Millard.[55]

As it turned out, Kahn's greatest achievement in designing the slab was not the structural engineering at all, but the integration of the mechanical systems. What made the slab most memorable, however, was the intricate play of shadows on the three-dimensional form, an effect that created a powerful visual counterpoint to the refined works of art that were to be displayed beneath it. Not for the last time, Kahn retained a form that fell short of the level of theoretical rigor that Tyng or Fuller might have hoped for but conveyed an emotional message that he felt was essential to his architecture. Nicholas Gianopulos, a Philadelphia structural engineer, reviewed the issues with Kahn, who in turn conveyed Gianopulos's recommendations to Pfisterer. Gianopulos, who would later become a regular consultant to the Kahn office, remembered the architect saying of the gallery slab, "I know it's not pure, but I'll buy it."[56] That did not mean he overlooked the details of construction. Peter Millard remembered seeing Kahn on the roof of the gallery as a workman was installing electrical conduits, which were soon to be covered by concrete. Kahn suddenly began berating the workman for doing a sloppy job. "Lou cared about order, and the way the conduits were installed was part of that order, even if the result was invisible," said Millard. "He was not a nice man that day."[57]

The process was far from over, however. As Kahn would do for the rest of his career, he labored over virtually every aspect of the design. One of the most important was the way the interior of the gallery would be lit. In this

ABOVE Although its visual impact may have been Kahn's basic reason for retaining the sculptural slab, it was easier to justify when the architect found that wires and ducts could be threaded through the voids. ARCHIVES, YALE UNIVERSITY ART GALLERY

LEFT The harshness of the raw concrete walls of the stair tower was mitigated by the delicate fretwork of the railings. ARCHIVES, YALE UNIVERSITY ART GALLERY, THE COLEMAN PHOTO SERVICE,

LEFT Responding to the university's requirement that the building be able to accommodate various functions, which might change over time, Kahn settled on large expanses of open space. The complex ceiling slab, designed with Anne Tyng's help, had originally been justified as structural, but when its strength was questioned and stiffening was required, Kahn nevertheless retained the basic shapes, which had undeniable ornamental appeal. ARCHIVES, YALE UNIVERSITY ART GALLERY he was aided greatly by Richard Kelly, a Yale-trained consultant on architectural lighting. Charles Sawyer remembered: "One night I sat up until 3 in the morning with other members of the Building Committee and the architect and went to bed confident that we had reached a satisfactory solution for a rather complicated problem of interior lighting. When I came to work at 9 the next morning, I discovered that Lou had sat up until 6 rethinking the whole problem, and that we were 'back to square-one' again."[58]

Even with so many internal constituencies to please—the building committee, the advisory council, the president of Yale, and the donors—Kahn had to face additional challenges to his vision. An example was a proposal from Robert Lehman, the senior partner in the Wall Street firm of Lehman Brothers and head of the University Council Committee on the Art Gallery. Lehman was so upset by the blank wall Kahn proposed to present to Chapel Street that he argued strenuously for a Classical frieze and cornice. The idea was gently deflected.

Lehman's proposal was not the only alteration suggested for the design. Earl Carlin remembered picking Kahn up one afternoon at the New Haven railroad station and noticing that the architect was carrying an unfamiliar cardboard model. It turned out to be an entirely new scheme for the gallery: an equilateral triangle with each corner resting on a circular drum. The triangle would have housed the teaching and exhibition spaces, and the three drums would have contained the mechanical services. The idea was, thought Carlin at the time, "brilliant," and perhaps even more appropriate than the approved version. But the gallery was already under construction, and there was no chance that the client would start over again at such a late stage. "It took guts to come up with that idea so late in the game," said Carlin. "It showed both how tough—and how naïve—Lou was."[59]

Howe remained involved in the design throughout. Perhaps his most significant contribution, after the program, was an apparently small one that nevertheless had a major impact on the way the exhibition spaces were used. It was what came to be known as the "pogo-panel," a floor-to-ceiling movable wall, 5 feet wide, on spring-mounted, rubber-tipped poles that allowed curators to create new "rooms" merely by moving the panels to different locations in the gallery. Yale's engineers, who had grown steadily more annoyed by with Kahn's revisions and delays, and could be abusive to him in person, ran out of patience when the pogo panels were delivered. They insisted that each one would take four men a half-hour to move and

therefore should be scrapped. During a meeting on the matter, Alvin Eisenman, the head of the school's new graphic design program, loudly disagreed. To prove the panels were as mobile as advertised, Eisenman and Kahn picked one up and conducted a demonstration, nimbly moving the panel around the gallery. Kahn, who at 5 feet 6 inches was dwarfed by the 6-foot-2 Eisenman, declared to the doubting engineers that he and his colleague had just showed that the panels, far from needing four men to move, could be handled by "one-and-a-half" men.[60]

Fundamental to Kahn's emerging aesthetic was a wish to "tell" the story of how his buildings were made. The concrete members at the base of the Yale gallery's stair tower leave no doubt about how it is supported.

The building opened on November 6, 1953. No doubt partly because the gallery was at Yale, it drew predictable attention from the world of academic architecture. But the wider design community also took note. *Progressive Architecture* ran seven columns of letters to the editor in response to coverage of the building. Among the correspondents were the heads of the architecture programs at Columbia, Harvard, Penn, and Princeton. Penn's G. Holmes Perkins declared that Kahn's gallery was "a creation in the tradition of freedom and fearless intellectual exploration for which Yale stands."[61] While the *New York Times* was lukewarm in its response, the *Herald Tribune* pronounced the gallery to be "the outstanding academic building thus far produced by the modern movement in architecture."[62] In a matter of months, Louis Kahn had gone from obscure teacher to something approaching a design star. But as his reputation grew, his relationship with Yale began to deteriorate. When Yale's regulations obliged Howe to retire as chairman in 1954, he offered the post to Kahn. Kahn turned it down, perhaps sensing that Howe's departure would mean unhappy changes for Yale. And it did. Howe's second choice was Paul Schweikher, who had taught under Howe and Hauf. Kahn had already described Schweikher to Tyng in a 1953 letter, saying that he was "far from stupid but somehow I find it difficult to warm up to him."[63]

The strain opened Kahn to other options. In early January of 1954, he had received a letter from Perkins inviting him to teach at Penn's School of Fine Arts. Kahn wavered. As he wrote to Tyng in Rome: "Over-confidence could make me accept but I really should not and I think I will not."[64] A week later, he had changed his mind and began a tentative reacquaintance with his old school. Having given Schweikher the benefit of his loyalty, Kahn eventually realized that he would never have the sort of close personal relationship with the new chairman that he had had with Howe. Kahn was not alone in his reservations about Schweikher, who resigned in 1956. Nalle, whose insistence on fundamentals was increasingly thought to be out of date, and who could no longer call on Howe for protection, soon left as well. "He was not a diplomat," remembered Sawyer.[65]

After a brief teaching stint at MIT in the spring of 1956, Kahn (with Vincent Scully's backing) was again offered the post of chairman at Yale, but he was now on the brink of the kind of practice that he had wanted for so long, and his hopes of doing more buildings at Yale were clouded by the administration's irritation at the delays in completing the gallery, so he

When Anne Tyng became pregnant by Kahn, she traveled to Rome to have her baby away from the inevitable criticism at home. She returned to the United States by boat in January of 1955 with her daughter, Alexandra Tyng. COURTESY ALEXANDRA TYNG

declined. Kahn continued as a part-time professor of architecture, but finally left New Haven after Paul Rudolph, who became chairman in 1957, and the gallery's director, Andrew C. Ritchie, approved changes to Kahn's building without consulting him. (The changes included enclosing the stair tower and erecting fixed walls, actions that infuriated Kahn, who felt they destroyed the spatial character of his design.)

As he would do so often throughout his remaining career, Kahn in the Yale Art Gallery had absorbed a host of influences from a variety of sources—the Beaux-Arts, Modernism, ancient Rome—and found a way to make the final consolidation of them something entirely his own. And there was probably no better place at the time than Yale for Kahn to make those connections. Between Sawyer's emphasis on the integration of the arts and Howe's unflagging personal and professional patronage, Kahn had experienced an environment uniquely suited to his own pluralistic search for an architectural language that went beyond the confines of what had been done before. The gallery set Kahn on a course that drew on his deep concerns for both architectural continuity through history and a clear acknowledgment of modernity.

But as Kahn moved on from the Yale Art Gallery to what was to be an almost uninterrupted series of masterworks, he was not above giving credit—if characteristically less than full—to one of his muses. In a letter to Tyng in Rome, he wrote: "My faith in you made me take your advice and courage which led to some of the things I did."[66]

CHAPTER FOUR

BACK HOME TO PHILADELPHIA

THE RICHARDS MEDICAL RESEARCH BUILDING

1957–64

In the mid-1950s, the University of Pennsylvania's School of Fine Arts was going through much the same sort of upheaval that had transformed Yale a decade earlier. And just as Yale had relied on Charles Sawyer to guide the process, Penn also turned to a seasoned outsider. He was G. Holmes Perkins, a graduate of the Phillips Exeter Academy, Harvard College, and Harvard's graduate architecture program, where he took his degree in 1929. Perkins had taught city and regional planning at Harvard under Walter Gropius, and made enough of a name for himself to attract the attention of Penn, which invited him to become its dean. Perkins arrived in Philadelphia in 1950, at the age of forty-six. Over the next two decades, he would develop the architecture program—which had slumped badly since Kahn's day—into what a prominent former faculty member recalled as "the most vibrant architecture school in the country."[1]

Howe's retirement from Yale in 1954 had been a severe blow to Kahn. Perkins said he sensed that with Howe gone, Kahn no longer had a strong reason to stay at Yale, especially under the leadership of Paul Rudolph, and invited him to join his own faculty.[2] Kahn had been teaching as a visitor at

Penn since 1955. He now accepted Perkins's offer of a position as professor
of architecture and would remain a member of the school's faculty for the
rest of his life.

Mindful of Kahn's powerful reputation as an unorthodox teacher,
Perkins created a special program for his new hire, telling Kahn to "do it
your way."[3] The class, known as the "master's studio," was limited to
advanced students who were pursuing a second professional degree. It met
twice a week for four hours in the upstairs studio of Frank Furness's flam-
boyantly ornate red-sandstone building near the center of the Penn campus.
Kahn was joined in his teaching by Norman Rice, his friend and former
schoolmate, and Robert Le Ricolais, a French engineer who taught structures and was best known for his interest in the more theoretical and creative dimensions of his famously dry subject.

On the surface, the alliance of Kahn and Perkins reminded some colleagues of the relationship between Kahn and Howe. Like Howe, Perkins
was a paragon of the WASP establishment, and not merely because of his
gold-plated education. "For Holmes," wrote a colleague after Perkins's

G. Holmes Perkins, who brought Kahn back to Penn from Yale, may have felt that he had taken on too large a talent, and later failed to provide the professional support that others thought the architect deserved. © G. HOLMES PERKINS COLLECTION, THE ARCHITECTURAL ARCHIVES, UNIVERSITY OF PENNSYLVANIA

death, "elegance was a logical, ethical, aesthetic way of thinking and acting."[4] But at least one observer felt the Howe model was wrong. "Lou and Perkins had a strange relationship," said Thomas (Tim) Vreeland, who had studied at Yale and went on to work for Kahn and teach at Penn. "They were always at loggerheads. Perkins considered Lou a dreamer, impractical. The Penn department never had a chairman; it was run by Perkins as the dean along with the other arts departments. Lou was the obvious choice for a chairman if it was going to have one, but Perkins wouldn't give it to him, and he never passed Lou the design work he had access to."[5] John (Jack) MacAllister, who was a student in Kahn's Penn studio before going to work for him, felt that, despite his initial support for Kahn, Perkins eventually found "Lou too much of a star to handle."[6]

Despite their different personal profiles, Perkins and Kahn became more than professional colleagues, and spent considerable time off campus together. The dean was notorious for his lunch routine, which reportedly included three whiskey sours, a bag of potato chips, and a slice of apple pie.[7] Kahn preferred martinis. At one late-night party off-campus, the slightly tipsy Kahn noticed a Ping-Pong table in the house, and unsuspectingly challenged Perkins to a game. He did not know that Perkins had been a champion tennis and squash player at Harvard. Perkins won effortlessly, and Kahn never brought up the subject again.

Kahn's teaching at Penn extended the same combination of close attention to student work and free-form lecturing that had made him so popular at Yale. "He treated his students like puppies," recalled a Penn alumnus. But, as at Yale, Kahn had little patience with orthodoxy of any kind. The same alumnus remembers Kahn repeatedly urging one student to abandon his dutiful imitation of Le Corbusier's style in the design of a particular roof detail. When the student showed no signs of exploring the problem in a creative way, Kahn strode to the display wall, tore down the offender's drawing, crumpled it into a ball, and stomped on it.[8] Such rare outbursts may have contributed to the sense of awe, if not fear, that was developing around Kahn. Another former student, Charles Dagit, remembered that when Kahn entered the studio, the room grew instantly "hushed." The architect "walked with a sort of a less exaggerated Charlie Chaplin

When Kahn returned to the University of Pennsylvania from Yale, he made his classroom work with students virtually inseparable from what went on in his professional office.
© THE ARCHITECTURAL ARCHIVES, UNIVERSITY OF PENNSYLVANIA. PHOTO BY EILEEN CHRISTELOW

side-to-side swaggle," recalled Dagit. "He constantly had his hands on his thick glasses, adjusting them on his nose. The glasses were as thick as the bottom of a Coke bottle. He wore a black suit with a black bow tie, the knot bigger than the remains of the tie. He had a sort of Santa Claus twinkle in his eyes that was constantly alighting on the room and the students. Suddenly, he pointed to one of us and said, 'You there, what have you been thinking about this summer?' "[9] Kahn had a sense of theater as well as humor in dealing with his students. When Dagit's turn came to report on his summer, he said that he had visited Frank Lloyd Wright's Fallingwater, which he described as "a cathedral of housing." Curiously, in light of Wright's extraordinary stature in the architecture world, Kahn had little overt interest in the man. He certainly knew Wright's published work and at different times visited the Robie House, Unity Temple, and the Johnson Wax Building, but, according to Kahn's former student Duncan Buell, Wright's "organic stuff didn't register with him at all. In ten years in the office, I never heard Lou mention Wright's name once."[10] Kahn's daughter, Sue Ann, supported this view. "Lou talked about Le Corbusier often, but he never mentioned Wright to me, ever," she said."[11]

Accordingly, then, Dagit was not surprised when Kahn proceeded to "tear the building apart." Then he paused for dramatic effect and said, "But it's pretty damned good, isn't it?" The point, Dagit said, was that "you could criticize architecture, but you had to respect it. He had set me up."[12]

Perkins thought Kahn's frequent tendency to wander from the students' own material into architectural abstractions may have been advanced at least partly by his deteriorating eyesight. "Lou would have the students pin their drawings up on a wall behind him and then start to philosophize," Perkins recalled. "It didn't have anything to do with the drawings; his eyesight was so bad that he couldn't see them." Perkins said that when Kahn finally had his eyes operated on for cataracts he declared to the dean that "I haven't seen colors in years!"[13]

As at Yale, the teaching at Penn was far more than an academic exercise for Kahn. Indeed, he used his weekly studio to explore themes in his own professional work, and the results were put to immediate effect in his practice. Duncan Buell recalled that "his teaching at Penn and his work in the office were a continuum. He could go home in the afternoon, and then come back and start a new day at 10:30 at night."[14] When he got tired, Kahn would occasionally sleep on a bench in the office for a few hours before going back to the drafting table. He even sent his laundry out from the office. The work continued through the weekends, except for Saturday afternoons in the fall. Kahn had season tickets to Penn football games and attended as many as he could. Employees were never sure when Kahn would get back from a game, but usually stayed in the office until he did. The motivation was not so much fear that Kahn would think badly of them for "quitting early" as it was a desire to be around the architect whenever they could. For the young and unmarried, the routine was thrilling. "You picked up on Lou's enthusiasm," recalled Vreeland, "and became someone other than yourself."[15] William Huff remembered harboring a "hope we might see him during the night."[16] One employee recalled that there was a joke often repeated in the office that overtime began at 81 hours, or slightly more than twice the standard work week.[17]

But for those with spouses and families, the nonstop nature of the office routine created predictable tensions. One night, a draftsman who had stayed well past what would have been the normal closing hour in other architecture offices finally slipped away to be with his wife. Kahn noticed the departure and said to those who remained at their drafting tables, "I guess he's not very interested in what we're doing."[18] The statement was apparently not intended to be critical; it merely reflected Kahn's view of the importance of the work at hand. In Kahn's defense, Vreeland explained that "Lou had so much energy that it was hard for him to see that other people might not have as much."[19] Despite Kahn's intensity, few resented the working conditions. "No matter how hard we worked," recalled MacAllister, Lou worked harder."[20]

As one of his consultants remembered it, "Kahn's office was more like an artist's study or studio than an architect's office."[21] Indeed, dressed most often in a rumpled suit jacket or shirtsleeves, with his signature bow tie carefully askew, Kahn "looked more like an art or philosophy professor than an architect," said a colleague.[22] And he communicated like one as well. Charles Dagit recalled that in both the office and the Penn studio Kahn often "spoke in parables," using language that puzzled outsiders.[23] ("Therefore a stripe painted horse is not a zebra"; "A street wants to be a building.")[24] He would invoke precedents from architectural history, references to nature, and technical comments on the project at hand, often in no apparent sequence. But Buell insisted that the students and the employees alike seemed to understand what he was trying to say. "Nobody ever left say-

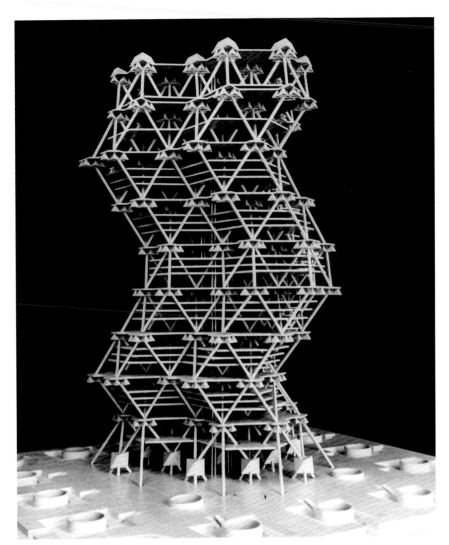

Anne Tyng's role in Kahn's work reached a peak in the late 1950s with City Tower, a high-rise scheme for Philadelphia based on complex geometry. From this point on, Kahn began to move towards a less theoretical, more intuitive approach to design.
© LOUIS I. KAHN COLLECTION, UNIVERSITY OF PENNSYLVANIA AND THE PENNSYLVANIA HISTORICAL AND MUSEUM COMMISSION

ing, 'That guy's nuts,' " Buell said.[25] But there was never much doubt when Kahn was displeased by work done under his direction. Although he is remembered as almost always charming and smiling, Kahn did not overlook poor work. "He didn't say much, but you could tell by his face when he didn't like it," recalled Vreeland. "His face would wrinkle up as if he were looking at a piece of cow manure."[26]

Since his unemployed days during the Depression, Kahn had retained his interest in city planning, and in the early Penn period he was able to return to the subject. But it proved a frustrating interlude in his career. He

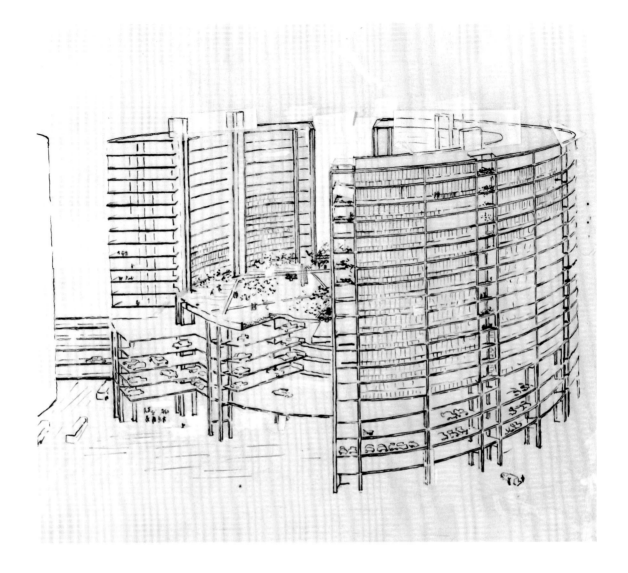

was at first encouraged by the dynamic and irascible Edmund Bacon, a Cornell-trained architect who in 1949 had become the director of Philadelphia's City Planning Commission. Bacon—a tall, lean, combative autocrat who enjoyed his image as an iconoclastic thinker—had big plans for his city. At first, Bacon insisted, Kahn seemed like an ideal collaborator. "As an executive," Bacon said, "I needed a very good architectural designer to work with me. I said to myself, 'I will see whether I can get the great Louis Kahn to join me in my life's work.' When we met, I liked him so much that I decided that I would devote my life to working with him. I would

Kahn never learned to drive a car, and he tried in 1957 to protect downtown Philadelphia from the assault of the automobile by proposing a series of enormous parking garages that would leave the streets largely free for pedestrians.
© THE ARCHITECTURAL ARCHIVES, UNIVERSITY OF PENNSYLVANIA

do the planning, and he would do the detailed designing."[27] But even if the relationship was foreordained, it soon foundered. As Bacon remembered the situation, "I was always interested in the larger picture, and Lou was always saying, 'Wouldn't it be nice to put a little curving staircase here?' Or, 'How about a pointed tower there?' He was unwilling to be stultified by the practical requirements of the program. So finally, I said, 'Lou, we have to part company.' "[28]

Jack MacAllister felt that the break was not so simple. "Bacon stood in Lou's way at every turn," he said. Comparing Bacon's relationship with Kahn to the one he had with Perkins, MacAllister claimed that the planner was afraid of being outshone by the obviously brilliant architect. "Ed wanted to prove that he had a bigger mind than Lou," MacAllister said.[29]

Disappointed by the separation, Kahn nevertheless persisted in his plans for Philadelphia, many of which were hardly small-scale. Indeed, some were almost gargantuan, including enormous towers for parking cars, complex traffic pattern studies, and an enormous structure dubbed "City Tower," a zig-zagging column constructed of triangular elements that resembled nothing so much as a child's monstrous Tinkertoy fantasy, but struck a generation of architects as a way to break out of the conventional high-rise "box." In this design, Kahn owed another debt to Anne Tyng, whose fascination with geometry had contributed to the Yale Art Gallery ceiling slab but now threatened to consume Kahn. "Anne was very bright," remembered Buell, "and geometry was her religion. She got Lou focused on its power." The hold she had on Kahn caused some resentment in the office, however. "If he got going on a scheme of hers," said Buell, "Lou would be shut off from the rest of us. He played along, because they were in love." It could also cause some embarrassment. On one occasion when Kahn's wife was visiting the office, Buell found himself walking toward the elevator just as Esther and Tyng started in the same direction. Buell, who was well aware of Kahn's affair, remembered that "I was terrified of getting on. I don't know if I did."[30]

The break with Bacon ended what might have been a productive opportunity for Kahn in Philadelphia, and some have suggested that social differences, even anti-Semitism, may have accounted for the lack of subsequent commissions more than Kahn's disagreements with the planning director. But if such issues occurred to some as a contributing factor, Bacon—another pillar of a WASP establishment that took "polite" anti-

Semitism in stride—was quick to dismiss them. "I never thought anybody attached any importance to his Jewishness," said Bacon. "I'm not kidding. There was no feeling of that at all."[31] Bacon's sentiment was supported by Holmes Perkins, who used to take Kahn for lunch at the frosty Rittenhouse Club, which at the time did not admit Jews as members. Kahn didn't seem disturbed by the discrimination. "It was never an issue," said Perkins. "I don't know how he overcame it."[32] MacAllister, who as an employee might have been on the alert for slights to his mentor, insisted that he "never even thought of Lou as Jewish."[33]

In the wake of the frustration over the lack of large-scale work in Philadelphia, Kahn was offered what turned out to be a small commission that would, however, have a major impact on his subsequent career. It was a community center for a social service organization in Ewing Township, on the edge of the New Jersey city of Trenton. Although only a portion—and a small one at that—of the original plan was executed, it had a powerful effect on the architectural community. Charles Moore, who became a leading figure in the Postmodernist movement and chairman of the Yale architecture department in the 1970s, declared in a 1986 interview, "I wouldn't put it on a list of the ten most beautiful buildings in the world, but I would put it on the list of ten most important."[34]

Although Kahn had grown up in a Jewish household and married a Jewish woman, he never made an issue of his religion, either to celebrate it or reject it. And as Bacon and MacAllister confirmed, it was something they were hardly aware of. Nevertheless, Kahn's ethnic background may have given him an advantage with some clients, among them the board of the Trenton Jewish Community Center. Like many such social organizations, the JCC was struggling with a steady loss of members to the suburbs. Eager to follow its congregation, the organization located a site outside the city and invited Kahn to design a new facility for them. He got the job in July of 1954.

The commission was an auspicious one. The chairman of the Trenton building committee was H. Harvey Saaz, a Yale Law School alumnus, who may have been drawn to Kahn because of the architect's earlier advisory role on a Jewish community center in New Haven. (The *Yale Alumni Magazine* had also done a story in December of 1953 on the Yale Art Gallery.) According to Susan Solomon, the author of a book on the Trenton commission, Kahn "romanticized how JCC members would be able to frolic in abundant nature, and he saw the Trenton complex as a picturesque com-

The Trenton Bathhouse, finished in 1955, was only a fragment of the original commission, but it proved to be a milestone on Kahn's architectural journey, consolidating and clarifying his approach to organization and function. © LOUIS I. KAHN COLLECTION, UNIVERSITY OF PENNSYLVANIA AND THE PENNSYLVANIA HISTORICAL AND MUSEUM COMMISSION

The Trenton plan was deceptively simple, incorporating a variety of uses within the structure of the building while conveying a sense of formal inevitability. © LOUIS I. KAHN COLLECTION, UNIVERSITY OF PENNSYLVANIA AND THE PENNSYLVANIA HISTORICAL AND MUSEUM COMMISSION

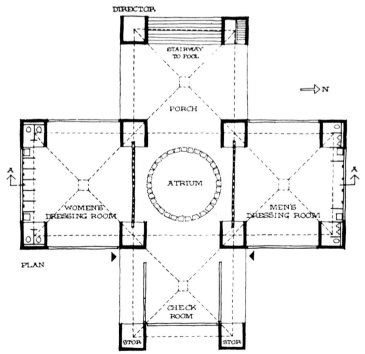

munity that could define suburban life."[35] But the scale of Kahn's concept quickly exceeded that of the board members, and—in a progression that would become steadily more familiar—internal disputes and financial shortfalls ultimately reduced Kahn's role to the completion of a bathhouse and four small pavilions adjacent to the swimming pool.

The pavilions had scant architectural distinction, but the bathhouse, while measuring only 97 feet across, far exceeded its size in impact. Much of that was due, again, to Anne Tyng. According to Tim Vreeland, Kahn was having trouble with the design. As the story goes, late one night, while the office was still humming as usual, Tyng was heard calling from her side of the room that she "had something." Kahn walked over to have a look and, according to Vreeland, "immediately saw that Anne's design was *it*."[36] When fully developed by Kahn, the scheme comprised four hollow squares abutting a central courtyard—a simple cross in plan. The courtyard was left open to the sky, and the outlying volumes were covered by shallow pyramidal roofs raised slightly off the supporting walls and pierced at the top. The openings permitted sunlight to penetrate the interior spaces from above and on all sides. Two of the squares were devoted to dressing rooms—one for women, one for men. A third served as a checkroom, and the fourth as a porch giving onto the pool area. The smaller squares—or "hollow columns," as Kahn called them—served as supports for the roofs, and provided space for toilets and storage. The dressing-room walls facing the court ended near the midpoint of the support structures, allowing bathers to walk around the edge of the walls out of sight of other bathers, thus avoiding the need for doors but ensuring privacy.

The design could not have been simpler. Indeed, it was almost primitive, recalling the brooding character of the Yale Art Gallery ceiling slabs, but with no need to apologize for any structural sleight-of-hand. And the allocation of functions to each of the spatial elements perfectly satisfied the functional demands of the program. Moreover, the overall composition gave the building a sense of serene resolution: Virtually nothing could have been added to the design to make it better, and almost anything taken away would have diminished it.

The clear distinction in this tiny structure between the main volumes and the lesser ones supporting them appears to have watered the seed of what Kahn had begun at Yale and soon began to articulate as "served" and "servant" spaces. But while the geometrical clarity may have owed much to Anne Tyng's mathematical rigor, it was both tempered and amplified by an arrangement of forms that was at once modern and ancient—and perhaps, as at Yale, even a touch theatrical. Kahn himself in later years insisted that the building had been a crucial moment in his development as an architect. He told an interviewer for the *New York Times* in 1970, "I discovered myself after designing that little concrete block bathhouse in Trenton."[37]

Perhaps the greatest virtue of Trenton is that its geometry was not oppressive, reflecting a subtle touch with space, form, and light that was to mark Kahn's buildings from then onward. He was once again absorbing information and deploying it in a new synthesis, but he was also moving on. Indeed, a 1960 commission for a dormitory for Bryn Mawr College began to create tensions in the office between the more theoretically inclined Tyng advocates and the more lyrical approach that Kahn was developing. "I realized that there was a competition growing in the office," recalled Vreeland. "Lou was struggling with Anne's system, and was beginning to see its limitations, that its repetition of small geometric patterns would never produce the more monumental architecture that he was after. Anne was not interested in that, and they began to diverge aesthetically. Bryn Mawr was the beginning of the rift."[38]

Although his ambitions as an urban planner had been stalled by the failed partnership with Bacon and the Trenton commission—which, for all its aesthetic success, had been truncated—Kahn's ambition to design large-scale work in Philadelphia got a significant boost with an invitation from the University of Pennsylvania for a science building. Although Eero Saarinen was also a candidate, as he had been for the Yale Gallery, he was given a women's dormitory. And on the advice of Holmes Perkins, whose support of Kahn was still strong, the medical building commission was awarded to him in February of 1957.

The building, which would be officially named the Alfred Newton Richards Medical Research Building after a prominent Penn faculty member, was intended for the study of medical procedures of many sorts. The site, amid existing Penn buildings, precluded a large footprint, but that seemed to suit the architect. According to Vreeland, Kahn disliked the most familiar laboratory type at the time—a one-story box with a long corridor down the middle. Returning with Vreeland on the train to Philadelphia one night, Kahn dismissed the standard laboratory scheme as "not a building." Pulling out a used envelope, Kahn promptly began to sketch stacked horizontal forms among slim towers.[39]

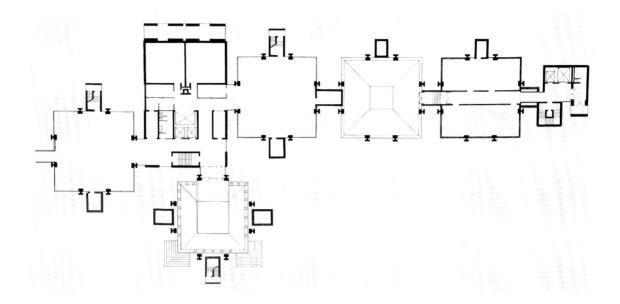

Welcome as it may have been, especially to a Penn alumnus, the commission was hardly a plum. Although the university at the time was embarking on a major expansion of its research facilities for surgery, radiology, and other scientific specialties, the Richards building was to be shared by the departments of public health, microbiology, physiology, and research surgery. It was also to house the animals used in much of the research.

Not surprisingly, there were problems from the start. Because the building was intended to serve several departments, each was given a say in the programming. Their recommendations had to be cleared by assorted deans and vice presidents. "The client was a committee," recalled Perkins. This was both an advantage and a disadvantage. "Lou could talk a committee into anything," Perkins said.[40] The problem was that no one on the committee was in overall control. Indeed, a memo reporting on a September 19, 1957, meeting noted the attendance of the architect, as well as the vice president in charge of medical affairs, the dean of the medical school, the chairman of the planning committee, and heads of the departments of surgery and preventive medicine, as well as representatives of physiology, botany, and zoology.[41] "Penn never put a man of its own on the project full time," reported an observer.[42]

Making matters worse, one of the main figures in the Penn hierarchy was an ex-military man. "Lou couldn't stand him," recalled Vreeland, "so he had to go through all the individual chairmen."[43] Nevertheless, Kahn

The plan of the Richards Medical Research Building at the University of Pennsylvania advanced Kahn's concept of served and servant spaces, but was flawed by a belief that medical research could be conducted on a studio model like that used for architectural design.
© LOUIS I. KAHN COLLECTION, UNIVERSITY OF PENNSYLVANIA AND THE PENNSYLVANIA HISTORICAL AND MUSEUM COMMISSION

took on the challenge with enthusiasm. He considered his design "the outcome of the consideration of the unique use of its spaces and how they are served."[44] The concept—rooted in his Beaux-Arts training under Cret—had begun to reassert itself in the Yale Gallery, and more clearly in the Trenton Bathhouse. In Philadelphia, Kahn began to use it as a way to guide the design from the beginning.

The scheme was relatively simple. From the outset, Kahn provided for a cluster of towers that would house the scientific laboratories. To these was added a fourth element for the animals. Arranged in a pinwheel pattern, the towers were linked to smaller shafts on their periphery. These contained fire stairs as well as ducts to vent hazardous fumes. At the center of the vertical elements was a core for the elevators, the main stairs, and corridors leading to the labs. The layout was eminently rational, concentrating the work spaces away from the utilities and the animal quarters, and presumably leaving the researchers complete freedom to arrange their laboratories as they saw fit. Kahn's description of his concept was at once practical and poetic: "These research men will be infecting animals with germs. They will be working with isotopes and noxious gases. My solution was to create three great stacks of studios and attach to them tall service towers which would include animal quarters, mains to carry water, gas and vacuum lines, as well as ducts to breathe in the air from 'nostrils' placed low in the building and exhaust it out through stacks high above the roof."[45]

Attractive as the concept was in the abstract, its construction was another matter. The final design was heavily indebted to one of Kahn's consulting structural engineers, August Komendant. Like Kahn, Komendant was born in Estonia, but he was of German descent and had been educated in Dresden before returning to his homeland. When Germany attacked Russia in 1940, it also invaded Estonia. Komendant was sent back to Germany and spent the war there developing military projects. Komendant was interned by American forces during the closing weeks of the war, but when his talents became known, he was contacted by General George S. Patton himself. As Komendant told the story, Patton, the legendary tank commander, was worried that a damaged bridge that lay in his path might not support his armored columns. He ordered Komendant to investigate, and the engineer promptly called for a bucket of white paint and a brush. He then proceeded to trace a wavy white line down the middle of the bridge and told Patton that if his tanks followed it they would be in no danger of

The Estonian-born, German-educated August Komendant became one of Kahn's most important (if combative) collaborators, transforming many of the architect's concepts into buildable reality through innovative structural engineering. © AUGUST KOMENDANT COLLECTION, THE ARCHITECTURAL ARCHIVES, UNIVERSITY OF PENNSYLVANIA

dropping into the river.[46] No tanks were lost, and Komendant crossed the river with Patton.

After the war, Komendant was assigned to study the German submarine shelters on the French coast to find out how they had survived so well under Allied air attack. The lessons he learned about wartime concrete construction techniques proved valuable for his civilian career when he emigrated to the United States and went into practice on his own. He first met Kahn during preliminary work on the Trenton Jewish Community Center. Impressed with his obvious talents, Kahn asked Komendant to join in the Richards project to augment the work of the other consulting engineers, the Philadelphia firm of Keast & Hood.

An opinionated man who was not above expanding on his share of the credit for shared projects, Komendant enjoyed demeaning his less technically inclined collaborator. In Komendant's view, Kahn was "completely ignorant of engineering. He lacked the basic knowledge of structures and structural materials, and their special physical characteristics." But Komendant was willing to concede that Kahn was teachable. His "attitude about engineering changed drastically after close association with Robert Le Ricolais and myself," Komendant wrote.[47] It was a measure of either Kahn's need for Komendant's expertise, or his tolerance for those with egos larger than his own, that the relationship continued. As William Huff remembered the exchange, "They fought from time to time and said they'd never work on another job with each other. They'd call each other an 'idiot' two or three times. But Komendant could fascinate Lou with his knowledge, and Lou was always open to new ideas. He'd listen to people and learn from them. That was an excellent trait Lou had."[48]

With Komendant's assistance on technical matters, the shape of the building began to assume a powerful identity. At the heart of the engineer's contribution was a complex system of precast concrete columns, beams, and Vierendeel trusses. Named for their nineteenth-century Belgian inventor, these are not actually trusses, which include diagonal members, but perforated structural frames through which conduits could be threaded in much the same way Kahn had done at the Yale Gallery. The elements were assembled on the site with a precision that impressed even industry experts. "Kahn insisted on craftsmanship," wrote *Architectural Record*, "and he got it: the exposed members fit together with a deceptive simplicity more typical of fine cabinetwork than of concrete construction."[49]

But the allocation of spaces proved disturbingly unrelated to the intended functions of the building. "He had had no contact with scientists, their work and habits," insisted Komendant.[50] But the engineer went on to detect another influence on the design, and its eventual problems. Komendant suggested that Kahn was assuming that scientists and architects—as creative people—worked in similar ways and would therefore flourish in similar spaces. "The studio image, to start with, was very attractive" to Kahn, Komendant noted, "and he thought it would provide the best environment for scientific work."[51]

The building's shortcomings became apparent even before it was occupied. The worst problem was that by wrapping the laboratories' exterior with so much glass, Kahn allowed far too much sunlight to penetrate the workspaces. Many of the researchers later had to resort to draping the windows with aluminum foil to protect their chemicals and equipment from

The construction of the Richards building was a marvel of engineering, but a lack of clear guidance from the university and a series of financial cutbacks left both the users and the architect frustrated by the result. © AUGUST KOMENDANT COLLECTION, THE ARCHITECTURAL ARCHIVES, UNIVERSITY OF PENNSYLVANIA

damage. (One researcher cited another disadvantage to what was called the "fishbowl effect": "When a man kisses his secretary, he doesn't want the whole world to know about it.")[52] The large windows also cut down on wall space, meaning that research equipment had to be clustered at awkward locations in the labs, and storage space was in short supply. Because the ceilings had been left open for pipes and lighting, sound traveled freely from one lab to the others on the same floor. No provision had been made

for secretaries and other assistants, so their desks quickly began to clog the already narrow corridors.

In Kahn's defense, Penn's scientific population was expanding faster than anyone had anticipated when the building's needs had been projected. One prominent biophysicist complained that his lab was too small, only to learn that the university had assigned him space in what Kahn had laid out as a corridor.[53] Such problems with the design were further aggravated by budget cuts. As construction moved forward, Penn became tangled in a labor dispute, which put pressure on its finances. As a result, according to one observer, "the university simply tried to build too much building for its budget."[54] In attempts to reduce the cost, the architect was forced to replace the original KoolShade sun-protection system, which would have mitigated the problems of glare and heat. He also had to cut back on insulation, and take out the panels that were intended to seal the ceiling slabs and prevent air and noise from moving from one lab to another. "The design had plenty of problems," said MacAllister, who had been hired in the middle of the job to oversee the site work, "but the university was brutal; it was responsible for at least half of them."[55] Marshall Meyers, Kahn's former student who was now working in his office, felt that some of the problems Kahn encountered had been almost inevitable. "The client for that project was not focused," Meyers said. "He worked with a kind of institutional bureaucracy that did not challenge him sufficiently. This gave him a freedom to elaborate on ideas that never were thoroughly tested."[56]

The troubles could not all be laid at Penn's door, however. A disturbing pattern was emerging in the way the architect made buildings. Kahn regularly submitted drawings and other documents late. Even though costs began to climb, Kahn—without someone at the university to resolve the inevitable conflicts—perhaps naturally succumbed to the temptation to "fine-tune" the design past a reasonable point.

Whatever the explanations for the building's shortcomings, they did not convince Reyner Banham, a prominent English architectural historian and advocate of the school of British architecture known as the "new Brutalism." Unimpressed by Kahn's rising reputation in American architectural circles, the famously cranky Banham found "nothing in the conception of Louis Kahn's Richards Medical Research Building in Philadelphia that marks any useful advance on the position reached by Le Corbusier thirty years earlier."[57] Banham pointed out that the brick towers of Richards conveyed an impression that they supported the laboratory slabs, when in fact they did not. He also noted that the towers' massive appearance was compromised by the open tops of the stair towers, which had been raised to match the exhaust towers in height for transparently aesthetic reasons. With withering sarcasm, Banham dismissed Kahn's "big brick schnorkels" and "pseudo-monoliths" as unconvincing elements in a "picturesquely heroic visual format," and dubbed Richards "Duct Henge."[58]

In retrospect, even some of Kahn's loyalists conceded that Richards was more image than substance. Romaldo Giurgola, later a colleague of Kahn's at Penn, felt that the architect and his team had been too absorbed by the technical aspects of the project to explore its design fully. "They were too much taken by the engineering, the construction," recalled Giurgola.[59] But these critics were overwhelmed by a chorus of praise from the upper echelons of the design community. New York's Museum of Modern Art mounted a show dedicated entirely to Richards, giving it the sort of imprimatur and exposure that would guarantee success in the academic and artistic wings of the profession. In the brochure for the show, Wilder Green, the former student of Kahn's at Yale who had become a MoMA curator, described Richards as "probably the single most consequential building constructed in the United States since the war."[60]

In his *Modern Architecture*, published in 1961, the Yale art historian Vincent Scully, who had been a Kahn advocate from the architect's earliest days in New Haven, declared that "Kahn's design enforces human recognition of an environment both meticulously realistic and heroic in itself: one which is intended to make the scientist feel not in command but both mysteriously and comprehensively challenged."[61] In his monograph on the architect published a year later, Scully called Richards "one of the greatest buildings of modern times," "entirely successful," an "urbane sequence," a "mighty assertion," "not just San Gimignano but the modern brotherhood of work."[62]

The invocation of the romantic towers of the Tuscan hill town was almost irresistible, especially since Kahn had visited it in 1929 and painted several images of it. But he also knew the fortified city of Carcassonne and Scottish castles, and if his appetite for text was not large, his ability to absorb visual imagery from photographs was ample compensation, and Kahn regularly referred to historical monuments, whether famous or obscure, in talking with his staff. "We were always working in the past," recalled Vreeland, adding that Kahn would leave illustrated architectural

books on the employees' drafting tables to provoke them.[63] The San Gimignano "stamp" on Richards would seem to be another early example of how the interpreters of Kahn's work were drawn to an apparent source as definitive, when in fact it was probably one of many. In any case, the imagery was always more evocative than imitative.

Whatever the precise origin—if there was one—the image of the Richards towers created an immediate sensation in the elite architectural world. The reason was that Kahn had found a way to design a thoroughly modern building that simultaneously touched something historically familiar in its admirers. Indeed, the key problem of Modernism up to Kahn's Philadelphia building had been the creative dead-end that the Miesian aesthetic had created. Driven by rationality and a dedication to new materials and "honest" expression of structure, the orthodox Modernists had perfected the form. There was really nowhere to go from the elegantly reductive principles of Mies van der Rohe's Seagram Building.

The decorative experiments of such contemporaries as Edward Durell Stone and Philip Johnson, who turned to embellishing their buildings with columns and grillwork, did little to solve the problem. While Kahn's solution could be detected in retrospect as early as the Yale Gallery, and even more in the Trenton Bathhouse, the Richards towers offered the tantalizing possibility that "heart" could be restored to the "mind" of Modern architecture, largely through the acknowledgment that history—at least in abstracted form—still had something to offer.

One of the people who may have played a part in Kahn's growing appreciation of history was a Princeton graduate named Robert Venturi. Venturi had studied under Jean Labatut, a revered Princeton teacher who had defied the Modernist dicta of the 1940s and '50s by insisting that his students be well versed in architectural history. Kahn had served as an enthusiastic critic on Venturi's thesis and later made him a teaching assistant at Penn. In 1951, Kahn recommended Venturi, first for a job with Eero Saarinen, and then in 1954 for a fellowship at the American Academy in Rome. When Venturi returned from Rome, in 1956, Kahn hired him, and although he spent only nine months in the office, the two became personally close. In 1961, Kahn wrote a recommendation for Venturi for membership in the Philadelphia Art Alliance, and the endorsement was more than ringing. In his letter, Kahn called Venturi "one of the most thoughtful and deeply understanding architects in this country."[64]

Not surprisingly perhaps, Venturi—like Tyng, Komendant, and so many others before and after them—felt that he had a defining effect on Kahn's work. Indeed, nearly forty years after he had left Kahn's employ (by which time he was a major architectural figure himself), Venturi took a substantial share of the credit for Kahn's original interest in architectural history. As Venturi put it, "Kahn's use of historical reference in the fifties and sixties is usually attributed to the influence of his early Beaux-Arts training and his time at the American Academy in Rome in the early fifties. But I think it derived more from me when I was close to Kahn in the late fifties and early sixties—during the end, let's not forget, of his fifties geometric-structural period dominated by the ideas of Buckminster Fuller and Anne Tyng."[65]

Whatever the sources of Kahn's aesthetic inspiration for Richards, the building vaulted him to the highest ranks of his profession. No longer was he an "architect's architect," a designer accessible only to the academy. Richards also put Kahn in the public eye and immediately made him highly desirable to a new range of clients across the country—everywhere, that is, but at the University of Pennsylvania. Still smarting from the delays and the problems with performance that were nearing scandalous proportions in the Richards labs, a university vice president was heard to mutter, "He will never do another building at Penn."[66] In fact, Kahn had already been asked to do a biology building adjacent to Richards, but when completed it had little of the power of his first effort, and he would get no more offers from the university.

Fortunately, the developer of the vaccine that freed the world from polio was willing to give Kahn a fresh chance.

CHAPTER FIVE

THE CLIENT CONNECTION

THE SALK INSTITUTE FOR BIOLOGICAL STUDIES
1959–65

If a single image conveys to the public what Louis Kahn accomplished as an architect, it is surely the view west to the Pacific Ocean through the plaza of the Salk Institute for Biological Studies in La Jolla, California. The austere expanse of stone, bounded on either side by the serrated profiles of study towers and split down the middle by a narrow channel of water, immediately evokes resonant visual references. If the Richards labs recalled Italian hill towns or Scottish castles in the eyes of some, the Salk complex suggested a host of other imagery: Greek temples overlooking the Aegean, the villas of Rome, and—most often—Thomas Jefferson's graciously expansive Lawn at the University of Virginia in Charlottesville. Like these durable monuments, Kahn's composition has an almost irresistible appeal to the eye and to the camera lens.

In fact, the plaza—which is mercilessly exposed to the midday sun—is the least important functional element of the Salk facility and is not often visited except by photographers and architects; the scientists and staff members may scurry across it, but they rarely linger. Nevertheless, the Salk courtyard has become the icon for the building, and the building has

become an icon for Kahn's career. One writer has described the plaza as "a cosmic void" that is "perhaps the most sublime space in the twentieth century."[1] Fair enough. There is indeed something otherworldly about this man-made enclosure that makes such seamless contact between the natural world and the high aspirations of its inhabitants.

However, the contrast between the visual impact of the space and its "uselessness" marks a shift in Kahn's architecture. Like Richards, the Salk Institute became a classic of American twentieth-century architecture, but unlike Richards, it succeeded admirably not only as an architectural image, but also in its functional purpose. And if Richards was the building that consolidated Kahn's concept of served and servant spaces, Salk was the building in which Kahn began to clarify his affinity for the role of institutions in society—and the role of architecture in advancing those institutions.

At the heart of the Salk saga is that, unlike Richards, where he had to grope among department heads in search of decisions, Kahn in La Jolla had a client, Jonas Salk, with not only professional credentials, but also a romantic vision of human potential that matched his own. As Jonas Salk's

The Salk Institute.
© GRANT MUDFORD

The celebrated polio researcher Jonas Salk became Kahn's best client, and their collaboration produced one of Kahn's best buildings. The reasons for their close relationship included their remarkably similar background as children of immigrants who had flourished against the odds.
© W. W. NORTON

eldest son, Peter, said, "They were kindred spirits; they spoke the same language."[2] Kahn himself wrote, "There are few clients who can understand philosophically the institution they are creating. Dr. Salk is an exception."[3] Elsewhere the architect said: "When you ask who has been my favorite client, one name comes sharply to my mind, and that's Dr. Jonas Salk. Dr. Salk listened closely to my speculations and was serious about how I would approach the building. He listened more carefully to me than I did to myself."[4]

What Salk was listening to was an emerging sense of purpose in Kahn's architecture. From his early training under Paul Cret, Kahn had been steeped in the physical nobility and cultural importance of institutions, whether the Pan-American Union or the memorials to the American dead of World War I. The institutions Kahn himself had been involved with reinforced that sensibility. As a student at Penn, he learned what a great university could do for an immigrant like himself, and at Yale he began to realize that institutions were more likely to have a positive role than low-income housing in improving the human condition. But Kahn sensed something more about institutions—that they need not function only as independent entities, but could also integrate larger social concerns. In Jonas Salk, Kahn found a soul mate, a scientist who believed that his scientific specialty of biology was only a fragment of a cultural effort that should include the humanistic as well as the technical. Salk wanted to create an institution that would advance that philosophy, and in Kahn he discovered an architect whose emerging worldview was almost totally sympathetic to his own. In Salk, Kahn found someone with whom he could not only empathize, but also struggle. "I think Lou was only really effective as an architect when he had a very responsible and even difficult client," recalled Jack MacAllister. "Lou could not design in a vacuum. He really needed a solid, constructive and critical client to do a good building."[5] If George Howe had been a sort of personal and professional godfather to Kahn for the Yale Gallery, Salk became his first true client. Not the least of the reasons was that Salk also had the will and the authority to transform the vision he and Kahn shared into a reality.

There was more than shared philosophy to the bond that would develop between Kahn and Salk. Indeed, there was an almost uncanny symmetry in their personal backgrounds. Jonas Salk was born on October 28, 1914, in New York City to a family with striking similarities to Kahn's own. His parents, Daniel and Dora Salk, were East European Jewish immigrants. According to one biographer, Salk's mother, like Kahn's, "had designed him for fame."[6] Like Kahn's family, the Salks began their life in America in poverty. Their first home was the storied ghetto on New York City's Lower East Side, the big-city equivalent of Philadelphia's Northern Liberties. The Salk family later moved to a tenement at 106th Street and Madison Avenue in East Harlem, and then to Crotona, a Jewish section of the Bronx; the orthodox Salk parents felt more comfortable in a community whose older residents still spoke Yiddish.

Salk's early education—also like Kahn's—benefited from a strong public school system. At the age of twelve, Jonas entered New York's demanding Townsend Harris Hall high school. He finished in three years rather than the usual four by enrolling in a program that identified promising candidates for the College of the City of New York. Salk was admitted to City College at fifteen with plans to study law, but a course in chemistry proved more interesting, and in 1934 he went on to New York University's medical school on scholarship, finishing in 1939.

So well did Salk perform in medical school that he was offered an internship at Mount Sinai Hospital, something that was considered the medical equivalent of "playing ball for the New York Yankees."[7] But his two years at the hospital confirmed Salk's growing sense that he was more interested in research than in the conventional practice of medicine. "From childhood," Peter Salk said, "he had wanted to help society."[8] In 1942, Salk accepted a position at the University of Michigan in Ann Arbor to work on the study of viruses. After helping to develop an influenza vaccine that was used by the American forces during World War II, Salk in 1947 left for the University of Pittsburgh School of Medicine to become a research professor of bacteriology.

The move surprised Salk's professional colleagues, many of whom had advised him against it. "Pitt" was considered a lowly perch after Michigan, but Salk was encouraged to defy his advisers by the offer of a virus research laboratory of his own. Once established in Pittsburgh, Salk began work on ways to combat a devastating disease known as poliomyelitis, which had become a worldwide scourge. In the early 1950s, it infected some 30,000 people a year in the United States, and many more in other countries. Victims often recovered, but some died, and many more were left paralyzed. Polio's victims were most often children, some of whom were condemned to living in "iron lungs," coffinlike metal tubes that assisted the victims' breathing. Parents began to shun public pools, movie theaters, summer camps, and beaches where they feared the mysterious virus might lurk.

Salk dedicated himself to battling the disease, but his methods were not universally admired. According to one account, many of his colleagues "had been annoyed for years by his unconcealed desire for professional independence and recognition. All of them had been propelled by the same ambition and many had satisfied it, but few had ever seemed as inexorable about it as Salk. They were uneasy about the self-assurance with which he tackled major problems, the speed with which he offered his solutions, the glibness with which he defended them, the stubbornness with which he refused to be deflected from whatever course he had mapped for himself, the nimbleness with which he altered course when ready."[9] Salk was wounded by the sniping, but conceded that it was not entirely unfounded. "My striving was strong and unconcealed," he said, "I wanted to do independent work and I wanted to do it *my way*."[10]

If Salk's go-it-alone attitude had put off professional competitors, it attracted the respect of the National Foundation for Infantile Paralysis

(NFIP), an organization that had been founded by Franklin Delano Roosevelt, himself a polio victim, and its fund-raising arm, the March of Dimes. With the help of NFIP, Salk by 1952 had developed a vaccine that seemed likely to prevent polio. Rigorous testing ensued on thousands of volunteer subjects. (Salk was so sure of his work that he himself, his family, and his coworkers were inoculated.) On April 12, 1955, at a news conference packed with reporters, Salk's vaccine was pronounced safe and effective. Within several years, the epidemics of polio that had terrified millions were a thing of the past. In recognition of his achievement, Salk was later awarded the Congressional Gold Medal. Nevertheless, he was dogged by complaints that he was a mere medical doctor, not a properly credentialed scientist, and had exploited the work of others without giving them proper credit. Albert Sabin, Salk's chief rival in the race for a polio vaccine, famously described Salk as "a kitchen chemist" who "never had an original idea in his life."[11] Keeping his own counsel was John Enders, a Harvard researcher who had discovered how to grow the polio virus in test tubes, thus giving others, including Salk, the raw material with which to work in pursuing a vaccine. In 1954, Enders's pioneering work won him the Nobel Prize, an honor that would elude Salk.

Although the vaccine made Salk famous, it did not make him wealthy. While he could have made a fortune from the fruits of his research, he chose not to patent his development, and he earned no income from its discovery, deciding to see the vaccine production technique made available freely to others. Meanwhile, according to his son Peter, "something else was going on" in Salk's mind: "He was beginning to think about what would come next, perhaps a cancer cure. He was looking for new horizons."[12] As it turned out, the polio breakthrough itself was enough to attract additional support. The man most responsible for it was Daniel Basil O'Connor, then the director of NFIP, who in 1960 promised Salk enough money to create his own research institute in hopes that other ailments might fall to his type of independent research.

The Salk Institute for Biological Studies was to be no ordinary scientific organization. Salk had been fascinated by C. P. Snow's influential 1959 book *The Two Cultures and the Scientific Revolution* about what the author saw as a dangerous and growing gulf between science and the humanities. Snow argued: "The non-scientists have a rooted impression that the scientists are shallowly optimistic, unaware of man's condition. On the other hand, the scientists believe that the literary intellectuals are totally lacking in foresight, peculiarly unconcerned with their brother men, in a deep sense anti-intellectual, anxious to restrict both art and thought to the existential moment."[13] In the view of his biographer, Salk was determined to bridge this intellectual gap and "resolved to encourage cross-fertilization of the sciences by creating an environment favorable to collaborative interchange."[14] The chairman of Salk's board of trustees, Warren Weaver, declared that "essential in the structure of the Institute from the very beginning are scientists who are interested not only in science but in the whole range of the humanities, the creative arts, the whole artistic and esthetic and philosophical side of man's life."[15] As O'Connor understood Salk's mission, "he insisted that these individuals, working under the same roof, would be uniquely compatible with each other, complementing each other, inspiring each other, getting more done in that way than any other group could. He called them a 'critical mass' from which a chain reaction would come."[16]

The leading humanist in the original group was Jacob Bronowski, a Polish-born scholar who later created the British Broadcasting Corporation television series *The Ascent of Man*. In the book that accompanied his series, Bronowski wrote: "The recent findings in human biology have given a new direction to scientific thought, a shift from the general to the individual, for the first time since the Renaissance opened the door into the natural world. There cannot be a philosophy, there cannot even be a decent science, without humanity."[17] Other early Institute fellows included Leo Szilard, an expert in theoretical and nuclear physics who had collaborated with Enrico Fermi on the first self-sustaining nuclear chain reaction, and Francis H. C. Crick, a British scientist who would share the 1962 Nobel Prize with Maurice Wilkins and James Watson for discovering the double-helical structure of DNA. Clearly, Salk's institute was not to be limited to routine experiments.

Although not known for his aesthetic taste, Salk had an architectural as well as an idealistic concept for his institute. On a trip to Italy in 1954, he had been captivated by the ancient Umbrian town of Assisi. He was particularly moved by the town's thirteenth-century Monastery of St. Francis, which centered on an intimate cloister of the sort Salk thought would be ideal for the contemplation of life's larger questions. It was a religious space, made famous by Assisi's most famous son, a former knight who was beatified for his service to others, especially children. Salk, having defeated a crippler of

Kahn and Salk reviewing a site model of the Salk Institute. From the outset, the men were drawn to each other by their shared quest for ways to bring art, science, and philosophy together for the benefit of a greater community.
PHOTOGRAPH © BILL EPPRIDGE

so many young people, may have sensed a personal connection to the home of St. Francis, for it was there that the saint-to-be had experienced his epiphany. Although Salk could not have known it, Assisi was also well known to Kahn, who had sketched it on his 1929 trip to Europe.

Salk needed an architect worthy of his vision, and called Kahn on the suggestion of a friend who had heard him lecture at the Carnegie Institute of Technology in Pittsburgh on "Order in Science and Art." Salk might have composed the title himself. The hope was that Kahn might help Salk select an architect for his California institute. The two men met in Philadelphia in December of 1959, and Kahn showed Salk through the Richards laboratories, which were still under construction. Salk was reportedly interested in the building but not moved by it. He was far more impressed by Kahn himself and the way the architect described his underlying concept for the Penn project as a place for research that would benefit mankind. Salk promptly suspended his search for an architect and invited Kahn to design his institute.

According to Kahn, "When Salk asked me to do the laboratories in San Diego, he said that he wanted a hundred thousand square feet of space to give to ten scientists who wanted each ten thousand square feet of space. The space requirements were roughly those of the Richards building, but Salk had something more in mind than mere square footage. He said, 'I would like to add one more requirement. I would like to be able to invite Picasso to the laboratories.' "[18] The reference to Picasso was not Salk's originally. In a not uncharacteristic gesture, Salk had picked it up from a remark Kahn made during the Pittsburgh lecture and adopted it as his own, but the architect never insisted on his authorship. "Lou wanted to let Jonas feel that he was part of things," recalled Sue Ann Kahn. "That was part of his strategy."[19]

At the time, Kahn was engaged in two other major projects. One was an American consulate building in Luanda, the capital of the West African nation of Angola. The architect had been offered the job in 1959, but it was in trouble, due both to local political tensions and Kahn's failure to produce the required work on the government's schedule. In the process of developing the design, however, Kahn had taken careful note of the punishing impact the sun had on local buildings and their users alike. As Kahn later described his experience in Africa, and his thoughts about a solution to the problems posed by the sun: "When you are on the interior of any building, looking at a building was unbearable because of the glare. . . . Now, placing a wall in front of a window would cut the view and that is not pleasant . . . so I thought of placing openings in the wall; the wall then becomes part of the window. When that wall got the light—even the direct sunlight—it would modify the glare."[20]

In developing his designs for both Luanda and Salk, Kahn was eager to avoid the sort of applied devices, such as the brise-soleils, or sun-breaks, that Le Corbusier had used in so many of his buildings, or the more overtly decorative grilles of such architects as Edward Durell Stone. In August of 1961, the Luanda commission was withdrawn. But now that he was working in another sun-drenched area, Kahn quickly found a use for what he had learned in Africa.

The other project on which Kahn had already embarked was the First Unitarian Church in Rochester, New York, a commission for which he had been selected over Walter Gropius, Carl Koch, Paul Rudolph, Eero Saarinen, and Frank Lloyd Wright. Begun in the spring of 1959, the design would eventually be anchored by a near-square form with offices and facilities for a church school surrounding a central space for worship. The brick exterior projected an austere rectilinearity, relieved only by deep-set slots for windows, but the interior was another matter. The frequently gloomy climate of northern New York State was nothing like that of Luanda, but Kahn was nonetheless eager to make use of controlled natural light as an element in his design. For the Rochester sanctuary, he employed a massive concrete ceiling shaped rather like the underside of a ship's hull and recalling the powerful sculptural effect of the Yale Art Gallery slab. So weighty, both

physically and visually, was the ceiling, however, that the client felt it would make the congregation feel oppressed. Accordingly, Kahn decided to lift his concrete "hull" above the surrounding walls and place four towers at the corners. These towers were faced with glass on the inward-facing sides above the level of the roof, allowing indirect sunlight to penetrate and wash down the concrete-block interior walls into the space below.

While rather simplistic, this device of lifting the roof off of the walls marked a pivotal moment in Kahn's serious investigation of the use of light to animate the severe masses of concrete and brick that were, increasingly, his chosen materials. To further mitigate the chill of those materials, Kahn for the first time in Rochester also began to use expanses of finely detailed wood for doors and cabinets, a technique that would become familiar in his subsequent designs, especially Salk. The result was a powerful setting for

The First Unitarian Church, in Rochester, New York, revealed Kahn's growing interest in the manipulation of natural light to enrich the experience of his often austere interiors. It was also the first time he made extensive use of wood on the interior, a device that would inform Salk and all of his subsequent designs. © GRANT MUDFORD

The Esherick House, built between 1959 and 1961, was one of only a few residences designed by Kahn. He used them as opportunities to explore geometric and spatial relationships, the juxtaposition of materials, and the role of landscape in his architecture.
© GRANT MUDFORD

spiritual reflection, but one that, consistent with Unitarian tradition and Kahn's own pan-religious inclinations, avoided overt sectarian gestures.

The site for Jonas Salk's own ambitiously idealistic undertaking was one of the most beautiful in southern California and certainly the most spectacular Kahn would ever encounter. Spreading out over 27 acres on a bluff 350 feet above the Pacific Ocean in La Jolla, it provided a setting that was as inspirational as it was unencumbered. The weather was mild and sunny year-round, the sea was ever-present, and the land was free; it had been donated to Salk by the city of San Diego, whose mayor, Charles Dail, was a polio survivor.

Salk and Kahn visited the Institute site for the first time together in early 1960. It presented a new challenge to the architect, who had never had to deal aggressively with topography. Although the few private residences he designed in this period near Philadelphia, particularly the Esherick House and the Fisher House, respected their natural settings, most of Kahn's other buildings up to this point had been on flat sites. Engaging the land, however, only added to the richness of Kahn's California opportunity.

Kahn responded both to Salk's ambitions and to the irregularities of the site, which was split by a ravine, by proposing what he apparently sensed might become an ideal community of mind and spirit. Speaking of his conversations with his client, Kahn said, "I came up with the idea that what he wanted was a place of the measurable, which is a laboratory, and a place of the unmeasurable, which would be the meeting place."[21] He also intended to include a library (for reference books, but also for the mystery novels Salk felt were important as a way to relax), a 500-seat amphitheater for concerts and plays, and a swimming pool—all the amenities that one might hope to find in a place dedicated to the ideal of a healthy mind in a healthy body. To house visiting researchers and guests, the plan included a cluster of small residential units.

The meeting house was to be located at the western end of the site, closest to the sea, to provide a constant reminder to the researchers of the vastness of the natural world they were investigating. The residences would have their own precinct across the ravine to the south. The labs, meanwhile, would be located at the eastern end of the site, adjacent to the public road, and therefore easily serviced by suppliers of research materials and equipment. All the elements would be within easy walking distance of each other.

The design team included Carles Enrique Vallhonrat, an austere Spaniard who served as Kahn's chief assistant on the early phases of the project; Fred Langford, a specialist in architectural concrete; and Jack MacAllister, who would eventually open a San Diego office in a trailer on the site to see the Salk building through to completion.

Although the design changed significantly over the life of the project, the idea of locating the meeting place, the residences, and the laboratories in discrete areas remained constant. This was the beginning of what would become in Kahn's later projects on the Indian subcontinent a cluster of "citadels," each devoted to functions that would improve the human condition, and all interrelated.

The meeting house was initially the most appealing of the elements to Kahn, no doubt because its potential merged with his own—and Salk's—ideas about liberating the human imagination from the conventional limitations of science and architecture. As the design developed, the portions of the complex devoted to the reading room and dining room became either circular forms set within a square enclosure, or squares set within a circular enclosure. The outer walls stood free of the inner ones and were pierced by large geometric openings. The shape of the openings in the walls can be traced to Kahn's Luanda design, and to his plan for the largely utilitarian

Tribune Review Building in Greensburg, Pennsylvania. But in La Jolla they began to subtly take on the look of masks, giving the facades a mysteriously anthropomorphic look.

As the design proceeded, Kahn seemed uncomfortable with the plan of the meeting house. Tim Vreeland, who was working on the project in the Philadelphia office, casually superimposed a sketch of a portion of Hadrian's Villa on the meeting house scheme. When Kahn saw it, he missed the specific reference, but redrew his original plan. Much has since been made of the way Kahn apparently relied on this "lifting" of a classical precedent to solve his design problem. But while Kahn never made a secret of his fascination with architectural history, he was irritated by suggestions that he was consciously or even unconsciously borrowing his material. Referring to Vincent Scully, his longtime advocate on the Yale faculty and author of the first monograph on Kahn, in which he mentioned the Hadrian's Villa episode, Kahn declared, "Scully, who is an historian, sensed the desire, saw these pictures, and then put things down like that, but it's completely the opposite."[22] According to Kahn's daughter Alexandra Tyng, her father was "annoyed by conjectures that the Salk Institute . . . was directly influenced by Hadrian's Villa. . . . When the similarities were pointed out to him, he was struck by them, but the idea of direct influences was to him ridiculous."[23]

The housing was characterized as a "village" from the start. The early drawings show a cluster of low buildings aligned along a curving pedestrian corridor that gently rose and fell like a narrow street in a medieval European city. One can easily imagine researchers dreamily strolling among these spaces at the end of a day, relieved to be away from the demands of the laboratories and the meeting house, but not too far separated from them.

While visiting La Jolla to review progress, Kahn's preference for his own housing also ran to the traditional. "He liked the La Valencia because he walked everywhere," recalled MacAllister about Kahn's choice of hotels. "And also the Del Charro, because of its kind of charm. It was an old stable remade."[24]

The first scheme for the laboratories involved two research towers supported by a pair of service buildings. This was soon replaced by a series of four two-story rectangular buildings set parallel to each other and separated by two open courtyards.

The simple geometry of the plan made complete functional sense, but Salk was having second thoughts. Peter Salk recalled that late one afternoon

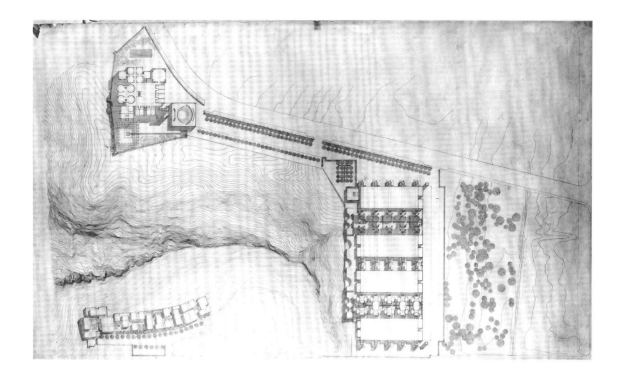

his father, having mulled over the original scheme for the complex, "went out on the cliff and looked back, and realized that something was wrong."[25] The next day, on a flight to San Francisco with Kahn, Salk broached the possibility of reducing the four buildings to a pair with a single court between them. A construction contract for the original solution had been signed, and to make such a radical change at such a late date involved enormous financial and creative risks for both men, but Kahn agreed. When he informed his design team that they would have to start over, his shocked listeners told him that he was "crazy," to which Kahn replied, "It's an opportunity to build a better building."[26] In fact, the change produced a simpler relationship between the buildings and eliminated a possibility that the four-building scheme might encourage a division of the researchers into separate, even competing, groups.

No doubt smarting from the shortcomings of the laboratory spaces at Richards, Kahn was surely eager to do better with the rather similar program at Salk. Here again, he was fortunate in his client, a working scientist who knew exactly what his kind of research required and had the authority to make decisions on how it was served. He also understood the research in

Salk's concern that the original four-building design for the laboratories shown here might have produced competing cultures among the researchers fueled a fundamental reorganization of the scheme, reducing the elements to two. The meeting house and the curved residential component, which would have completed the idealistic complex, were never built. © LOUIS I. KAHN COLLECTION, UNIVERSITY OF PENNSYLVANIA AND THE PENNSYLVANIA AND HISTORICAL AND MUSEUM COMMISSION the symbolic terms that so appealed to Kahn. Salk called the relationship between the served and servant spaces "mesenchymal," a scientific term describing the relationships among branching cells.[27]

In a fundamental way, the design of the Institute provided Kahn with an opportunity to address the problems that had plagued the Richards labs. Where the utilities had been organized vertically at Richards, Kahn's solution at Salk was to run many of them horizontally. Such a scheme might normally have required enormous amounts of space in either an attic or a basement, but Kahn decided to distribute that space between the laboratory floors, rather like the alternating layers of a sandwich. In executing this, he was aided again by August Komendant, the structural engineer who had made such a contribution to the Richards labs and was also heavily involved in the Rochester church. "Kahn told me the task was so tremendous that it would be impossible for him to accomplish it alone," Komendant recalled some years later with his characteristic lack of modesty. "He needed me to discuss the ideas, to help create a proper image, and to carry out the structural part."[28] But Komendant was no less aware than Kahn of the failings of the program for the Richards labs, and set himself to understanding the needs of Salk's scientists. The main one was for large expanses of uninterrupted space that could be reconfigured as needed for new equipment and changing staff. As was the case in Philadelphia, both Kahn and Komendant wanted to isolate the servant spaces from those that were being served, but this time they took a radically simple approach. They proposed that the labs be totally open, and that the spaces for the mechanical equipment be given floors of their own. An original idea of using "folded plates," or large hollow concrete members, for the structural system was rejected, at which point Komendant came up with a series of thirteen modified Vierendeel trusses that were strong enough to support the laboratory floors without the normal columns. This would give Salk the uninterrupted space he required for the laboratories, but, at 9 feet in height, the trusses were tall enough to allow walk-through room for the pipes, ducts, and wires that carried water, steam, chemicals, heating and air-conditioning, and exhaust fumes to their destinations. The interstitial mechanical floors (which the designers dubbed "pipe space") with all their machinery looked much like the engine rooms of enormous ocean-going vessels.

More than mere mechanical services was required for the people who were to use the labs. Both Salk and Kahn were drawn to meeting the needs of intensely creative individuals when they were alone with their thoughts.

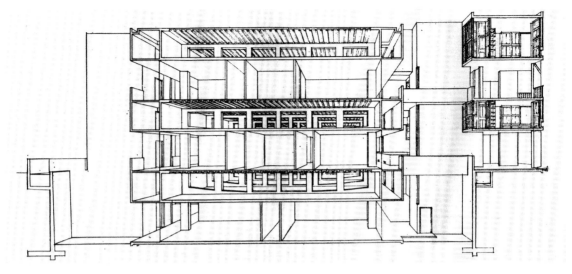

The physical expression of that wish became a series of study towers positioned adjacent to the laboratories themselves. Kahn said that the scientists should have a refuge from the hardware of science and should be provided with an environment that he equated with contemplation: "I realized that there should be a clean air and stainless steel area, and a rug and oak table area."[29] Salk and Kahn both wanted each scientist to have a private "study unit" removed from the laboratories but still accessible to them. The idea was a shamelessly romantic one, suggesting that great thoughts would emerge from tranquil refuges away from the mess of the labs. In fact, some of the scientists themselves had limited interest in the idea; they were apparently happy to spend their days at their benches, even eating lunch among their beakers and tubes. But Salk and Kahn prevailed.

Although the disposition of the buildings and their structural system had changed, the study spaces remained, suggesting a high-rise variation on Jefferson's "hotels" for the UVA faculty. The studies were housed in ten towers, five on each side of the court. One wall of each study was set at an angle so that each occupant would have an unobstructed view of the Pacific. Recalling the service towers at the Richards labs, Kahn positioned eight shorter versions on the outside walls of the two main buildings to accommodate elevators, bathrooms, and storage areas. Two additional elements for offices were attached to the western end of the buildings.

Once the basic functional scheme had been approved, Kahn began to address the materials from which the building would be made. The basic one was concrete, but it was concrete of an unprecedented sort. Indeed, the care

Again relying heavily on August Komendant's creative engineering, Kahn at Salk solved the problems of the cramped laboratories at Richards by using deep trusses that created three separate mechanical "floors" and left the laboratory spaces entirely open, to be arranged as the scientists wished. © AUGUST KOMENDANT COLLECTION, THE ARCHITECTURAL ARCHIVES, UNIVERSITY OF PENNSYLVANIA

The study towers, each of which had private views of the Pacific, appealed to the romantic image Kahn and Salk shared about scholars pursuing their work in monastic isolation.

© GRANT MUDFORD

Kahn's treatment of the concrete at Salk reached unprecedented levels of precision. Numerous mixtures were tested to ensure the desired color and texture, and the surfaces were inflected by subtly exploiting the joints of the wooden forms into which the concrete was poured.

lavished on what Kahn liked to call "molten stone" was as great as that on the engineering. Special forms were designed by Fred Langford, whose efforts were described by Jack MacAllister as "almost maniacal."[30] The aggregate was repeatedly examined and adjusted to make sure the color was exactly what Kahn and his client wanted. Even the practical steps had a philosophical dimension. To test the various concrete mixtures, Kahn had trial pours used as walls for the building's basement. Marshall Meyers remembered that the architect wanted these steps to "remain in the building as the history of its making. They would be like 'fossils,' he would say."[31] The wooden forms into which the concrete was to be poured were coated with six layers of polyurethane resin to guarantee a smooth finish. But Kahn decided to retain what minor marks were left on the concrete when the forms were removed. Not only did they serve as a sort of ornament, but they also testified to the way in which the building was made.

Rather than patch the inevitably messy joints between the levels of concrete as they were poured, Kahn recessed them, creating a sharp shadow line on the surface of the walls. The points where the plywood panels used in the forms joined each other were also exploited for visual effect. Kahn called attention to them by having the edges of the panels beveled so that they would leave narrow, V-shaped protrusions once the concrete was poured behind them. These V's cast shallower shadows, adding further to the visual texture of the walls, which might otherwise have been merely harsh planes, and creating a visual hierarchy to the joints that explained the construction process. The surface of the concrete was then "punctuated" with lead plugs inserted in the holes formed by the steel bolts used to secure the wooden forms. Filling the holes was necessary, because leaving them open would have allowed water to rust the steel stumps and stain the walls. But patching the holes with concrete was, in Kahn's view, a cosmetic act of concealment. The lead plugs were at once simple, effective, attractive to look at, and actually accentuated the process by which the wall had been made. According to MacAllister, Kahn derived the device of the lead plugs from his study of the way the material had been used in medieval times to tie blocks of masonry together.[32] But it was yet another subdued form of ornamentation based in necessity, Kahn's favorite kind.

While Kahn insisted on the highest possible level of quality for the concrete, there was a brief period when he was not able to test it himself.

The architect's attention to details extended to handrails of the exterior stair connecting the study towers and the laboratories. Rather than have the rails assembled from parts, Kahn had them extruded from steel as a unit. He insisted that the scratches created in the process be left unpolished as evidence of how the railings were made.

MacAllister remembered that during the work on Salk, Kahn had to undergo an operation for cataracts. After the operation, he would visit the site, but, according to MacAllister, "he was just totally blind." The young architect would have to "walk him to the site and hold him by the hand. And he'd whisper in my ear, 'Tell me when something's bad so that I can really scream about it.' And so I'd walk up and say, 'Lou, there's a really poorly laid concrete wall in front of you.' And Lou would stand there and wave his arms and say, 'That's not acceptable! I won't accept that kind of concrete work!' And he couldn't see a damned thing."[33]

Although his eyesight may have provoked some diversionary theatrics at the early stages of construction, Kahn's attention to detail at Salk was never affected. An example was the way the architect dealt with the handrails for the exterior staircases serving the study towers. The original design called for a round, inch-wide steel rod to be welded to a thin rectangular support, rather in the shape of an inverted exclamation point. Kahn didn't like the welded joint, and asked whether the entire railing could be extruded as a single form. The fabricator said he would try. He succeeded, but the process left deep scratches on the metal. When Kahn found the installers buffing the scratches down, he immediately told them to stop. Once again, the architect was insisting that the marks of making something be left as evidence of the process, and not tidied up in any way.[34]

While Kahn had used wood in his residential projects and in the interiors of the Unitarian Church, the Salk project was the first one in which he combined it with concrete on exterior surfaces with such positive effect, using it for the window surrounds and sun shades of the study towers. In La Jolla, the architect specified a high grade of Burmese teak, which resisted rot and could be expected to weather to a soft brownish-gray. The juxtaposition of the industrial concrete and the organic wood made a powerful visual statement about the presence of the natural as a companion to the industrial.

Although Salk himself had provoked the most dramatic change in the original design by arguing for the two-building scheme, Kahn's own increasingly familiar pattern of changing details that had been considered final delayed the start of construction. And past a certain point, delay triggered tax penalties under the local laws. So Galen Schlosser, one of Kahn's architects, persuaded a member of Salk's office to hire a bulldozer to move enough earth around on the site to convince the city that construction had begun.[35]

As the labs began to rise, the area between them remained unresolved. Kahn had originally planned to plant poplar trees in the open space to create a shady area that would encourage interaction among the scientists. But he was not happy with the idea, and the solution to the problem came from an unusual source. Some time earlier, Kahn had seen an exhibition at the Museum of Modern Art of the work of Luis Barragán, a Mexican architect who was known for his austere buildings in stone and stucco. Kahn was impressed with Barragán's work, especially by his designs for gardens, and invited him to La Jolla to advise him on the Salk open space. Although Kahn was always ready to listen to the ideas of others—and absorb them with ease—it was rare for him to call on another artist to solve a specific problem. Barragán responded to the opportunity with grace and a simplicity that must have appealed to Kahn's own appreciation of the elemental. The visitor, having surveyed the space between the buildings and its majestic view of the ocean, advised his host to abandon the garden scheme that had been part of the design from the beginning, and to leave the space open. "There should be no garden," Barragán said. "It should be a plaza." By creating a plaza, Barragán observed in the sort of inspirational language that Kahn himself so enjoyed, the architect would be creating "a façade to the sky."[36]

The key to the change was as much verbal as it was architectural. "Lou was very concerned about the meaning of individual words," recalled MacAllister. "He had been thinking of the open space as a 'garden' from the start, and he couldn't get past that because of the word. When Barragán said 'plaza,' Lou was free to make the change."[37]

Kahn followed Barragán's counsel. But he went beyond it by inserting a narrow channel to carry water down the middle of the plaza, and allowed the stream to cascade into a sculptural cistern at the western end. By this time, Kahn had been spending considerable time on new commissions in India and Pakistan, and had seen examples of Mughal gardens that employed water elements. (See Chapter Six.) This may have been the source for the channel and the fountain at the Institute. But the inspiration may just as well have been the fountains of the Alhambra. (Kahn had laid a book on the Moorish landmark on MacAllister's desk one night and later sent him to Spain to see the real thing.) The plaza was to have been paved with a Mexican stone, but to save money Kahn switched to Italian travertine, which he discovered he could get for less than the cost of American vinyl tile.[38] Despite such economies, concerns about money that had shadowed the project from the early stages intensified. Indeed, planning for the meeting house and the residences was halted in the late summer of 1963.

Meanwhile, things were not going well in the Tyng household. Sue Ann was in her twenties, and on her own as a musician and teacher. But Alexandra Tyng, called Alex, was not yet a teenager and was suffering a special form of childhood pain. While Kahn's wife and most of his colleagues knew that Kahn had a second daughter, she existed in a sort of limbo, acknowledged but not recognized. Alex came to the office frequently with Anne and made drawings on the yellow tracing paper that littered the desks, but she never felt as if her father was a major presence in her life with her mother. "I saw him about once a month," Alex remembered. "That was the way it was. I didn't think about it, but I realized he wasn't the kind of father other kids had."[39] Alex said that her father was generous with presents, and always "picked the best of everything," including a painting set that she would use for years afterward.[40] But she did not remember her father ever visiting her at elementary school. He did not sign her report cards. Even on the rare occasions when Alex and her father went out together, they remained apart. Alex remembered a concert by the Vienna Choir Boys during which a colleague of Kahn's came up to greet him. Kahn introduced his daughter as Alex Tyng, not "my daughter, Alex." She remained stoic about the experience, but conceded, "I was so upset."[41]

There was one incident when Alex got her father's full attention, but for an ironic, and potentially disastrous, reason. "He came over for my birthday party," she recalled, and I started to blow out the candles on the cake. My hair was in braids, and as I leaned over, one of them caught fire. My father grabbed it and put it out." The flames could only have reminded

Kahn was unsure about how to deal with the space between the twin laboratory wings until he consulted with the Mexican architect Luis Barragán, who advised him against creating a garden and urged him instead to make a plaza that would be a "façade to the sky." © GRANT MUDFORD

Kahn of his own near-fatal encounter with fire as a young boy. But to Alex, the moment sent a mixed message. "It was one of the few times he paid attention to me instead of to his theories," she said.[42] The effect was lasting. After college, Alex became briefly an illustrator of children's books. She found it especially hard to draw pictures of fathers. "I didn't really know what they did," she said.[43]

Although Kahn continued to visit Tyng for Alex's sake, the romantic relationship had come to an end. In 1964, Tyng wrote, limiting herself to their professional association, that "although Lou had plenty of work in the office, he 'let me go' by simply not giving me work."[44] New women would continue to drift in an out of Kahn's life. In 1959, Kahn had begun a liaison with Harriet Pattison, a thirty-two-year-old aspiring landscape architect whom he had met through Robert Venturi, but the relationship proved no more exclusive than that with Esther or Anne. Former associates remembered Kahn taking admiring young women home from parties; he reportedly invited at least one comely associate to the office late at night to review "something I'd like you to see" before making a pass (which she rejected).

Excuses were made for Kahn, even by those closest to him. In Philadelphia, his social community was made up of artists, architects, and other creative people. "It was very Bohemian," said Sue Ann.[45] In that environment, marriage was considered somewhat bourgeois, and love affairs on the side were not uncommon. "We expected it of an artist," said MacAllister.[46] David Rinehart, a Penn architecture alumnus who had been MacAllister's roommate during their student days, had another theory about why Kahn did not leave his wife. "Lou would never commit himself to any family," he said. "His home was where his architecture was. But by the same token, he could never have taken responsibility for leaving Esther."[47] Nevertheless, Kahn would instruct his secretary not to tell Esther where he was when she called, even if he was out of town. He even had the secretary put his correspondence upside down on his desk so that Esther would not see anything she was not supposed to see on one of her unannounced visits to the office.[48] However troubling such behavior was to those around him, MacAllister felt that Kahn's marriage gave him more than memories of happier times and Esther's many years of financial support. For one thing, it was a ready excuse if pressed for a commitment by a lover. "Lou could always say he was a married man," MacAllister said.[49]

The conflict within the marriage must have been wearing, but Kahn almost never mentioned it. Rinehart learned to his surprise that one person Kahn talked to about his home life was a Philadelphia cabdriver. Kahn had still not learned to drive, and took taxis when he couldn't be driven by a friend or colleague. But he didn't like sitting in the back seat, apparently because he felt it created a class distinction between him and the cabbie. Sitting in the front seat, however, was technically against Philadelphia law, so Kahn went so far as to get a letter from the taxi bureau allowing him to sit in front if the driver agreed. One who did, and drove Kahn regularly, picked up Rinehart one day at the office and asked about his other customer who worked in the same building and looked like a "wizard." Rinehart recalled the driver saying that Kahn had asked him whether he was married and whether he was happy. The driver said he was both, to which Kahn replied, "I got the short end of the stick."[50] MacAllister was not surprised by the story. "Lou told me at dinner one night that he knew the morning after he got married that he had made a mistake," he said.[51]

The affairs may have filled some void in his marriage, but Kahn may well have been dealing with other, deeper forces in himself. Even though he was by this time a nationally renowned architect, he would never have the social stature of a George Howe or a Holmes Perkins. "Lou was a homely little Jewish man," said MacAllister. "I think the women were his way of saying, 'Maybe so, but I'm still OK.' "[52]

Work was clearly a refuge from his romantic entanglements, but the growing amount of it was stretching even Kahn's formidable capacity. His delays on the Salk project were creating a crisis for both Salk and Kahn himself. According to MacAllister, the architect had run so low on money that he was not able to pay his consultants. David Rinehart remembered that during the Salk project, Kahn would be in the office "for days at a time, and take baths in the men's room sink."[53] Nevertheless, the delays continued. Finally, remembered MacAllister, who was in the Philadelphia office at the time, "the Salk people called Lou and said, 'We're going to fire you!' Lou said, 'What can I do?' The Salk people said that he should 'put Mac in charge.' To which Lou responded, 'I should have thought of that myself!' "[54] MacAllister was indeed given the management responsibility for the rest of the project, and it turned out to be the only building Kahn ever designed that made a profit. But that was not an achievement that MacAllister was especially proud of. Kahn was no spendthrift, he insisted. "Lou struggled over budgets, he took them very seriously. He stripped $2 million out of the Salk project in five days after bids came in too high. But he just couldn't change. He would just throw out more drawings the day before construction began and say, 'We can't afford to do a second-best building.' "[55]

Salk said that the main reasons for the reduction in the scope of the project were financial, and there was much to his argument. The federal government, which had poured millions into scientific research following the Russian advances symbolized by the launch of their *Sputnik* satellite in 1957, was pulling back now that the perceived threat had eased. Moreover, the original funding for the complex had been intended to provide an endowment as well as to cover the cost of the buildings. When construction costs began to run over budget, the Institute was faced with a choice between completing one laboratory building and starting the second, or abandoning the second to protect the endowment. Salk decided to push forward with the second building. "If it had been left up to the accountants, the Institute would never have been built," he said later.[56] All involved hoped that more money would be found to finish the entire complex. It never was.

Finances were by no means the only source of strain in Salk's life. He had always considered himself a man of vision, and his fame was secure, but according to his son Peter, he was still affected by the lack of acceptance of his accomplishments within the scientific community. "I think that because of this 'rejection,' my father continued to carry the feeling that he had something more to prove," Peter said.[57] Whether this affected his ambitions for the institute is not clear. Some members of Kahn's staff were uncomfortable with Salk's insistence on being involved at virtually every level of the project. "Show me how you arrived at that decision," he would tell the young architects, sending them searching through wastebaskets to retrieve rejected versions of design solutions. "The team hated it," recalled MacAllister, "but Jonas was as interested in the process as in the result. And Lou loved it because the result got better each time."[58] Salk's determination to oversee every aspect of the institute was perhaps not surprising. Peter recalled the time his mother asked his father to clean their stove and later found him with the appliance pulled out from the wall so that he could clean around the screws in the back. "My father was obsessed with the details," Peter said.[59]

The relationship with Kahn seemed to be enriched by the constant probing and questioning, a process Kahn himself relished. But Salk was beginning to encounter resistance to his large-scale ideas from other quarters. "The scientific 'stars' he had gathered at the Institute were finding themselves embarrassed by his musings about man's place in the cosmos," Peter said. "The people around him were beginning to foreclose the possibility of further exploration in those realms. It had been a bold initiative, but it became difficult for my father to be fully himself within the institution he had created."[60] Making matters worse, Salk's marriage to his wife, Donna, was in difficulty.

The buildings that emerged from the alliance of Salk and Kahn were, at best, a truncated version of the men's original shared vision. The passage of time has placed the laboratories and their plaza among the monuments of modern architecture, but the component that most embodied the pancultural ambitions of the scientist and the architect—the meeting house—remained unbuilt. So did the residences, which would have completed the communal goal based on the image of the monastery at Assisi. One can only speculate about whether the completion of the original scheme might have functioned in the integrated way Salk and Kahn had hoped, and whether the science produced in the laboratories might have advanced still further.

Nonetheless, the Salk Institute represented the emergence of a masterly confidence in Kahn's architecture. If structure had been his main concern in the Yale University Art Gallery and the Richards labs, space (both interior and exterior) and light now began to play equally important roles. Here were all the elements that would distinguish Kahn's best future work: a profound interest in the way a building was made; a fascination with the manipulation of natural light; and a commitment to the role of architecture in the support of institutions that could have a positive impact on the human condition. Salk, who had had to see his original hopes cut back so drastically, pronounced himself happy with the core that survived. "I would say the building is as close to perfection as anything possible," he said.[61] According to Salk's son Peter, the Institute was "as pure a creative undertaking as one might imagine."[62]

Of course, it could not have been done had Salk not been someone who so shared Kahn's worldview and had the commitment and the resources to see it into built form. A series of similar relationships would sustain Kahn through the design of the most ambitious projects of his entire career, two institutions on the opposite side of the globe.

CHAPTER SIX

"A DEGREE OF UTTER PURITY"

THE SUBCONTINENT 1962–83

By early 1962, the publicity surrounding the Trenton Bathhouse and the Richards Medical Research Laboratories had made Louis Kahn a major force in the American architectural community, and the Salk Institute and a number of lesser commissions had increased the load on the firm. On March 19, Kahn moved his office from 138 South Twentieth Street, where it had been since 1951, to a five-story building at 1501 Walnut Street. It was not an impressive work of architecture, but it was located in the bustling heart of downtown Philadelphia, and the top two floors provided enough additional room to handle new commissions. Suddenly, there were two very large ones.

On June 6, 1962, Kahn was contacted by representatives of the Indian Institute of Management in Ahmedabad, in the northwestern Indian state of Gujurat, asking him to design a graduate school of business administration. Slightly less than three months later, on August 27, Kahn received a telegram from the Pakistani Department of Public Works inviting him to design nothing less than a new government center for East Pakistan in the city of Dhaka. Louis Kahn was now not only a leader within his profession, but an architect of international stature.

The Assembly. COURTESY
RAYMOND MEIER

Although located halfway around the world, the new commissions had a powerful appeal to Kahn. First, they offered him opportunities for the sort of large-scale planning that had eluded him in the United States. Beyond that, he had been increasingly attracted to architecture that would go beyond the limitations imposed by individual buildings. Quite possibly, both of these institutions on the Indian subcontinent could, in their different ways, "change the world," something Kahn had been hoping to do since his youthfully idealistic days with Stonorov and Howe.

But just as his career began to soar, Kahn's already tangled personal life grew even more complicated when his affair with Harriet Pattison intensified. A graduate of the University of Chicago, Pattison had studied theater at Yale and in addition to her landscape work had wide-ranging interests in philosophy and music. In November 1962, Harriet gave birth to a son, Nathaniel. As Nathaniel recounted it many years later, when Kahn learned from Harriet that she was pregnant, his response was a stunningly insensitive "Oh no, not again."[1] But as he had done after the birth of Alexandra, Kahn set his increasingly messy family issues aside and turned fervently to his new architectural opportunities.

When he made his first trip to India, in November of 1962, to see the IIM site, Kahn also went to visit Le Corbusier's sprawling government center at Chandigarh in the Punjab. Kahn had been at once fascinated and haunted by Le Corbusier at least since the stay at the American Academy in 1950–51 and considered the Swiss-French master to be something of an idol. Kahn was impressed by the massive sculptural forms that Le Corbusier had executed in concrete for the new city, which was not finished until 1963, but the visit confirmed a judgment he had made in a speech a year earlier on the basis of photographs that the buildings of the complex were alien to the Indian environment. As Kahn described his feelings for the Voice of America, he concluded that while Le Corbusier's works for the capital were "beautiful," they were also "out of context."[2]

In both India and Pakistan, large-scale architecture had always been linked to authoritarian rule, whether by Mughal princes or colonial masters. Le Corbusier had avoided the challenge of developing a new vernacular by creating a Modernist complex that could have fit just as comfortably in France or the United States; India was merely the available site. Kahn hoped to exploit his own far-flung commissions to develop something unique, but he was well aware that it had to be expressed in a language accessible—and acceptable—not only to his clients, but to the people who would be using the buildings. He was to be helped to a better understanding of the local conditions in both Ahmedabad and Dhaka by a small cadre of highly unusual people.

Although conceived with the backing of the state and national governments, the Indian Institute of Management also benefited from the support of the Ford Foundation and the Sarabhai family, wealthy Indian industrialists who had earlier commissioned Le Corbusier to design several buildings in Ahmedabad. Determined to provide India with the sort of business training that had been developed in the United States, Vikram Sarabhai, a distinguished scientist and industrialist who was director of the project, in 1962 turned to a prominent young Indian architect named Balkrishna Doshi. Having trained with Le Corbusier in Paris, Doshi had come back to India in 1955 to oversee the construction at Chandigarh and at Ahmedabad, where he served as the project architect on the historical museum Le Corbusier had designed for the city. But Sarabhai also suggested that they find a distinguished foreign architect to help. Doshi recommended Kahn, whom he considered to be "the best architect after [Frank Lloyd] Wright."[3]

Balkrishna Doshi, who was instrumental in bringing Kahn to India, consulting with him on the site of the Indian Institute of Management in Ahmedabad. Doshi had worked with Le Corbusier on his government complex in Chandigarh, but found Kahn's architecture more appropriate to the local context. COURTESY BALKRISHNA V. DOSHI

Doshi's assessment of Kahn went back to 1958, when the young Indian was on a Graham Foundation fellowship and met Kahn while visiting Philadelphia. They liked each other immediately, and after a trip to Kahn's office during which Kahn showed Doshi drawings of the Trenton Bathhouse, the Richards labs, and the plans for Salk, they agreed to go out to dinner. Doshi was puzzled by the fact that such a distinguished architect first had to borrow money from his secretary.[4]

Two years later, Doshi, then teaching at Washington University in St. Louis, was invited by G. Holmes Perkins to lecture at Penn on his work with Le Corbusier, and he again met Kahn. Doshi returned to Philadelphia in 1962 to teach, and, as he put it, "my dream of spending more time with Lou became a reality."[5]

The architects were drawn to each other on more than professional grounds. Doshi remembered that Kahn's attitude toward architecture, history, and nature seemed refreshingly non-Western. Indeed, Doshi wrote later that "Lou was more Indian than a lot of Indians."[6] The friendship developed to the point that Doshi became one of only a few of Kahn's professional colleagues to be invited to his home, where he met Esther. (Kahn entertained his visitor by playing one of his medleys of classical and jazz on the family piano.) Kahn also held on to the key to Doshi's Philadelphia apartment while he was away, and would throw it down from the top floor of 1501 when Doshi returned to town.

Both Doshi and Kahn attended the Aspen Design Conference, the annual cultural retreat in the Colorado Rockies, in the summer of 1962, and Doshi took the opportunity to broach the idea of a building in Ahmedabad. Kahn said that he was interested, but got the impression that he was being asked to do the city's architecture school, which Doshi himself was already designing. When Kahn realized the mistake, he asked Doshi, "What am *I* going to do?" The misunderstanding was soon cleared up, but there was no discussion of a fee or even travel expenses. Nevertheless, in September of 1962, Kahn formally accepted the offer to design the institute.

Arriving in Ahmedabad two months later, Kahn toured the IIM site—a flat, dusty, 65-acre expanse on the edge of the city. At first, Kahn was officially identified as the "consulting architect," and Doshi as the "assistant architect," but Kahn's lead role was never in doubt. Doshi was content with the arrangement, considering Kahn at this point to be "like a brother."[7] (Doshi remembers that whenever Kahn came to Ahmedabad, he brought two bottles of vodka, one for his collaborator and one to use when brushing his teeth so that he would not have to risk catching something from the water supply.) They agreed on the architecture of Chandigarh. Although Doshi had been intimately involved in the design and construction of Le Corbusier's new city, even he had reservations about it. He later said, "I think that 20 years hence Chandigarh may not even be considered an Indian city because it gives us Le Corbusier's sense of the future, but not of Indian life. . . . you have streets, open spaces, houses—but you have no life!"[8]

The academic model for IIM was the Harvard Business School, the most prominent institution of its kind in the United States, and Harvard shared in developing the program. This included the standard academic components of classrooms, offices, and a library. But the institute was to be a self-contained campus with housing for both students and faculty, and as such promised to fulfill the communal ambitions that had been frustrated at Salk when the original master plan was cut back. In the case of the housing, Kahn was able to draw on his recent experience at Erdman Hall, the dormitory for Bryn Mawr College in Pennsylvania. But his inspiration went much deeper. Once again drawing on his past visits to European monuments, but also tapping a romantic image of an ideal learning environment, Kahn declared, "The plan comes from my feelings of monastery."[9]

Apart from the academic program, Kahn immediately began to focus on the physical form that IIM might take. He returned to the idea of the courtyard that had become the focus of the composition at Salk, as well as the cylindrical forms for the ill-fated Mikveh Israel Synagogue project in downtown Philadelphia. But the Gujurati climate—temperatures reached 120 degrees in summer—was a powerful consideration in the development of the design. And here Kahn was able to call again on the research he had done for the unsuccessful commission for a U.S. consulate in Angola. This was the beginning of the spatial layering that would distinguish both IIM and the Assembly building at Dhaka.

Beyond the requirements for classrooms and student housing was a need to find an architectural language that would be appropriate to India. Kahn's thinking on this subject was informed to a large degree by Doshi. As Kahn described the relationship at the time, "Mr. Doshi, wonderful architect of India, sees to the architectural interpretations in India when I am not there."[10] But Doshi also served as Kahn's introduction to Indian culture, architectural and otherwise. Among other sites, Doshi took Kahn to Sarkhej Roza, a summer retreat of the fifteenth-century Islamic rulers of Ahmedabad that included buildings blending Islamic and Hindu influences. Set around an excavated 17-acre pond, or "tank," the pavilions of Sarkhej are marked by deep galleries of columns that sheltered the rulers from the sun and made the most of the cooling movement of the breezes. The edges of the pond were lined with ghats, or stone steps, that provided access to the water for bathing and washing clothes. Another influential monument was the sixteenth-century Hindu "step-well" at Adalaj, a building with stairs leading down through ranks of columns to a below-ground reservoir. The segmented spaces, and the theatrical effect of the shadows moving as the sun changes position at Adalaj, could only have impressed on Kahn the potential for using the play of light as an element in his own design. Doshi also supplied Kahn with books on the history of Indian architecture. As a result of his visits and his reading, Kahn rapidly became familiar with the "citadel" form that distinguished so many Indian forts and temple complexes. Doshi was well aware of his new role as cultural mentor. "I was trying to explain what India is," he said.[11]

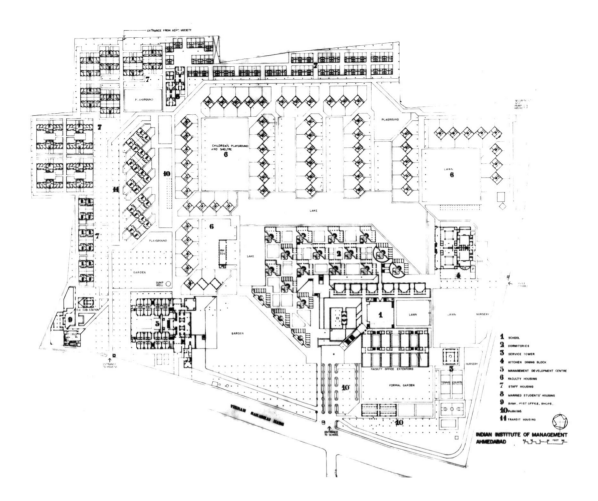

The following labels appear in the plan legend:

1 SCHOOL
2 DORMITORIES
3 SERVICE TOWER
4 KITCHEN DINING BLOCK
5 MANAGEMENT DEVELOPMENT CENTRE
6 FACULTY HOUSING
7 STAFF HOUSING
8 MARRIED STUDENTS' HOUSING
9 BANK, POST OFFICE, SHOPS.
10 PARKING
11 TRANSIT HOUSING

INDIAN INSTITUTE OF MANAGEMENT
AHMEDABAD

The Ahmedabad concept was based on the Harvard Business School and comprised classrooms, a library, and dormitories for the students as well as faculty offices and housing. Much like Salk, IIM was to be an ideal intellectual community that would improve society as a whole. © LOUIS I. KAHN COLLECTION, UNIVERSITY OF PENNSYLVANIA AND THE PENNSYLVANIA HISTORICAL AND MUSEUM COMMISSION

In its final form, the heart of the IIM complex was a U-shaped composition with a long courtyard at the center. At the closed end of the U was the library; a four-story wing of classrooms formed one arm, and faculty offices the other. Spreading out from the classrooms was a cluster of student dormitories and, beyond them, housing for faculty and staff. At the far end of the complex was a water tower, which served as a strong visual anchor for the lower buildings.

For all the geometric order of the overall scheme, Kahn also provided scores of gestures to the impromptu meetings that are so much a part of any successful campus. Walking the internal paths between buildings was not unlike a stroll through the complicated streets of an ancient city. "Schools," Kahn said many times, "began with a man under a tree, who did not know he was a teacher, discussing his realizations with a few others, who did not know they were students."[12] Kahn's subtle intertwining of pedestrian spaces compelled students and teachers to cross paths, and then provided eddies in which to pause, and low parapets that invited sitting and conversation.

Like Salk, the IIM design evoked Thomas Jefferson's "academical village" at the University of Virginia. Unlike UVA, however, the architecture was not meant to be directly instructive; there were no classical orders from which the students were expected to learn about the history of architecture. The language of IIM had been stripped to its essence, providing an environment for interaction without imposing on its nature.

A crucial participant in the development of the Ahmedabad commission was a young Indian architect named Anant Raje, who had met Kahn in Ahmedabad in 1962 and two years later went to work for him in Philadelphia as an "industrial trainee." As the Indian project grew in complexity, Raje took on a correspondingly larger role. After five years in the Philadelphia office, however, he announced to Kahn that he did not want to stay on in the United States. Even though Kahn then offered to recommend

The forms Kahn used at IIM encouraged speculation about Roman ruins as a source for the design. But he also immersed himself in traditional Indian architecture of the Mughal period, as well as the work done during the period of British rule, drawing on them no less freely and integrating all the elements into a unique whole. © LOUIS I. KAHN COLLECTION, UNIVERSITY OF PENNSYLVANIA AND THE PENNSYLVANIA HISTORICAL AND MUSEUM COMMISSION

Anant Raje, an Indian architect who had worked in Kahn's office, in Philadelphia, with a model of the Library building for the Indian Institute of Management. © THE UNIVERSITY ARCHIVES, UNIVERSITY OF PENNSYLVANIA

FAR RIGHT While Kahn had to adjust to the relatively crude construction methods of the Third World, he insisted on a high level of precision in the treatment of the masonry. He was not above instructing the bricklayers himself with tools he brought from Philadelphia. © LOUIS I. KAHN COLLECTION, UNIVERSITY OF PENNSYLVANIA AND THE PENNSYLVANIA HISTORICAL AND MUSEUM COMMISSION

him for a job that he knew of in Italy, Raje insisted that his "roots" were in India, and that he wanted to go home. Kahn's response was to give his assistant a big hug and invite him out for a drink.

Raje was rather surprised, and a bit wounded, that Kahn was so enthusiastic about his decision to leave Philadelphia. As it turned out, the architect was happy not merely for Raje's sake. Raje's return to India meant that Kahn would have a trusted associate who knew Kahn's way of working and could look after the execution of his design.

This was important for more than technical reasons. Not surprisingly, Kahn's long-distance relationship with Doshi had developed some strains. As Raje remembered the situation, Kahn felt that "Doshi had no depth in details" and did not communicate well enough with Kahn about some of his decisions.[13] The resolution was to have Raje set up a partnership with Doshi and take over the stewardship of the project. This relationship was also not without some tension, as Raje and Doshi were becoming professional rivals, and each had a strong feeling of personal kinship to Kahn. But the marriage of convenience was successful overall.

When Kahn himself was in Ahmedabad, he poured himself into IIM, sometimes working eighteen hours a day. On one visit, he decided to extend

Although built with primitive methods, the institute provided Kahn with a new scale of operations. It allowed him to experiment with abstract forms for their own sake, but also provide outdoor public spaces that were protected from the intense sun. © LOUIS I. KAHN COLLECTION, UNIVERSITY OF PENNSYLVANIA AND THE PENNSYLVANIA HISTORICAL AND MUSEUM COMMISSION

his stay an entire week just to teach the masons how to lay the bricks to his standards. Using a test arch erected for the purpose on the site, the architect himself took up the tools to demonstrate exactly how the work should be done. "Lou wanted the bricks laid as tight as possible," recalled Raje. "He always had stone in his mind."[14] To get the effect of horizontality that he wanted, Kahn insisted that the mortar be scribed along the horizontal joints, but not the vertical ones, and to help the laborers he supplied them with American-made trowels that had a thin ridge for creating just such an effect. The workers nevertheless had difficulty with the technique, and Kahn was not content until Raje found a way to snap a length of cord into the soft mortar, creating a reasonable facsimile of the indentation the architect wanted.

Raje's contributions extended well beyond such subtle solutions. When the main building was already well under way, the clients decided that it needed a more impressive entrance than Kahn had provided, and suggested that a ceremonial concrete canopy be erected in front of the main stair. With a fine appreciation both of the clients' wishes and his boss's romantic image of a school as a gathering under a tree, Raje came up with a deft proposal. There was an enormous mango tree growing almost exactly

Plans for an artificial pond were abandoned when IIM's director, who was religiously opposed to killing of any kind, objected to the prospect of spraying insecticide to eliminate mosquitoes. © LOUIS I. KAHN COLLECTION, UNIVERSITY OF PENNSYLVANIA AND THE PENNSYLVANIA HISTORICAL AND MUSEUM COMMISSION

FACING PAGE The clients had belatedly asked for a ceremonial concrete canopy to shade the main entrance to IIM, but Anant Raje, with Kahn's support, persuaded them that an existing mango tree would create the desired effect more naturally, even though foundations had already been poured and the library had to be realigned. © ROBERTO SCHEZEN/ESTO. ALL RIGHTS RESERVED

where the canopy might have gone, and Raje pointed out that its spreading branches produced the same sheltering effect, but in a natural way. The problem was that it was located slightly wide of the preferred location. Raje boldly suggested that the library—which was to go up to the left of the tree—be moved to accommodate it. Even though the library's foundations had already been poured, Kahn (and the clients) agreed that the rest of the building should be repositioned to gave the mango pride of place.

Helpful as Raje was, he could not break Kahn of what now seemed to be an almost pathological penchant for delay. Deadlines were repeatedly missed. Drawings did not get from Philadelphia to Ahmedabad when they had been promised. The situation got so bad that in the spring of 1969, the clients threatened to turn the entire job over to Doshi. Kahn promptly flew to India to salvage his commission. But, perhaps because of his growing involvement with the work in Pakistan, he was apparently losing his passion for the project. The refinement and execution of the campus fell increasingly to Raje, who set up a field office on the site.

There were disappointments. From the outset, Kahn had planned to provide an artificial lake between the faculty housing blocks and the student dormitories. The water element would have made a dramatic contribu-

tion to the composition, invoking the traditional "tanks" like the one at
Sarkhej while providing both a practical and a symbolic separation between
the senior and junior scholars. But persistent complaints from the clients
about how the water would create a breeding area for mosquitoes finally persuaded Kahn to abandon the idea. (Kahn had proposed that the area be
sprayed with insecticide, but the director of the school was a Jain, a member of a religious sect that opposed killing of any kind, and he refused.) A
plan to put a broad flight of steps at the head of the austere main courtyard
would have added a welcome gathering place for students, especially if the
planned fabric roof had been included. That, too, was canceled.

Nevertheless, the end result was impressive by any standard. The complex projects a restrained elegance, calling on the Beaux-Arts examples Kahn had studied at Penn as well as the majestic buildings of the Indian past. Yet the complex geometry and welcoming warmth of the brick create a humane counterpoint to the formal order that underlies the plan. The unembellished, open-ended main court (which Kahn had originally intended to close off with another building) lends itself to the pomp of commencement ceremonies, while the small scale of the faculty residences evokes the intimacy and unpredictability of the streets of Ahmedabad's old city. As would be the case with all of Kahn's work from

Filled with students, the IIM campus provided an inviting environment for academic interaction. With the students gone, it suggested the timelessness of the monuments Kahn had admired across Europe and the Middle East, as well as the ancient architecture of India to which Doshi had introduced him.

this point forward, the references were sensed but not literal, understood but not identified.

IIM provided a testing ground for architectural ideas that Kahn's work in America could not. In Ahmedabad, he began to experiment with the frankly theatrical geometry of oversized openings in his exterior walls. While they could be justified technically as a way to control the sunlight coming into his buildings, they also asserted a link to the elemental and timeless forms that had intrigued Kahn in Europe, but had been amplified by his exposure to the architectural history of the subcontinent. Indeed, as in the design for the Salk meeting house, some of the cutouts began to suggest human faces or tribal masks. The architect's deft inclusion of intimate public spaces among these abstract flourishes gave the buildings a unique flexibility, making them visually powerful when empty but vigorous and inviting when filled with people.

Not the least of Kahn's innovations in Ahmedabad were the concrete ties that he used repeatedly to support the shallow arches above openings in both the main buildings and the residential quarters. Like the exaggerated sun shades, these elements could be explained as functionally necessary. But just as he had with his surface treatment, Kahn used the technical justification as an opportunity for visual delight and structural explication. The expressed triangular "ears" at the ends of the ties were added to resolve the forces at the joint, "hooking" the bricks on both sides together, and adding an ornamental touch in the process. These small elements recalled Kahn's retention of the tetrahedral elements in the Yale Art Gallery slab as decoration even after their structural role had receded. And they were among the touches that gave the buildings a feeling that they had been designed with the users' visual pleasure in mind.

Although Doshi's relationship with the project had cooled somewhat, at least on Kahn's end, the Indian architect remained loyal to Kahn throughout. Doshi also continued to feel that the architect had achieved something at IIM that resonated with Indian architectural history. During one of Kahn's last visits to Ahmedabad, Doshi pointed out to him the resemblance of the buttressed walls of one portion of IIM to those at a ruined temple at Mandu, built in the fifteenth century. Doshi recalls that Kahn was "thunderstruck," but the similarity only added to Doshi's conviction that Kahn was working at some suprahistorical level of sensitivity.

The process in Ahmedabad, for all its delays, proved tidier than the one in Dhaka, which was proceeding almost simultaneously, but where pol-

Like Balkrishna Doshi at IIM, Muzharul Islam was an accomplished architect, but was eager to have Kahn as the lead designer for the Dhaka complex in order to advance his country's architectural standing at an international level. Islam was also a seasoned politician and became Kahn's protector as well as his mentor on local culture. COURTESY STANLEY TIGERMAN

itics would come to play an almost fatal role. From the beginning, the scope of the Dhaka commission had dwarfed that in India. This was to be a vast complex that included not only a center of government, but also housing for the legislators and their staffs, as well as a supreme court, a library, a school, a hospital, a meteorological station, and a center for the study of tropical diseases. And it had enormous symbolic importance to the Pakistanis, especially to those who would within a decade become Bangladeshis.

In the late seventeenth century, Dhaka had been ruled by the Mughals, and was one of the largest cities in the world. It declined dramatically in the following two hundred years, but following the British partition of India and the creation of a divided Pakistan in 1947, Dhaka became the governmental center of the eastern portion of the country. The military ruler of the country, General Ayub Khan, was no friend of democracy, but he was eager to retain the loyalty of his eastern constituency, and decided that in addition to the western administrative capital in Islamabad, there should be a "second capital" in Dhaka that would, according to the government's program, "bind East Pakistan more firmly to the nation by conducting the nation's business for half of each year."[15]

Ayub offered the job of designing the Dhaka complex to Muzharul Islam, a young but forceful individual who was the only formally trained architect in all of Pakistan at the time of independence. (Virtually all building design at the time was done by engineers.) After undergraduate studies in Calcutta, Islam had gone to the United States, where he earned a design degree at the University of Oregon, and went on to the Architectural Association in London for a diploma in tropical architecture. He then returned to the United States to attend the Yale School of Architecture, earning his master's degree in 1961. The head of the Yale program at the time was Paul Rudolph, but Kahn was still teaching there as a member of the visiting faculty, and Islam spent his single year in New Haven toiling on the top floor of Kahn's addition to the art gallery.

Well aware of the impact that Chandigarh had had on India, and eager that his own country should have a comparable monument to help establish its new status in the world, Islam told Ayub that they needed the assistance of an architect of international stature. Ayub reluctantly agreed, and Islam extended invitations to Le Corbusier, the Finnish master Alvar Aalto, and Kahn. Le Corbusier responded that he was too busy with other work (Chandigarh was not yet finished), and Aalto missed his flight to Pakistan. (The official explanation was that he was sick, but a story began to circulate that the famously bibulous Finn was recovering from an excess of consumption.) This left Kahn.

Islam's decision to engage another architect was not greeted with universal support. The time lost in negotiating with a foreign designer would be substantial, and once hired, Kahn would have to be paid roughly six times what Islam would have commanded as a Pakistani. Neverthless, Islam was so committed to having Kahn that he even turned down a suggestion by the government that they share responsibility for the job, something Kahn's colleagues thought he might well have accepted just in order to land such a plum assignment.[16]

Kahn made his first trip to Pakistan in late January of 1963, staying for six days. While there, he met with Islam, who, like Doshi, set about introducing Kahn to the local conditions. Traveling by jeep, boat, and occasionally by helicopter, they crisscrossed the country, Islam making sure that Kahn was immersed in the Bengali building and cultural traditions. Together, they toured the major architectural sites, including Dhaka's venerable Lalbagh Fort, a walled complex with a mausoleum at its core. Traveling or not, Islam and Kahn met almost daily for tea in Islam's leafy garden in the heart of Dhaka, where they would discuss culture, history, and the progress of the design.

Even without Islam's prompting, Kahn had observed on his flight into Dhaka the way the eastern part of the divided country was laced with waterways. Situated in the delta where the Ganges and the Brahmaputra rivers meet, East Pakistan was subjected to annual floods when the Himalayan snows melted, and sometimes these could be devastating to the flimsy structures that made up most of the region's architecture. For centuries, the local farmers had battled the problem by digging out portions of their land and creating mounds, or earthen plinths, on which to raise their houses above the floodwaters. (The residual excavations were preserved as fishponds.) Islam pointed out to Kahn that this system of isolating buildings was a part of the local building tradition and discussed with him the idea of treating the assembly complex in the same way, setting it on raised ground and surrounding it with water. Islam also emphasized the Mughal tradition of providing outdoor gathering spaces around forts and palaces, suggesting that the assembly complex should have space for the populace to congregate. In addition, Islam took Kahn through the turbulent streets of Dhaka's old city, where life spilled out into the right-of-way with colorful and cacophonous abandon. As in Ahmedabad, the urban hurly-burly could have reminded Kahn of his childhood, living on the stoops of the Northern Liberties.

Nevertheless, the contacts with Pakistani officialdom were not at first encouraging. In addition to the Dhaka complex, Ayub Khan wanted an architectural statement of his own in Islamabad and invited Kahn to design a presidential estate as well as an Assembly building for the western capital. The president and his advisers, eager to give the buildings an appropriately "Islamic" flavor, pushed for a design embellished with minarets and domes, which Kahn studiously ignored. "The insistence of the Islamic touch is plaguing," Kahn wrote.[17] Finally, the Islamabad offer was withdrawn. Some of Kahn's colleagues remember officials whispering at the time that Kahn simply couldn't understand what was needed, at least in part because he was Jewish.[18] The job was transferred in 1966 to Edward Durell Stone, known for his rather prissy surface decoration. Stone's Islamabad building had the requisite dome and pointed arches, but no power as a work of architecture.

The Dhaka commission was another matter, and there Kahn had a skilled protector. Muzharul Islam was not only a trained engineer and architect, but also a dedicated and wily politician. Indeed, he was a convinced Communist, and his office was filled with revolutionary tracts that included Maoist texts and manuals on wars of national liberation. A physically power-

The architect studying a site model of the Dhaka complex. More than any other commission, this one gave Kahn an opportunity to fulfill his earliest idealistic ambitions to change the world for the better. While at heart a government center, the original goal was to embrace facilities for education, health, housing, and research—the ideal human community he had always hoped to create.

ful man with a prominent brow and a fearsome temper, Islam shielded Kahn from the bureaucrats and insisted that the architect be left alone to develop the Dhaka design without the sort of interference he had suffered in Islamabad. Since this project was in East Pakistan, the scrutiny from the central government was understandably less intense. But Islam was not above exploiting Ayub's political agenda. A government architect who took part in the project commented that "the whole thing was politically motivated. The Ayub government must have communicated the message clearly to the architect to do everything at monumental scale, as an eyewash. The scale was conceived to impress the people of Eastern Pakistan that the big brothers of the West care and have great plans for them."[19] Whatever the degree of political maneuvering, the backers of the project were aided throughout by a cadre of skilled professional bureaucrats led by Kafiluddin Ahmad, a Pakistani engineer and veteran of the World War II Burma Road project, who helped keep the various participants in the Dhaka commission in line.

The site of what was to become known officially as Sher-e-Bangla Nagar, or "City of the Bengal Tiger," was an expanse of farmland near a military airport, presenting no obstacles to construction. Although Kahn was assigned at first only 200 acres, he was eventually able to persuade the government to increase the allocation to nearly five times that size. Drawing on all he had absorbed from Islam (as well as from Doshi) and his own research into Mughal and other indigenous examples, Kahn concentrated on the concept of "citadels" as his organizing principle, this time making it explicit.

One portion of the site would be devoted to the Citadel of Assembly, comprising the main governmental structure and located on the original 200-acre site. The Citadel of Institutions would rise on land beyond the Assembly and be made up of a school of arts, a school of sciences, and a sports complex. The "institutions" were never built, but they remained central to Kahn's ambitions for the project as an integrated urban complex.

At Ahmedabad, Kahn was employing perforated walls as sun screens, but in Dhaka they assumed a scale that evoked the fantastical images of the eighteenth-century Roman architect Giovanni Battista Piranesi, whose drawings Kahn knew and admired. Here, too, could be found echoes of Kahn's training in the Beaux-Arts tradition of grand municipal monuments. The Assembly building design was a basically symmetrical, diamond-shaped cluster of cubic and cylindrical forms rising ten stories. But here—

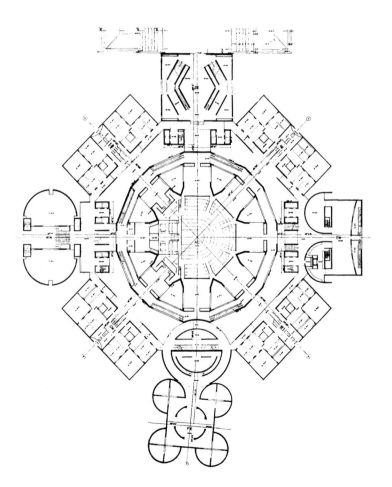

The final plan for the Assembly building was a massive enrichment of Kahn's many earlier institutional schemes that clustered supporting services around central cores, or sanctuaries. Kahn said that he had deliberately skewed the prayer hall, with its cylindrical towers, off the axis of the main building to align it more closely with Mecca.

again as in Ahmedabad—the architect leavened his enormous forms with intricate interior passages that recalled the turbulence of the urban street, whether in the Northern Liberties of the early part of the twentieth century or the much older but spiritually similar lanes and alleys of medieval communities in Europe and on the subcontinent itself. Flanking the main building was to be an enormous artificial lake, fulfilling the ambitions Kahn had entertained for IIM but in this case calling up the ancient Bengali traditions of building above the floods.

The original scheme went through numerous changes, many of which Kahn was able to explore with help from his students at Penn's architecture school, to whom he had assigned the Dhaka commission as a studio problem. But the fundamental idea of a great governmental building served by and integrated with a community of smaller residential structures survived all the iterations. Dhaka had become at once the reborn city plan for Philadelphia and a fulfillment of Kahn's longstanding ambitions for an ideal urban community.

Kahn's involvement in the project grew steadily more intense, and no doubt helped him overcome one of the major disappointments of his career: losing his bid to design the John F. Kennedy Library. President Kennedy had been assassinated on November 22, 1963, and his widow, Jacqueline, organized a much publicized search for an architect to design a memorial, which was originally to have risen near the Harvard University campus. Mrs. Kennedy interviewed six of the leading designers of the day: Mies van der Rohe, Paul Rudolph, Gordon Bunshaft, Philip Johnson, I. M. Pei, and Kahn. The visit of the president's widow to the Kahn office was something of a disaster. Kahn had failed to do much to tidy up the shabby quarters, which were entered past a drywall partition that was covered with notes and numbers scrawled in haste by members of the staff using the main office telephone. Those members of the staff who were present for the visit remember Kahn taking an eraser to the drywall, but to little avail. In any case, the office was still littered with juice cans overflowing with cigarette and cigar ashes.[20]

The job went to the relatively untried Pei, and a downcast Kahn had to content himself with a handwritten note from Mrs. Kennedy saying: "I know you could have done something so beautiful—and that you understood President Kennedy. Please understand how terribly hard it is. I'll always remember you and the help you gave."[21] Kahn concealed his disappoint-

August Komendant had planned to streamline the construction of the Assembly along American lines, but the local government officials wanted to employ as many unskilled workers as possible, so the engineer was replaced. © LOUIS I. KAHN COLLECTION, UNIVERSITY OF PENNSYLVANIA AND THE PENNSYLVANIA HISTORICAL AND MUSEUM COMMISSION

ment in a remarkably warm telegram to Pei, writing, "I know you have the love and the energy that it will take to do this work."[22]

Construction on the Dhaka buildings began on October 6, 1964. The engineer for the project was at first August Komendant, who had done so much to save the Richards laboratories and to make a success of the Salk commission. In early March of 1963, Kahn, Komendant, and Carles Vallhonrat flew to Dhaka to present their preliminary designs. The combination of talents worked well at first, but Kahn soon found Komendant's Teutonic efficiency—which had been so helpful at Richards and Salk—to be a disadvantage in Dhaka. Komendant wanted to organize and train a relatively small team to do the work, which would have been carried out in an on-site plant built for the purpose. As a colleague described Komendant's approach: "He was bragging that ten to 15 men could run the whole operation."[23] The clients, however, were eager to employ as many of their impoverished people as possible, declaring, "We want 500 men on this job, and every one laying a brick!"[24] Komendant was still heavily engaged on the Salk project, and the difference of opinion on how to run the Dhaka job gave him an excuse to withdraw, leaving the rest of the work to Keast & Hood, the Philadelphia firm that had first advised Kahn on the Yale Art Gallery ceiling slab.

The separation from Komendant was not a happy one. The engineer later claimed that "Kahn became arrogant and acted like an immature primadonna."[25] In his autobiography, Komendant recalled: "As far as I was concerned, our close association was finished. All the fame had raised Kahn to the status of 'celebrity' and he acted like one. So it was high time for him to have another engineer."[26] Keast & Hood's Nicholas Gianopulos, who took over the job, suggested that Komendant shared responsibility for the split. "Gus was charming, but he was steely and intolerant," Gianopulos recalled.[27] (The rift was not permanent. Kahn contacted Komendant in 1969 to discuss the design of the roof for the Assembly building, and although in his autobiography the engineer leaves the impression that he was the sole author of the solution, it was actually developed by Harry Palmbaum, the structural engineer who succeeded Keast & Hood in 1964.)[28]

With Islam's continuing protection, Kahn pressed forward, taking the need for a large but unskilled labor force in stride. The main building was centered on the Assembly chamber, which in addition to seats for the delegates also had galleries for the press and visitors. The first scheme for the chamber provided 300 seats for delegates, but Islam, always focused on the future of his region, persuaded Kahn to increase the seating to 500, in anticipation of a bigger role for the capital. Outside the chamber was a continuous hallway, or ambulatory, that gave in turn onto offices for the delegates and their staffs. A system of openings in the roof brought natural light into all the major interior spaces. Beyond the office ring was a thin shell of concrete pierced by enormous openings in basic geometrical shapes: triangles, rectangles, and circles. These not only admitted sunlight to the offices, but also created a powerful design motif for the building, one that could be seen from great distances.

The geometric cutouts were similar to the ones that Kahn was designing at the same time for Ahmedabad, but here their greater scale gave them a much more monumental effect. Asked whether his sources for the enormous forms might lie in ancient Rome or the abstract inventions of such eighteenth-century French architects as Étienne-Louis Boullée and Claude-Nicolas Ledoux, Kahn was heard to say, "I did it for the hell of it!"[29]

The main plaza, which faced the city, reflected Kahn's desire to provide a place consistent with the Bengali tradition of open public gatherings. It was here that construction began, largely because Kahn's team was under pressure to have something under way before Ayub Khan's first visit to the site. ("We had to get something in the ground," recalled a team member.)[30] Beneath the plaza, officially known as the Presidential Square, was a catacomb of low

spaces for parking cars. (The brick arches supporting the plaza were out of sight of the public and provided a welcome area for the local masons to raise their bricklaying skills up to Kahn's level of expectation.)

Fanning out at an angle on both sides of the main building, and separated from it by an artificial lake, were the so-called "hostels," two-story structures with roof terraces and deep porches that served as outdoor rooms (and places to dry laundry). The more spacious hostels were intended for the ministers and senior officials, while the smaller ones were for the assembly members who were expected to visit the complex from all parts of the country during Assembly sessions.

Kahn decided to make his main building of concrete, a material that would have to be imported and with which the local workers had limited experience. It was a risky decision, not least because the damp climate tended to coat exposed concrete with mold over time. The architect had seen enough concrete buildings in Dhaka to know this well, but he was apparently determined to make a monumental statement with his central building, and he felt that brick, even if treated in the "stone-like" fashion he was then using in Ahmedabad, was not up to the task. "I knew concrete would be a complete failure," Kahn said rather dismissively in an interview published in the Penn architecture journal. "But still my love for concrete couldn't be denied, so I tried to make these people make a purse, let's say, out of a sow's ear."[31]

Kahn assigned Gus Langford, the brother of the construction engineer who had overseen the Salk project, to train a workforce that eventually numbered some 2,000 laborers. Using bamboo scaffolding lashed together with lengths of crude jute rope, they formed human chains that operated continuously throughout the construction. The scaffolding, which eventually enveloped the structure, was so flexible that one kick would send a ripple around the entire building.[32] As Kahn described the scene when the walls began to rise: ". . . they have no machines. They just have a swarm of bees, people, and you don't see what the work has been during the day until they leave!"[33]

The conditions were primitive. The workers carried the concrete in metal pans balanced precariously on their heads, and the maximum amount they could pour on a given day raised the walls only about five feet. The joints between one pour and the next were all too evident, so Kahn nimbly chose to celebrate the imperfections by marking the gaps with thin strips of marble. The technique had the added advantage of camouflaging the slight variations in color from one pour to the next caused by the differing sources

Working by hand, the laborers could pour only a limited amount of concrete each day, leaving exposed recesses at the gaps. Kahn took advantage of the problem by inserting thin strips of white marble, which both concealed the flaws and created a pattern that broke up the monolithic impact of the exterior. COURTESY RAYMOND MEIER

of the concrete. (The material came from Korea, China, Poland, and the Philippines.) So pleased was Kahn with the effect that he extended the marble strips vertically, creating a frankly decorative grid that also served to break up what would otherwise have been an overwhelming mass.

Nicholas Gianopulos, the Keast & Hood structural engineer, went to Dhaka in 1963, but the job required still more local oversight, and Kahn was determined to exercise complete control of the project, so in January of 1964 a field office was set up to oversee the work. Kahn's team was represented first by Roy Vollmer from the Philadelphia office, and Gus Langford, the specialist on concrete. Another key member of the Dhaka team was Henry Wilcots, an Iowan who had been working in Karachi for an American firm when the Dhaka project began. Uncertain about the practical skills of their celebrity architect, the Pakistanis had called on Wilcots to review Kahn's early drawings. The two had met in Dhaka during Kahn's initial visit. The plainspoken Wilcots was amused by the way Kahn was addressed as "Professor," and kidded him about assuming academic airs. Kahn replied that, "In the office, everyone calls me 'Lou.' " With that, the two established a bond, and when Wilcots returned to Des Moines, he found a telegram from Kahn reading simply, "Come when ready. Lou." Wilcots immediately transferred to the Kahn office and would remain on the Dhaka team until the building was finished.

Kahn's own visits to Dhaka could be trying for all involved. Muhammed Rashid, a young architect in the Public Works Department, remembered sitting with Kahn in the waiting room of a ministry for what seemed like hours. Embarrassed that his government would treat a distinguished guest so cavalierly, Rashid began to complain. Kahn quietly told him not to worry. "Why are you so upset?" Kahn asked his young minder. "Haven't you read Kafka's *The Castle*?" The following day, Rashid located Kafka's classic novel about bureaucratic frustration and concluded that he had much to learn about patience from this American.[34] Rashid was also impressed by Kahn's willingness to make major changes with a speed that contrasted with his chronic delays in most areas. Once, while they were going over the plans for the hostels, Rashid realized that the orientation of one of Kahn's buildings would expose the occupants to direct sun during much of the day. Kahn left the office that afternoon and came back the next morning with an entirely new scheme. Rashid, who had spent the night fearing he might he fired for questioning "the Professor," was much relieved.[35]

But there were some points on which Kahn would not yield. Henry

FACING PAGE The primitive construction techniques and the shortage of skilled laborers did not deter the architect from pursuing abstraction at a monumental scale.
COURTESY HENRY WILCOTS

The "hostels" housing delegates, visitors, and staff were executed in brick, which set off the concrete of the Assembly, creating a hierarchy of materials and making the entire complex resemble a medieval European town with a castle or cathedral at its core.

Wilcots remembered Kahn's reaction to a proposal that steel reinforcing rods be inserted in some of the brick elements to protect them against earthquake damage. The local engineers protested that the area was not prone to earthquakes, but the Americans had researched the seismic history of Pakistan and insisted that there was indeed a danger. The Dhaka engineers relented, but Kahn rebelled against the idea of putting steel rods through brick. "It was foreign to his concept of masonry construction," Wilcots said.[36] Thomas Leidigh, an engineer in the Keast & Hood office, recalled that "we struggled to get things to work structurally."[37] Leidigh and Gianopulos joked at the time about how the architect would describe his drawings as "unsullied by information," meaning that they embodied artistic concepts without reference to how those concepts could be executed in reality.[38]

And there were the increasingly familiar delays. Abdul Wazid, an engineer with the Public Works Department, recalled: "I had to be often quite hard with Lou due to government pressure to continue the work with no delay. Kahn often made painstaking delays in completing drawings. I went to Kahn's office with a $50,000 check in my pocket and told him that it was his if he finished the drawings. After two weeks, the situation remained unchanged."[39] In 1968, a member of the Public Works Department complained that "the selection of Louis I. Kahn as the Architect has been the biggest mistake Pakistan has made since 1947."[40]

A lingering problem was how to design a place of worship to be included in a building for a nation that embraced several faiths. The solution was to design a meditation space acceptable to all the religious groups that would be using it. But since the dominant religion in the region was Islam, all involved thought that the space should be oriented toward Mecca. However, Kahn had already aligned the Assembly building on a north-south axis to take advantage of the prevailing breezes. The architect's solution was to rotate the prayer hall slightly off-axis toward the west. It was not until after the foundations had been poured that someone noted that the new orientation was well short of pointing toward Mecca. "Lou actually believed he had done the right thing," recalled Henry Wilcots, "but it was an error, and nobody pointed it out to him."[41]

The adjustment of the axis of the prayer hall is hardly noticeable to the uninformed visitor. What is immediately apparent is how the main building relates to the hostels on either side, and to the plazas at front and back. Although some photographs can make the Assembly building appear to stand alone, they fail to include the rest of the architectural context. The main building is in fact inseparably related visually and functionally to the structures around it, much like the buildings of a medieval European city clustering around its cathedral. The hierarchy of the relationship is clarified not just by the difference in size of the different buildings, but also by the contrast between the gray concrete of the Assembly and the deep red brick of the hostels.

Back in Philadelphia, the pace of work on the design was unrelenting. Reyhan Tansal Larimer, a Turkish-born architect who had begun as a summer intern in the Kahn office before winning a full-time position, was young enough to find the punishing schedule exciting. "This was not just doing toilet details," she recalled. "The nature of the work was so absorbing that you never thought about quitting time. Time in the office was unending. You didn't notice if the sun was going up or coming down. There was no drop-dead date. There was a lot of burnout among the older employees; they never saw their children."[42] One durable member of the office was David Wisdom, who served as the closest Kahn had to an office manager. A Quaker, Wisdom had been with the architect for years and was the one person who could persuade Kahn to lay down his pencil and leave for a meeting. "David tried to keep things on track," said Larimer.[43]

As the plans went forward in Philadelphia, political conditions in Dhaka grew tense. East Pakistan had always seen itself as culturally separate from the western part of the country. The Bengalis shared a common language that was written in a script different from that used in West Pakistan, and they considered themselves artistically superior to their western counterparts. (Rabindranath Tagore, the author and philosopher, was a Bengali.) They also had a slightly larger population, and therefore considered themselves underrepresented in the divided nation. On March 26, 1971, a war of independence broke out, pitting the East Pakistanis against their countrymen in the west, who were supported by the United States. The Kahn field office was promptly closed, leaving the unfinished buildings exposed to the very real possibility that they would be destroyed. Nevertheless, Kahn and his team never stopped working on the design.

During the nine-month war, during which East Pakistan was allied with India, the Assembly building was used variously as an ammunition depot and as quarters for the Indian troops. A story persists that it was not bombed by the Pakistani air force only because their pilots thought it looked

Even though much of the original Dhaka plan was not completed, the parts that were built went far to satisfy Kahn's longstanding ambition for a citadel that would serve as a symbol of the ideal human community. While the main building and the supporting structures were separated physically, they formed an integrated composition of form, materials, and use. CARTER WISEMAN

The Assembly was flanked by large plazas and gardens for official and public gatherings. Complaints that the complex was insufficiently Islamic in style were met by surprise by the local population, which quickly embraced it as a national symbol. COURTESY RAYMOND MEIER

as if it had already been reduced to ruins. (One warplane did crash on the main plaza within yards of the building's walls.) Whether that tale is true or not, the war produced untold brutality, culminating in the roundup and murder of hundreds of Bangladeshi intellectuals by the Pakistani forces only three days before they retreated. As the most distinguished architect in Dhaka, as well as a leader of the independence movement, Muzharul Islam himself was forced to go into hiding to avoid execution.

When the war ended, the Kahn buildings had not only survived, but had been suddenly elevated from the status of a "second capital" to one of the primary seat of government. Muzharul Islam, who had become treasurer of the victorious separatist party, insisted to the new administration that Kahn be brought back and that work on the capital continue. Islam was so powerful that by this time he would deliberately make government ministers wait for long periods outside his office, so he got his way. In August of 1972, contact between Dhaka and Philadelphia resumed, and the following January, Kahn returned to the city with a new master plan requested by the government of a new nation. Those plans included a greatly expanded secretariat, which Kahn immediately began to design. The additional structures were never built, and those already under construction were finished after Kahn's death by David Wisdom, along with Reyhan Tansal Larimer and Henry Wilcots, who continued to serve as project architect through 1983, when work on the capital complex was considered substantially complete.

The symbolic impact of the building was immediately clear. In the midst of one of many subsequent government crises, a referendum was held on continuing with a parliamentary system of government based on the British model, or switching to a presidential system led by a powerful executive. The ballot was printed with a NO to be checked if people opposed parliamentary rule, but there was no corresponding space for supporters to mark YES. Where that space should have been was an image of the Assembly building itself. "It was waiting there like our conscience," said an architect who was present at the time.[44] Added a colleague: "Democracy would not have survived without that building."[45] It is a tribute to the role the building occupies in the Bangladeshi consciousness that Kahn's citadel now appears on the currency in the same way the White House appears on American money.

When the building was first nominated for the Aga Khan Award—the premier honor for architecture in the Muslim world—Nurur Rahman Khan, an energetic young architect and scholar in Dhaka, and his colleague

Khondokar Shabbir Ahmed were asked to canvass a sampling of the populace for their opinions about Kahn's work. Feeling from their earlier contacts with the jury that the members were prejudiced against the building—again perhaps because its architect was not sufficiently sensitive to the Islamic traditions the award was meant to advance—Khan and Ahmed were pessimistic about the outcome. They discovered, to their delight, that the building was universally beloved, the high cost not withstanding. As more than one Dhaka resident told Khan, "We may be poor, but that is no excuse to have a cheap building."[46] The sentiment was confirmed by Muzharul Islam, who concluded: "Basically the fuss over the expenditure is entirely meaningless. Some projects because of their importance in national life can afford to be slightly extravagant. . . . We wanted a building all can be proud of, and we think we got that at quite a modest price."[47]

Not everyone was so pleased with the result. August Komendant concluded as early as 1973 that "the parliament building, first so perfectly conceived, fails in design. The arrangement of elements is accidental and they do not relate to each other in form or function. . . . Maybe artists and critics will consider it great art and architecture. I don't, because these types of buildings do not talk to me or stand the test of reason."[48]

Komendant's blanket condemnation of the Assembly would seem to reflect some resentment over having been separated from its construction. Nevertheless, the building is not without its serious flaws. The acoustics in the Assembly chamber have never been right; the sounds of the speakers' voices reverberate jarringly off the concrete walls. The original teak window frames leaked and finally rotted, and had to be replaced with aluminum substitutes. David Wisdom and Henry Wilcots answered the concerns about rain penetrating the building by adding solid glass blocks that kept the weather out while admitting maximum natural light. In addition, the exterior concrete soon had to be cleaned of surface mold before every meeting of the delegates. Ironically, Kahn had explained to his colleagues during construction that he selected concrete as the "stronger" material more suited to the Assembly, while cladding the lesser structures in the "weaker" brick. Decades later, the brick has proved more durable and looks less weathered than the "stronger" concrete of the main building.

Some critics have accused Kahn of overreaching in his buildings on the subcontinent. The historian Lawrence Vale, in his book *Architecture, Power, and National Identity*, cited what he saw as Kahn's "near-obsession

Although thoroughly orderly in plan, the Assembly on the interior was a three-dimensional maze of interlocking spaces that obliged the members of the parliament to interact with each other, their staff, and the public as if they were traveling the streets of a densely populated indoor city.
COURTESY RAYMOND MEIER

with the interconnectedness of architectural beginnings and architectural ruin. . . . Kahn's vocabulary of Forms seems very limited; what the building 'wants to be' always seems somehow to fit with recognizable elements of Kahn's other buildings."[49] He went on to criticize Kahn for "taking poetic refuge in an idealized view of the primal origins of democracy," and said that "Kahn did little to adapt to the contingencies of a rapidly changing and decidedly undemocratic place."[50]

Such criticisms may have some merit, but they tell only a relatively small part of the story. The work in Dhaka, like that in Ahmedabad, consumed Kahn. But it also extended him as an architect. Always searching for fundamental and timeless values, he seems to have felt especially welcome on the subcontinent. As Doshi analyzed it, "For those, like Lou, who came from another culture, the preference could be for black and white rather than greys, because the distinction between the two extremes is very clear. But to us, the greys matter because without the greys, the extremes do not exist."[51] Doshi went so far as to suggest that Kahn had been an Indian in an earlier incarnation.

That seems more than a little extreme, but Kahn certainly felt a kinship in India and Bangladesh. Kahn's closest collaborators there—Doshi, Raje, and Islam—agreed that Kahn's willingness, indeed eagerness, to forgo overt signs of "auteurship" in his buildings was best understood in the context of a society in which the abandonment of self is respected, and egotism is shunned. "We respect people who renounce, who do not show any ownership," explained Doshi.[52]

Raje recalled that when Kahn had scheduled a trip to Ahmedabad, he would say, "Now I am going to India, where I am understood."[53] Perhaps partly for this reason, his way of speaking began to change more noticeably after he began work abroad, shifting gradually to the aphoristic utterances that seem odd to a Western ear, but are common in subcontinental conversation. Kahn's colleagues in India and Bangladesh even seemed to put his romantic complexities in a different context. In a land where marital infidelity is rare and is severely punished, Doshi, who was fully aware of Kahn's affairs with Anne Tyng and Harriet Pattison, chose not to judge his friend harshly. "Lou was sharing different parts of himself with his different women," Doshi said. "Each was suitable to each."[54]

Whatever the merits of such analysis, Kahn clearly absorbed an enormous amount from his work on the subcontinent. If he had been intrigued by the ruins of Rome as formal devices, he was now steeped in a new understand-

ing of imagery, meaning, and even spirituality. India and Bangladesh exposed him to a different attitude toward life itself, one to which he had always been temperamentally inclined but which often seemed alien in his own country.

Kahn himself might not have said it, but if Chandigarh brought the Modern to the subcontinent, IIM and Dhaka brought something timeless. As the Aga Khan Award citation said of the architect's work in Dhaka: "Clear in form and composition, powerful in scale and siting, this building is widely considered a masterpiece. The architect drew upon and assimilated both the vernacular and monumental archetypes of the region, and abstracted and transformed, to a degree of utter purity, lasting architectural ideas from many eras and civilizations."

Although Kahn did not live to see his buildings in Dhaka and Ahmedabad finished, the construction was largely complete by the time he died. Nevertheless, even in the final stages of construction, Kahn went into the Assembly building only once, in 1973, with the Bangladeshi minister of planning. Reyhan Tansal Larimer suggested a reason for his reticence before that. "Lou dreaded to see the finished building for fear it would not match his vision," she said. "He was afraid that it wouldn't be good enough. For him, the design process never ended."[55]

That process was to move forward from the subcontinent, but what Kahn had learned there would infuse his subsequent designs with an aesthetic power and depth that might otherwise never have emerged.

CHAPTER SEVEN

A "TEMPLE FOR LEARNING"

THE PHILLIPS EXETER ACADEMY LIBRARY
1965–72

Having studied under Kahn at the University of Pennsylvania, and having worked for him for ten years, David Rinehart was an architect who knew him better than many of his other employees. More than thirty years after Kahn's death, Rinehart reflected that "for Lou, every building was a temple. Salk was a temple for science. Dhaka was a temple for government. Exeter was a temple for learning."[1]

The commission for the Phillips Exeter Academy Library, in Exeter, New Hampshire, might have seemed to be a relatively minor opportunity after the Salk Institute and the commissions in South Asia. Exeter was, after all, merely a boys' boarding school in the granitic recesses of New England. Its mission was not to cure a medical scourge, influence the business affairs of the world's second-most-populous nation, or establish a governmental focus for an emerging democracy. For Kahn, at this point in his career, the scale of Exeter was surprisingly small, and its culture was perhaps even more foreign to him than those of Ahmedabad and Dhaka. But his embrace of this boutique assignment was to produce one of his most complex and successful buildings.

The Phillips Exeter Academy, founded in 1781, was by the 1960s considered to be one of the leading secondary schools in the country. In 1957, Exeter had 763 students in four classes numbering roughly 200 each. Of the seniors, 80 went on to Harvard, 37 to Yale, and 26 to Princeton. Unlike many other such schools, which catered primarily to the sons of the socially and financially prominent, Exeter had a strongly egalitarian tradition. Its founder, John Phillips, was described as "a strict Calvinist" with "a strong aversion to every thing that had the appearance of splendor, pomp, and parade . . . always preferring the useful to the showy."[2] In his deed of gift establishing the Academy, Phillips laid out its purpose to be, "instructing youth, not only in the English and Latin grammar, writing, arithmetic, and those sciences wherein they are commonly taught, but more especially to learn them the great end and real business of living."[3] Phillips further insisted that in the "appointment of any instructor, regards shall be had to qualifications only, without preference of friend or kindred, place of birth, education or residence."[4] Exeter was to be about the essentials of intellect and character. Over the door of the main building was a Latin inscription, *Huc venite pueri ut viri sitis*—Come hither, boys, that ye may become men. The school's motto was, *Finis origine pendet*—The end depends on the beginning.

That sentiment was uncannily close to Kahn's frequent assertion that "what will be has always been." But whether or not Kahn ever dug deeply into Exeter's founding ideology, he needed only to glance around the campus to absorb the same message of intense educational intent. The Academy's rambling assortment of buildings lay at the edge of a typical old New England mill town. Although prim white clapboard houses dotted the grounds, many of the buildings were of red brick, having been designed by Ralph Adams Cram in the first three decades of the century, most in what Cram described as the "Colonial" style. They included the Davis Library, which was modeled on an English manor house and was completed in 1912. Cram, although a high-church Anglican who might have been considered "showy," even vulgar, by John Phillips, was nonetheless dedicated to the idea that academic architecture should express enduring moral values to match those of the curriculum. As he declared in his autobiography, "Education, in its real sense, has not changed in its impulse and its principles—and only in detail in its methods—since the Schools of Athens and Alexandria."[5]

In 1947, the Academy appointed William Gurdon Saltonstall to be its ninth "principal instructor," as the head of the school is known. Tall, lean, and craggy, with bushy white eyebrows and a paternal demeanor, this Exeter alumnus was the very model of a New England prep school headmaster, but he was no mere figurehead devoted to tradition for its own sake. He was an educator who was aware that he had not only to protect his school's reputation, but also to advance it, to help Exeter expand its role as a national school "in which each boy comes to know sons of liberals and conservatives, teachers and lawyers, farmers and bankers, doctors and union laborers, all up and down the land and from many foreign lands as well."[6] Exeter was a school at which Louis Kahn would probably have flourished as a student.

Three years into his job, Saltonstall hired a young Navy veteran named Rodney Armstrong to be the Academy's librarian, telling him that he should expect to oversee the construction of a new building. Although only a member of the faculty, Armstrong would become for all practical purposes Kahn's client on the library commission, communicating with the architect on the progress of the design and serving as liaison between Kahn's office and the school.

Rodney Armstrong, the Phillips Exeter Academy's librarian, took part in the selection of Kahn as the architect, and then went on to shepherd the design and construction of the building through what were becoming disturbingly familiar delays. BRADFORD F. HERZOG, PHILLIPS EXETER ACADEMY

A slightly gnomish native of Atlanta, Armstrong presented an almost Dickensian image of a librarian: bald, bespectacled, with wide-ranging knowledge and a naughty sense of humor expressed with a silky trace of a drawl. He had been wounded in a kamikaze attack on his aircraft carrier during the World War II battle of Leyte Gulf, a history that seemed totally inconsistent with his tweedy persona. But his sports jackets concealed a steely ability to see his wishes fulfilled, even if that involved some artful dodging and the occasional pounding of fists on the principal's desk. In the tradition of Jonas Salk, Balkrishna Doshi, and Muzharul Islam, Armstrong would become not only Kahn's client, but also his advocate and protector.

Arriving at Exeter in 1950, Armstrong took charge of the Davis Library and ran it contentedly for ten years until the school began to outgrow the building, largely as a result of his own efforts. (He tripled the book-buying budget and increased the collection from 35,000 volumes to 50,000.) Although Armstrong was eager to have a larger library, he was not choosy about its architecture. "I would have been happy in a Delano and Aldrich building," he recalled years later, referring to the socially prominent New York firm that catered to the well heeled, including the Astors, the Rockefellers, and the Whitneys.[7]

A Delano and Aldrich library would have made no waves on the Exeter campus, but a new dormitory suddenly did. It was McConnell Hall, opened in October 1963, a deliberately bland structure intended to avoid the controversy that had greeted what many considered the "far-out contemporary design" of a recently constructed music building.[8] But to many Exonians, McConnell evoked nothing so much as a suburban ranch house. Armstrong described it as "a Howard Johnson motel that had lost its way."[9]

By this time, Saltonstall had left the Academy to take charge of the Peace Corps operations in Nigeria, and had been succeeded as principal by Richard W. Day, a World War II paratroop officer who represented a substantial change from his courtly predecessor. Armstrong described Day as "impatient, ambitious, courageous and, sometimes, ruthless. No intellectual." Nevertheless, Day had enough taste to be no less appalled than Armstrong by McConnell Hall, and for that alone would win Armstrong's praise as the "unsung hero" of the library saga.[10] Day was determined to right the McConnell wrong, and when he was presented with plans for a new library that had already been drafted by the New York firm of O'Connor & Kilham, he was not satisfied. Matters were made worse when Day learned that the athletic department was having the school's old gymnasium renovated by the same firm. He took Armstrong aside in front of the offending dormitory and declared: "This is not good enough for *my* school! I'm going back to my office, and I'm going to fire these people and appoint you to head a committee to find the very best contemporary architect in the world to design our library!"[11] The Academy's treasurer, James Griswold, reluctantly but diplomatically wrote to O'Connor & Kilham: "Ever since the completion of McConnell Hall, I think there has been a feeling among the Trustees that the Academy should have an architectural consultant to help with the esthetic blending of the new buildings to be added to the present structures of the Academy." Griswold then got to the point: "I therefore need to request that you slow down or stop the work you are now doing on the present Library plans."[12]

There was more than architectural quality involved in Day's decision. An enormous concrete gymnasium, designed by the Boston firm of Kallman, McKinnell & Knowles (architects of the new Boston City Hall), was already under way, and Day was worried that students' parents might wonder why athletics was getting so much attention when books might not. The new library, as Day saw it, was to be the "center of the school."[13]

While Armstrong was officially head of the search committee, he was aided greatly by Elliot Gould Fish, a flamboyant teacher of French and the fine arts who was well versed in architecture. The entire search process annoyed the impatient Fish, who was known as an enthusiastic teacher but a "terror to the lazy"[14] who could "put a boy in the infirmary if he showed any sign of weakness."[15] Fish had learned about Kahn through a former student, Sidney Guberman, and took the recommendation seriously enough to visit the architect's office in Philadelphia. The visit persuaded Fish. "It was love at first sight," remembered Guberman. "They stayed up all night playing, 'Can you top this?' and nattering on, in and out of Eastern mysticism and God knows what else, Lou downing *aqua vit* and Eli gin."[16] At the first meeting of the selection committee, Fish declared to his colleagues, "I don't know why we are going through this. The best person is Lou Kahn." The response by all of his fellow committee members was, "Lou *who*?"[17]

Nevertheless, Armstrong and Fish were soon being urged to consider the work of several other architects suggested by influential members of the board of trustees, and dutifully traveled as far as Georgia, Iowa, and California to do so. It was a trying experience. At one truck stop, Fish, sweltering in his Brooks Brothers seersucker suit, ordered iced coffee, and was presented with a pot of dark liquid with several ice cubes rapidly melting on the surface. The obligatory visits over, the committee members turned to a list of more prominent practitioners. One was Edward Durell Stone, Kahn's successor as the architect of the president's house in Islamabad. ("His name never got out of my office," said Armstrong.) Then there was Paul Rudolph, who said to the chairman, "You know, Mr. Armstrong, I do not work well with committees." In a memo to Richard Day, Elliot Fish conceded that Edward Larrabee Barnes was "civilized," but "could be reduced to something quite as amorphous as our new mistake, McConnell, were he compelled to justify his every innovation before our stern trustees."[18] I. M. Pei was likely to produce "stunningly new concepts" that "would be both beautiful and habitable and culturally stimulating for generations to come,"[19] but committee members worried about the large size of his office and his reputation for spending his clients' money too freely.

The most entertaining exchange with a candidate took place with Philip Johnson, whom the committee visited in his New York office in the Seagram Building, the Modernist monument by Mies van der Rohe on which Johnson had collaborated and designed the ground-floor restaurant.

Armstrong recalled an elegant reception served by a cadre of strikingly beautiful secretaries. He also remembered that Johnson was so eager for the job that he "had his tongue hanging out." In the course of the conversation, Johnson asked Armstrong which other architects were being considered. When the architect heard the list, he replied, "Ah, all the greats—and me!" Put off by the haughty tone, if not the secretaries, Armstrong was further convinced he had the wrong man when one of Johnson's young employees tugged at Armstrong's sleeve during the tour of the drafting room and whispered, "Don't hire him. It will be awful!"[20] Fish agreed, concluding that "PCJ does a beautiful box, a reliquary, if you will, but one has the feeling of being forced into a tight boot."[21]

Writing to the principal, Fish explained that, while the other contenders all had their virtues, Kahn was "my current enthusiasm." In describing him, Fish continued, "There is some strange analogy which I simply can not work out here with Homer's Polyphemus, the One-Eyed Giant, tender, even gullible and yet fierce."[22]

To confirm the decision, Fish and his fellow committee members set off for Philadelphia. The corporate slickness of Johnson's office was nothing like the shabbiness of Kahn's Walnut Street quarters, but for the Exeter delegation, that was actually an advantage. Always wary of conspicuous display, the educators were immediately attracted to the atmosphere of hard work. "Obviously, this was a place with people who worshipped the man they were working for," said Armstrong.[23]

If they needed further convincing, they got it from a well-informed source. Peter Salk, Jonas Salk's eldest son, was a member of the Exeter class of 1961, and had been Armstrong's dormitory advisee for three years. When his father learned that Exeter was looking for an architect, he called Armstrong and said, "I hear you are thinking about a new library. Come out here right away!"[24] Armstrong spent two days in La Jolla, and what he saw left no doubt about the selection. In his official recommendation to Day, Armstrong declared that Kahn "is the architect most certain to create for the Phillips Exeter Academy a great building in terms of art and architecture," noting "the extraordinary fact that each of the other architects interviewed voluntarily acknowledged that Louis I. Kahn is a great architect."[25]

Nevertheless, Armstrong and the committee were "gloomy" about their chances of approval of Kahn from the school's trustees.[26] To their delight, the architectural consultant to the board, Nelson Aldrich, an architect who might have liked to have the commission himself, enthusiastically endorsed Kahn. The commission was awarded in November of 1965. Kahn made his first visit to the campus the following January 27 and 28.

All involved knew that the selection of Kahn was a risky move. He was becoming notorious for his delays, and the problems with the Richards labs in Philadelphia were a further source of concern. "Kahn's cerebral approach to the design process was unlikely to produce the library out of the magic hat pronto," observed Armstrong.[27] Looking back, an Exeter alumnus involved in renovating the building in the 1990s said, "When an institution hires a creative architect like Kahn, it is investing in a prototype."[28]

The program was developed over a period of six months by Armstrong, Fish, and a member of the history faculty, Albert Ganley, and went through more than fifty drafts. The final document read, in part: "The quality of a library, by inspiring a superior faculty and attracting superior students, determines the effectiveness of a school. No longer a mere depository of books and periodicals, the modern library becomes a laboratory for research and experimentation, a quiet retreat for study, reading and reflection, the intellectual center of the community. . . . Fulfilling needs of a school expected eventually to number one thousand students, unpretentious, though in a handsome, inviting contemporary style, such a library would affirm the regard at the Academy for the work of the mind and the hands of man."[29]

The sentiment—even the phraseology—could not have been more Kahnian. This was to be no mere warehouse for assigned readings, it was to be an institution at the spiritual level of Salk, a place for the advancement of knowledge and the intellectual focus of the school. However, while he had engaged related issues at Salk, and was including a library at IIM, Kahn had never done a freestanding building of this kind. Undeterred, he immersed himself in the concept, going, as he had so often, to the sources. Ironically, Kahn was not a reader himself, and although he often bought books, he was candid about never reading more than a few pages in any of them. The pictures, normally of buildings, held his interest more. But he had a deep respect for books and what they stood for. He considered a book to be "an offering," and the places where they were stored almost sacred. In reverential terms, Kahn said, "How precious a book is in light of the offering, in the light of the one who has the privilege of this offering. The library tells you of this offering."[30] Kahn's deeply personal appreciation for the idea of the book drove the design of the library at the deepest level.

No less important than the idea of the book was the idea of the monastic community, which had made such a contribution to the Salk design, as well as those for IIM and Dhaka. (Kahn was also working on two related but unrealized designs, St. Andrew's Priory in California, and the Dominican Sisters' Convent in Pennsylvania.) But if Salk was about investigation, IIM about the conveying of knowledge, and Dhaka the implementing of knowledge through government, Exeter was to be about contemplation. The fact that the scholars were teenagers, not monks or aged sages, made little difference. This was to be a place where respect for learning was to be instilled through built form.

As Armstrong recalled it, the early design for the library showed "a handsome building with a central section and two flanking towers, quite Palladian in spirit."[31] But even the librarian found the scheme too big for its site. Nevertheless, he and his fellow committee members felt that Kahn had captured the spirit of the Academy's program and were confident that the architect would make the appropriate changes.

They were right, but the development of the design was slowed by Kahn's recurrent trips to India and Pakistan. When he was able to be in Exeter, Kahn often stayed with Elliot Fish and his family in their eighteenth-century house on Front Street, near the campus. Nina Fish, Elliot's wife at the time, remembered Kahn arriving in snowy midwinter on his way back from Ahmedabad wearing a lightweight blue suit and thin-soled shoes. "He didn't seem to notice that he was not dressed for our weather," she said. "When he was involved in the design process, he was oblivious to his surroundings, so we went around the house collecting old sweaters and bundling him up." During the stays, which usually ran to two or three days, Nina was especially struck by how easily Kahn related to her eight-year-old daughter, Maude, who was already interested in music. Kahn would play the Fishes' baby Steinway grand piano for Maude, encouraging her own efforts. "Lou was a great talker," Nina said, "and he would roll out sketches in front of the fireplace in our kitchen and explain how he was using them in his design for Dhaka. But I was most impressed by the way he could bring in a little girl and make her part of the group."[32]

While the trips to the subcontinent may have frustrated his New Hampshire clients, they had a positive dimension, allowing Kahn to refine at Exeter many of the design ideas he was working on abroad. Not the least of them were the oversize geometric shapes like the ones he was using for the exterior walls at IIM and the Assembly building, and the brick detailing, which limited budgets were making so difficult in India and Pakistan.

The library program had called for brick as the primary material, and the type Kahn selected for Exeter came from the Eno brickyard on the outskirts of the town. For many years, Eno had supplied much of the brick used on the Harvard campus, and Kahn was attracted by its rough texture and rich dark color. However, the yard at the time was on the brink of bankruptcy. Kahn promptly traveled to New Hampshire and insisted that the Academy buy enough of Eno's bricks—some 2 million—in advance to complete the job. The bricks were duly bought, and hauled to the school's athletic fieldhouse in case the yard's assets might be seized. (Several local patios were soon paved with a suspiciously familiar material.) The brickyard indeed went out of business, but the key material in the library's construction had been secured.

Not surprisingly in a town dominated by two-story Colonial houses and modest commercial buildings, the proposed size of Exeter's new library sparked some concern from the citizenry. Fortunately, the school's treasurer at the time was married to a native of Exeter, which helped placate the protesters. But additional questions were raised by trustees worried about rising costs, especially of the extra labor involved in the brickwork, and various other aspects of the project. At one point, Armstrong felt that he had to apply some muscle. "I knew that if the school butchered the design, I would leave," he said. "I wasn't married at the time, so I knew I would survive. I wasn't going to go along with an inadequate building from a great architect."[33]

Armstrong's forceful defense of the project would be vindicated, but it took a toll on his schedule. The librarian found that he had to travel to Kahn's Philadelphia office roughly once a month, but the trips proved personally as well as professionally instructive for an academic of his background. "Kahn knew there was always another solution, that there was never one answer to anything," Armstrong recalled. "He was always calm. He would look at me and say, 'What don't you like, Rodney?' The response that 'We have to try again' never disturbed him. I never saw the ego of a great man, but I saw a great teacher."[34] Armstrong was also impressed by the architect's round-the-clock attention to the project; on one visit, he was surprised to learn that Kahn had slept on a small Oriental rug on the floor of his office the night before the Exeter delegation arrived.

The original proposal for the building included a roof garden and two open exterior towers containing stairs. These elements disappeared when

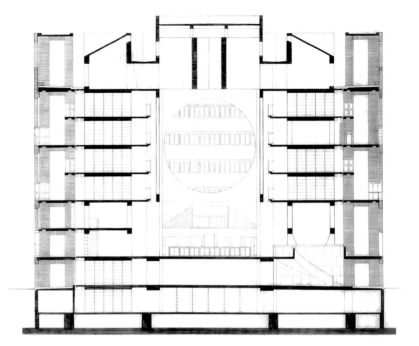

A section through the final design for the library shows the discrete zones Kahn created for circulation and the study carrels at the outside edge, the book stacks, and the atrium at the core.

the buildings and grounds committee reminded Kahn that winter temperatures could drop to 20 below zero in New Hampshire. More worrisome was the discovery of an underground spring running through the site and poorer-than-expected soil conditions. The solution was to "float" the building on a concrete pad and relocate the mechanical systems originally intended for a subbasement, while adding a floor to the top of the building.

A potentially disastrous development occurred in December of 1966, when the Town of Exeter passed a zoning law banning buildings over three stories in residential areas. Kahn reluctantly agreed to revisit his design and reduce it by one story, but he found he could not make the changes work, and finally wrote to Armstrong: "I will do anything necessary to convince the Buildings & Grounds committee that the only right way to build is to the height and proportions we so painstakingly worked out over so many months. . . . My fullest consideration has convinced me that my hopeful proposal of saving a story would have presented an intolerable condition that I must now firmly say I cannot accept. I must say that I have come to a stronger confirmation of my aesthetic judgement and I was misled by my willingness to make adjustments."[35] The town was persuaded to grant a variance.

Some other changes were made, however. Higher balustrades were added to the exposed roof promenade to satisfy the school's fears that students might be tempted to sit on the originals and fall (or jump) off.

The final design showed a brick cube measuring 111 feet on a side and rising to 85 feet with nine levels, including mezzanines. Echoing the Luanda consulate and the Salk meeting house projects, the library was a layered composition. Kahn had intended to use brick throughout the building, but to save money decided to use concrete on the interior. He described the building as a "brick doughnut" on the outside enclosing a zone for the book stacks, and a "concrete doughnut" at the center enclosing a large open space. Stairs, elevators, and toilets were located at the corners, but set in from the walls to allow circulation around the perimeter.

The library's exterior can be read in two ways—either as an enclosure of brick planes pierced by windows, or as a series of piers separated at each floor level by the windows and "jack arches," horizontal expanses of trapezoidal bricks laid vertically. The elemental simplicity of arches as an architectural form had always had a strong appeal for Kahn, and in this case he expanded on his oft-quoted remarks about "consulting" with his materials. "If you ask a brick what it wants to be, it would say 'an arch,'" he said. "Sometimes you ask concrete to help the brick, and brick is very happy. I could have souped up the brick with interior rods, but instead I allowed the brick to be brick and build the way brick wants to express itself."[36] That expression was amplified visually by allowing the exterior piers to grow narrower as the floors rose, a device that accentuated the building's height, but also symbolized the decreasing load they carried. "The weight of the brick makes it dance like a fairy above and groan below," the architect explained, with his characteristic appreciation of the trade-off between structural fact and fiction.[37]

For many critics of the library, the most obvious shortcoming of the design was the absence of an easily identifiable front door. Kahn had never liked the way conventional entrances dominated the composition of architectural façades, and from the Yale Gallery through the Trenton Bathhouse, to Richards and Salk, he had avoided the intrusion by banishing entrances to corners or recesses in the façades. At Exeter, Kahn totally concealed the main entrance by putting it behind the ground-floor arcade. To be sure, the original landscape plan included a paved forecourt that would have clearly announced the "front" of the building. But the only other clue to the entrance was a slight variation of the window treatment on the main façade,

Although at first glance a solid masonry cube, the library was revealed at its corners to be a far more complex, layered composition. The much-maligned dining hall lies behind the library to the right. ©

where four full-height windows interrupted the rhythm of openings on the other three facades, thus providing natural light for the staircase behind and a view of the campus from the staircase balcony. The architect explained his avoidance of an identifiable entrance rather weakly by saying that the arcade that circled the ground floor allowed a student to enter from any point. "If you are scurrying in a rain to get to a building, you can come in at any point and find your entrance," he insisted.[38] In fact, the reason was probably compositional. To make a traditional entry would have meant compromising the geometry of the cube.

If the omission of an obvious entrance preserved the geometry, the treatment of the corners relieved it. By chamfering—or cutting off—the corners, Kahn exposed the thinness of the exterior brick walls, making them appear like screens rather than massive bulwarks. In so doing, he was drawing on the "shells" that he had developed for the Salk meeting house, as well as those for IIM and Dhaka. Of course, in the New England climate there was no need for protection against sun glare, so here he used the device to lighten what might otherwise have been an intimidating bulk.

A further device to soften the impact of the building was the use of teak panels as part of the window composition. The panels recalled those at Salk, and had much the same effect, although at Exeter they complemented brick rather than concrete and made a correspondingly warmer combination.

Like many school and university libraries, which were anchored by central reading rooms, the Exeter design had a large open space—40 feet square—at the center. But Armstrong had insisted from the outset that the new building emphasize individual study spaces over a conventional reading room. Thus the void was not filled with the usual long tables lit by green-shaded reading lamps. Instead, it was left empty, forming a sort of "town square" at the heart of the academic activities going on around it.

Using a time-honored architectural technique, Kahn made the experience of entering this space a dramatic, almost theatrical, one. Having negotiated the ground-floor arcade and found the door, a student comes in under a low ceiling, then proceeds up a divided staircase (a gesture to the smaller one in the Davis Library), and suddenly encounters the atrium, a space that virtually explodes with spatial and tectonic excitement.

The many comparisons of the experience of entering Exeter's main space to that of entering a cathedral are not accidental. Kahn clearly wanted the students to be humbled by the sense of arrival, and he succeeded.

FACING PAGE At Exeter, Kahn transposed the large-scale geometry of Ahmedabad and Dhaka to the interior, creating a public space that allowed students to witness the activity of the entire building from almost any vantage point.
© GRANT MUDFORD

The librarian who followed Rodney Armstrong, Jacquelyn Thomas, insisted that the hormonally charged teenagers who used it tended to lower their voices and actually behave better once they were inside. (Nevertheless, Kahn had apparently paid no attention to the possibility that students might turn to mischief in the many areas of the building that could not be seen from the circulation desk. For instance, he did not foresee that students might enjoy tossing shredded newspapers from the upper floors late at night or trying to rappel on ropes from the balconies. A system of student proctors was soon established to police the areas out of sight of the librarians.)

One of the most striking aspects of the central space is the way the concrete enclosing it is treated. At each corner of the circular cutouts, the architect positioned rectangular columns on the diagonal. These supported the concrete members, but, as at Salk, the joints between the poured panels were deliberately recessed, creating a clearly legible diagram of how the pieces came together. This expression of the building's "joinery" was made so forcefully that any child who has ever used wooden blocks can instantly understand how the building stands up.

While such gestures appeared effortless, even simple, they involved complex interactions between Kahn and his engineers. Thomas Leidigh, the structural engineer who handled the commission for Keast & Hood, explained that some of Kahn's original ideas were difficult, if not impossible, to execute. So Leidigh and his colleagues would have to "get Lou to agree to what was buildable." The process could be frustrating, especially, said Leidigh, because "Lou didn't recognize that joints needed to be waterproofed." But the architect remained intimately involved in the process. "Lou *wanted* to understand the technical aspects of construction," insisted Leidigh. "He didn't want to build something that he didn't understand. He wanted what was there to work."[39]

Around the central void, Kahn wrapped a layer for the book stacks. But that layer was separated from the concrete by a circulation space. And by cutting enormous circles out of the concrete walls, he made the book stacks visible from almost every part of the building. At the edges of the balconies, he added inclined reading shelves, inviting students to spread books out, but also encouraging them to survey the activity going on in the stacks across from them, and in the "piazza" below.

The result was that students on all four sides of the atrium could see other students moving through the stacks across from them. One might

FACING PAGE The architect exaggerated the concrete members to illustrate how the building was put together and what held it up, but he softened the effect with wooden paneling and shelves that invited users to linger in intimate spaces. © GRANT MUDFORD

interpret this as a subtle incentive to the scholars to keep up with their academic competitors, but in any case it exploited the movement of people as a source of visual interest and entertainment. Kahn seemed to acknowledge the changeable balance between the academic and the social when he said, "I'm not sure the large reading room means very much any more because it is only a place where boy meets girl and nobody reads."[39]

In the space between the stacks and the outside walls, Kahn provided additional balconies at the mezzanine level overlooking spacious corridors, which were lit by windows facing out onto the campus. At each window was a study carrel made of white oak. The carrels had been specified in the program for the building, but Kahn designed them with shutters at desk height so students could shade their work from direct sun while still benefiting from the light coming through the upper portion of the window opening. Kahn often spoke of the ritual of "bringing the book to the light," and this was an especially graceful expression of the process. Again, as in the study towers at Salk, the *idea* of scholarship was given as much attention as the act.

Above the atrium hover two massive concrete beams, crossed in an X. While they appear to be—and indeed are—structural, they are far deeper than necessary; their no-less-important role was to diffuse the sunlight coming in from the surrounding clerestory windows and reflect it down into the atrium. The combination of expressed geometry, structural heft, and decorative effect harkened back as far as the work Kahn and Tyng had done on the ceiling slabs at the Yale gallery. (Even when the romance with Tyng had ended, the architect continued to acknowledge her influence. In a letter to Holmes Perkins dated June 21, 1968, Kahn urged the Penn dean to hire Tyng. Insisting that she was an architect of "utter genius" and "resourcefulness," Kahn told Perkins that it would "be a fine thing for the School of Architecture to have her serve as a teacher."[41] Perkins responded, "It's good news that her work is receiving its proper recognition."[42] Tyng was given a position on the Penn architecture faculty and went on to teach there for twenty-seven years.)

For all the evident power of the library design, Exeter's trustees were increasingly worried about the cost of building it. A recession had begun, and Richard Day had broken tradition by tapping the endowment to keep the project going; cost consultants were brought in to monitor progress. Armstrong had to employ all of his diplomatic skills to pacify the building's critics. Tensions rose to such a point that the librarian was also beginning

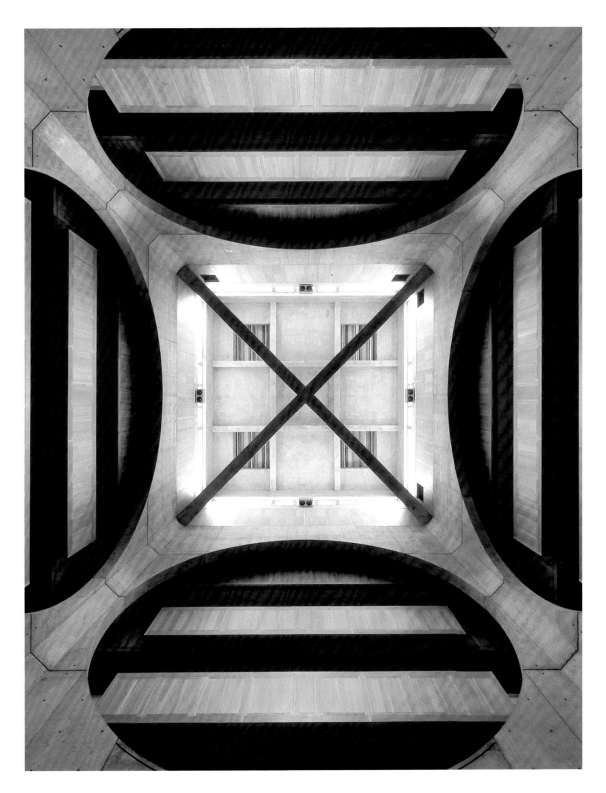

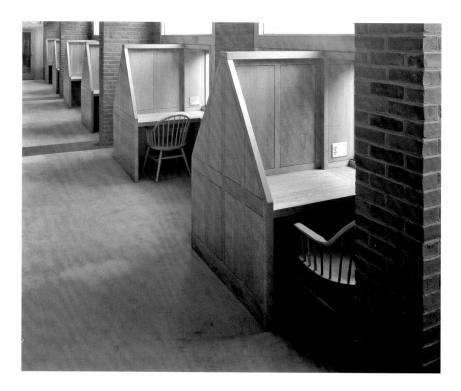

The individual study carrels were mandated by the program, but Kahn exploited them to reduce the monumental formality of the surrounding structure.
© GRANT MUDFORD

to worry about maintaining Kahn's trust in the school. In March of 1968, Armstrong wrote to Kahn: "Though I cannot report satisfaction among our Committee with the plans at this time, I can affirm our great respect, admiration, and affection for our architect and our belief that he will evolve changes in the building so that it will once again approach the ideal we have in mind for the school."[43]

Despite such gestures, the cutting continued. As with the stone for the plaza at Salk, the marble proposed for Exeter's main staircase was changed to travertine to save money. Winton Scott, the project architect, remembered a decision to widen the mortar joints on the exterior to save bricks. The furnishings budget was cut in half, and Armstrong recalled making an arrangement with a supplier of bargain sofas in Boston. On a trip to pick up the furniture, the librarian found himself hurrying into a building in a seedy section of town under the protection of a company strongman assigned to watch for trouble. "We were squeezing every penny we could," Armstrong said.[44]

Among the victims of the increasing economies was the landscape plan, which had included the paved forecourt. The cut was a special disappointment for Harriet Pattison, since she had worked on it in a fourth-floor room of the Kahn office behind locked doors so that Kahn's wife would not happen on her during an unscheduled visit. Armstrong wrote Kahn expressing his hope that the design would be built when more money was found. (It never was.)

Kahn absorbed the reductions with increasingly windy references to the original concept. In one interview he declared: "At no time could I have done this building if I hadn't had the absolute order dictation of the face around the periphery looking for a light, the interior space where the books were away from the light, and again the emergence of light in the center— placing books however in the section where there was no light so that they could be seen in borrowed light from the windows of the periphery."[45]

But the enthusiasm for the final result outweighed the unhappiness over the process. It also obscured the most curious aspect of Kahn's Exeter experience, the design of the dining hall that was built almost simultaneously adjacent to the larger building. In the summer of 1966, when the library project was in its early stages, the Academy realized that it also needed additional food service for its students, and that since the preferred site was next to the one for the library, Kahn should be asked to do it as well. Despite the "while-you're-up" nature of the second commission, Kahn accepted it, saying that he was "particularly interested in the architectural association of the Library with this building."[46]Perhaps he was thinking back to the dinnertime talks at the American Academy in Rome, or the original concept for the Salk meeting house, about which he had said, "I don't know of any greater seminar than the dining room."[47]

Kahn wrote to Richard Day in August of 1966 to express his interest in both Exeter projects, saying, "I appreciate the opportunity which both buildings, in wake of each other, give me to find the architectural order strong and resourceful to express each in its own use, yet architecturally in sympathy with each other."[48] The committee overseeing the dining hall was persuaded that without it, "the new library would stand awkwardly alone," and they were "delighted with the exterior of Mr. Kahn's new dining center."[49] The school was also pleased by the prospect of the savings projected by building both structures at the same time. Nevertheless, the dining hall clearly never occupied Kahn as much as the main building. The separation of the two projects was aggravated by the fact that the dining hall committee worked separately with the Kahn office in developing the design and never met with the library committee to coordinate their efforts. Rodney Armstrong was never even shown the plans for the dining hall.

The dining hall was distinguished by dramatic, overscaled gables, and chimneys that broke free of the building's walls. Both bear strong resemblances to elements of Robert Venturi's 1959 Beach House, and the house he designed for his mother. More than thirty years later, Kahn's former student was still certain about the influence. In a conversation with a former employee, he said, "There's no question it is Mother's-House-influenced (and then the chimney separate from the wall he got from me, too)."[50]

Whatever the origins of the dining hall's form, a key element in its design was that it was connected to the library by a tunnel, which allowed Kahn to consolidate the heating and cooling machinery that served both structures. The dining hall could thus 'feed' both the library and the students,"[51] a characterization that might be seen as completely consistent with the served and servant spaces that had become part of the Kahn liturgy.

Nevertheless, time has not been kind to the dining hall. Its acoustics were poor from the outset, and the arrangement of the serving facilities proved awkward. The building is rarely mentioned by Kahn scholars, who

Kahn and Harriet Pattison, who became the mother of his third child, Nathaniel. Harriet went on to become a landscape architect and worked in the Kahn office, but her landscape plans for the Exeter library were abandoned to save money.

seem to find it somewhat embarrassing and, accordingly, hard to accommodate among the architect's more substantial works. Most photographs of the library are carefully composed to eliminate the dining hall from the frame. But even if Kahn devoted less attention to this component of his work at Exeter, he clearly intended it as part of a larger composition, and in any case its role housing the utilities for both buildings freed the library design from the need to accommodate bulky chillers, heaters, and pumping systems. Moreover, even if it received less design attention than the library, the dining hall provided the sort of compositional counterpoint to its companion that the hostels and other outbuildings provided to the main buildings at Dhaka and Ahmedabad. Kahn was almost certainly thinking of his two Exeter structures—as well as the old Davis Library—as a communal grouping, a village within the campus.

The Exeter dining hall was conceived as an afterthought to the library, and the quality of the design suffered from Kahn's relative lack of immersion in the program. Nonetheless, the building serves as an important companion to the more prominent structure, providing both mechanical support and the sort of communal relationship the architect had explored in the secondary buildings at Ahmedaabad and Dhaka.
JOSEPH W. MOLITOR

As construction on both buildings neared completion, Kahn gave a lecture at the school and declared to the students, "I really believe that, what is, has always been, and that what was, was inevitable."[52] At least in the case of the library, the students must have heard the echo of their Latin motto.

To celebrate the completion of the library, the Academy suspended classes on November 16, 1971, and students as well as faculty and administrators—including Principal Richard Day—helped haul boxes containing the 60,000 volumes in the Davis Library to their new home, where they filled only a quarter of the stack space for 250,000 books. Kahn and Exeter were clearly planning for the future.

For the dedication ceremonies, Armstrong and his wife, Kitty, invited Kahn to stay at their house. "I told Esther about the feelings of gemutlichkeit of your house," he wrote back. But he went on with characteristic elusiveness whenever his personal life was involved to say, "but I am a sly one and I know that for this responsible occasion, the less duties Kit and you have the better. If you can find accommodations for us at the Inn, I think it will work out best."[53]

Other things did not work out so well. In November of 1972, Armstrong wrote to Kahn about "leaks which have appeared around the various wooden windows and other wooden framed parts of the library during a bad storm here this week."[54] Nicholas Gianopulos, from Keast & Hood, offered one explanation. "Lou would fall in love with certain bricks," he recalled. "He liked the imperfections and the shapes and colors they produced. The problem was that the flaws could be vulnerable to water."[55] But that did not explain the extent of the problems. They were so mysterious that the school's buildings and grounds people later had to engage in what they dubbed "forensic engineering" to establish the causes. Responsibility was never fully established, but some felt that Kahn's office had not monitored the construction firm well enough. Others noted that while putting wood directly against brick would have seemed to invite leaks, the thinking of the day was that caulk would be enough to permanently keep out water and wind, even without flashing, the metal sheets that were normally used to divert the flow of water. Why were the walls of a New England building left uninsulated? Winton Scott recalled specifying the material, which would suggest an error by the contractors. No one after the fact had a satisfying answer. But the problems were not at the core of the architecture, as they had been at Richards, and they were eventually fixed, albeit at enormous cost (roughly

$7 million). In 2005, the president of the Exeter board of trustees—himself an architect—having blunted complaints that the money might have been better spent on student aid, concluded: "The idea of the library trumped performance issues. We have a great work of architecture."[56]

Kahn had already pronounced himself well pleased with the building. "It appears simple and graceful," he concluded, "no decorative elements are resorted to, because I did not feel in the air the approval for decorative. I felt the striving not for severity but for the purity that I sense in a Greek temple."[57] Comparing this judgment with the spare language of John Phillips's original deed of gift establishing the Academy, one would have to agree that Kahn had captured the austere spirit of the institution, a classical commitment to the idea that history and continuity are basic to education—that "the end depends on the beginning."

Kahn had gone well beyond Exeter in his design. He had indeed given the institution a library well suited to its institutional character. But he had also tapped into the very concept of a library with such sensitivity and skill that his building had become virtually a definition of the term. It was indeed a temple to learning. In his next effort, Kahn would once again turn his search for the fundamentals of architectural meaning to the world of art.

CHAPTER EIGHT

LIGHT UNLEASHED

THE KIMBELL ART MUSEUM
1966–72

Throughout his mature career, Louis Kahn repeatedly referred to the qualities of "silence" and "light" as fundamental to architecture as he understood it. He explored their role in his work in a lecture first given in 1968 in which he said, describing his own experience of seeing the pyramids of Egypt, "There prevails the feeling 'Silence,' from which is felt Man's desire to express."[1] He went on to say, "I sense Light as the giver of all presences, and material as spent light."[2]

However woolly this pronouncement may have seemed in the view of some listeners, it went to the heart of his architecture as it had evolved over more than forty years. If *silence* was a key element of the Exeter library, *light* was the essence of his design for the Kimbell Art Museum in Fort Worth, Texas.

The setting for this building was almost as foreign to Kahn as the chilly lanes of Exeter, New Hampshire, the spectacular seafront of La Jolla, or the flat expanses of Dhaka. Fort Worth had been settled in 1843 and became the site of a frontier army post by midcentury. It flourished as a supply station for cattle drives on the Chisholm Trail after the Civil War, and

after the first railroad link was established, in 1876, the community's activ-ities expanded into shipping cattle, cotton, and other products. In the 1900s, it became a meatpacking and grain center. Oil was discovered in the area in 1919, and the city eventually became a hub of North Texas indus-try. But even by the 1930s, there were no dedicated art museums in Fort Worth; the only place one was likely to see a serious painting was at the public library or in the department stores in Dallas eager to attract cus-tomers with "exotic" attractions.

Nevertheless, Fort Worth had its share of residents eager to raise the cultural sights of their fellow Texans. Many were members of the Fort Worth Art Association, which mounted exhibitions for many years in the second-floor lobby of the Fort Worth Public Library. One of the visitors to these shows was Kay Kimbell, an entrepreneur who had gone to work at age thir-teen as a helper in his father's mill and had moved on to make a fortune in oil, food processing, and grain milling; he eventually became a director of some two hundred corporations. During an Art Association exhibition, Kimbell was so taken by one eighteenth-century English painting on loan from a New York art dealer that he decided to buy it. The purchase was the beginning of Kimbell's lifelong love of art, a love that was shared by his wife, Velma, as well as by his sister Mattie and her husband, Dr. Coleman Carter.

In 1936, this small cultural cadre formed the Kimbell Art Foundation to increase their holdings. But without a building of its own, the organization had to exhibit its works in local churches and in nearby colleges and universities, in many cases giving students their first glimpse of original paintings. The Kimbells treated their own home as a house museum, entertaining numerous visitors who wanted to see their pictures. When Kay Kimbell died, in 1964, the collection had grown to include roughly 360 items, ranging from jades and ivories to some distinguished paintings from the Italian Renaissance and western American works of the nineteenth century. The founder's wish had been "to encourage art in Fort Worth and Texas by providing paintings and other meritorious works of art for public display, study, and observation in suitable surroundings."[3] Soon after her husband's death, Velma turned over her portion of their common estate to the foundation with the purpose of establishing a museum "of the first class."[4]

After deciding to proceed with a museum to house the collection, the Kimbell trustees made pilgrimages to the Metropolitan Museum of Art and the Frick Collection in New York City, the Boston Museum of Fine Arts, the National Gallery of Art in Washington, D.C., and the Sterling and Francine Clark Art Institute in Williamstown, Massachusetts, as well as to museums in England and Europe. But the project did not come into sharp focus until the trustees agreed to hire a director.

After considering many of the leading museum executives in the country, they settled on Richard Fargo Brown, a craggily handsome scholar and administrator who was at the time director of the Los Angeles County Museum of Art. Brown was a great-grandson of the founder of Wells Fargo—a powerful legacy in Texas. He had been trained in art history at Harvard's Fogg Art Museum and had worked at New York's Frick Collection as a research curator. The Los Angeles County Museum hired him in 1954 and made him head of the institution seven years later. Brown was considered by friends to be reserved, even austere, and professionally demanding. Benjamin Bird, the attorney for the foundation and the trustee who conducted initial interviews with candidates for the directorship, described Brown in a memo as a man with "considerably dignity—formidable rather than impressive."[5]

Although Richard Brown (left, arm on hip), put Marcel Breuer and Mies van der Rohe ahead of Kahn on his preferred list of architects for Kimbell, Brown became one of Kahn's most loyal and protective clients, patiently putting up with the architect's repeated revisions of the design. He insisted that the building would be worth whatever problems were faced in its creation. KIMBELL ART MUSEUM, FORTH WORTH, TEXAS. PHOTOGRAPHER: BOB WHARTON

When he was approached by the Kimbell trustees, Brown was struggling with a number of weighty issues. On the personal side, his wife had been paralyzed by polio for years and was dependent on an iron lung. On the professional side, he had grown increasingly frustrated by the LACMA trustees over a variety of matters, beginning with their rejection several years before of his recommendation that Mies van der Rohe design a new home for the museum. Problems grew as some trustees insisted that works in their own collections be shown in the museum under attributions Brown could not accept. When he resigned from the Los Angeles County Museum, Brown explained his decision by saying that it was based on "irreconcilable policy and operational difficulties."[6] Having worked with the Kimbell trustees at long distance after his official hiring, in September of 1965, Brown moved to Fort Worth full-time in February of 1966.

The Kimbell collection was still small and did not yet have a clear definition. Most of the works were easel-size Old Master paintings of the seventeenth and eighteenth centuries, and the trustees did not expect—or wish—the collection to expand dramatically. Because the collection was never intended to include large-scale works of art, Brown understood that the scale of any building designed to house it would need to be relatively small. He was comfortable with this constraint, and after extensive reflection, research, and discussion with the trustees, he laid out guidelines for the future museum in a four-page document entitled "Policy Statement." The museum was to be "dedicated to the education, increased enjoyment and cultural enrichment of the public through the display and interpretation of definitive works of art." But the document went on to describe the proposed building as "a work of art itself," one that should be "a creative contribution to the evolving history of the art of architecture."[7]

Brown augmented the policy statement with a more detailed presentation of his ambitions in what he called a "Pre-Architectural Program," which was approved by the trustees along with the Policy Statement in June 1966. He wrote that while the building should indeed be a work of art in itself, he was against engaging in "architectural 'gymnastics' for their own sake." He felt that "among other experiences educational and personally enriching, a visitor to an art museum ought to be *charmed*." Well aware that he was no longer in the rarefied precincts of Harvard's Fogg Museum or New York's Frick Collection, Brown nevertheless insisted to the museum overseers that they create nothing less than "a gem as one of the Rembrandts or Van Dycks housed within."[8]

In pursuit of that goal, Brown wanted to make sure that "natural light should play a vital part" in the design. He was something of an expert on the subject, having written his doctoral dissertation at Harvard on nineteenth-century color science and the French Impressionist painter Camille Pissarro, and he insisted that "the effects of changes in the weather, position of the sun, seasons, must penetrate the building and participate in illuminating both the art and the observer."[9] Perhaps most striking was the director's declaration that "the form of the building should be so complete in its beauty that additions would spoil that form."[10]

In a partial reprise of the Exeter experience, Brown launched his search for an architect by reviewing the work of Max Abramovitz, Edward Larrabee Barnes, Marcel Breuer, Gordon Bunshaft, H. H. Harris, John Johansen, Pier Luigi Nervi, I. M. Pei, Paul Rudolph, and Mies van der Rohe, his unsuccessful candidate for the Los Angeles County Museum. Now in Fort Worth, Brown was no longer sure that the aging Mies was the right architect for this new opportunity. "I came to think," Brown told an interviewer, that "Mies would impose his great creative contribution on this building on his terms and in his tradition—in spite of a totally new situation with a different climate and light."[11]

Brown was on the advisory board of the La Jolla Museum of Art and was well aware of Kahn's work at the Salk Institute, which had impressed him. Brown learned more about Kahn through the exhibition of the architect's work in a one-man show at New York's Museum of Modern Art in the spring of 1966. Intrigued, Brown visited Kahn in his Philadelphia office later that spring. When he returned to Fort Worth, Brown strongly recommended Kahn to his trustees. At a meeting on June 6 that included a lecture on Mies by Brown, the director said that while he considered the architect of the Seagram Building in New York City to be the greatest architect of the first half of the twentieth century, he thought that Louis Kahn would become "the greatest of the second half."[12]

Nevertheless, Brown wanted to be absolutely sure that he had the right architect and contacted Charles Sawyer, Kahn's former client for the Yale gallery, about what it was like to work with Kahn. Sawyer later told a scholar that he replied: "Lou Kahn is one of the most creative people and one of the kindest and most generous human beings I have ever known. I would recommend him to you without any reservation whatever. I must warn you, however, that you must be prepared to sit up all night working with him, for otherwise you will find that he has changed his mind while you were sleeping!"[13]

Persuaded by Brown's confidence in Kahn's artistry, but evidently wary of his reputation as described by Sawyer, the Kimbell trustees quickly endorsed the recommendation and urged that Kahn associate himself with a local architectural and engineering firm. The firm they chose was owned by Preston M. Geren, who was known for doing well-executed buildings on time and on budget, qualities the trustees understandably felt that they needed so that Kahn would not indulge his increasingly well-known penchant for delays and cost overruns. Geren's responsibilities would include compliance with local regulations, preparing working drawings, hiring subcontractors, and sharing oversight of construction with Kahn's people. According to Frank Sherwood, who oversaw the job for Geren, his firm was known for its public schools—"good solid work that didn't leak."[14] The Kimbell trustees were assured that they would be getting high design under tight scrutiny. Kahn, who had worked well with Douglas Orr as associate architect on the Yale gallery, agreed to the condition and signed the contract for the Kimbell commission on October 5, 1966.

Influential as the Kimbell trustees would remain in the development of the museum, Brown was the motive force behind the project—the acting client—and would join the circle of intensely engaged individuals who had been so critical to Kahn's best buildings.

Some fifteen years had passed since Kahn had designed the Yale gallery. He had done no galleries or museums since, but his thinking on the subject had steadily evolved. Partly because the Yale building was originally intended to serve a variety of purposes, Kahn had created for it a totally flexible loft space. But in 1958 under Paul Rudolph, who had become chairman of the architecture department, and Andrew Ritchie, the new director of the gallery, the "pogo panels" intended to provide wall space for paintings had been abandoned. They had been replaced with fixed partitions, and the circular stair tower had been hidden by plaster-board to make the building look more like New York's Museum of Modern Art, where Ritchie had directed the department of painting and sculpture, and which was considered the finest modern gallery in the country at the time. Kahn was angered by the alteration of his original form, and declared, "If I were to build a gallery now, I would be more concerned about building spaces which are not used freely by the director as he wants. Rather I would give him spaces that were there and had certain inherent characteristics."[15]

Unlike the Yale building, which was intended to house the university's professional architecture program as well as the gallery but was expected to change uses over time, the Kimbell museum was to be dedicated entirely and permanently to art, and Brown's strong feelings about the sort of space in which that art should be seen coincided almost exactly with his architect's. Once again, Kahn was blessed with a client who spoke his aesthetic and philosophical language. The fact that Kahn had designed a building for the man who helped put an end to the disease that had crippled his new client's wife, who died in January of 1966, could only have intensified the bond.

Roughly two miles from the center of Fort Worth, the site for the Kimbell Art Museum was a trapezoid comprising approximately 9½ acres in a city park that already included three museums: the Modern Art Museum of Forth Worth, the Fort Worth Museum of Science and History, and the Amon Carter Museum, designed by Philip Johnson and completed in 1960 to house nineteenth- and twentieth-century art of the American West. A condition of the design of the Kimbell was that it not block the view from the Amon Carter Museum to the Fort Worth skyline, and thus it could not be more than 40 feet high.

Enthusiastic as Kahn was about the Kimbell commission, he was hampered by an increasingly demanding schedule of travel, which had already slowed the Exeter project; he was still traveling to Dhaka and Ahmedabad. Moreover, the First Unitarian Church in Rochester and the Exeter library were still under construction. He was also designing Temple Beth-El for a small Jewish congregation in New York's Westchester County, and struggling with the directors of the Mikveh Israel Synagogue in Philadelphia, who in 1962 had asked Kahn with great fanfare to design a new building but could not agree on the program; they eventually let the architect go. Adding to the workload in the office were a performing arts center in Fort Wayne, Indiana; the factory for the Olivetti-Underwood business machine company in Harrisburg, Pennsylvania; and a project for an office tower in Kansas City. Despite the added work, Kahn's staff had not expanded significantly.

On those occasions when he was in Fort Worth, Kahn stayed at the Fort Worth Club, where the offices of the Kimbell Art Foundation were located. One evening, the architect and several of the consultants were having drinks at the Petroleum Club, directly across the street. Kahn had asked for Stolichnaya vodka, which was not stocked at the bar, so a waiter was sent out to find some. After sampling the new bottle, Kahn was observed staring pensively out the window at the façade of the Fort Worth Club, which was embellished with a frieze of scantily-clad Roman gladiators, one of whom appeared to be urinating. Already concerned about what this unorthodox architect from Philadelphia might do, a security consultant in the group began to wonder if Kahn might insist on something similar for the Kimbell.[16]

The consultant need not have worried; there were other influences on the design that were more pressing. The climate in Fort Worth was a controlling element from the outset. The city was subjected to blazing sun and temperatures that ranged between 90 and 100 degrees for six months of the year or more, not to mention high winds and dust, which permeated the air. Thus a low structure with limited exposure to the weather was almost a given. The concern expressed by both Brown and Kahn for a building that made use of natural light in such an environment emerged as both the major challenge and the major opportunity.

The earliest concept for the Kimbell, sketched in the early months of 1967 and presented to Brown and the trustees that spring in two models, showed a one-story building with fourteen angular vaults of folded concrete plates running north-south with slits at the top of each to admit light. It was not unlike what Kahn had experimented with in the early phases of the Salk design, although in Forth Worth the folded form had more to do with illuminating the interior than with accommodating mechanical services. Indeed, reflectors were to be slung beneath the roof slots to diffuse the light and deflect it from direct contact with works of art. The reliance on natural light was a response to Brown's request but was a bold move nonetheless, rejecting the then prevalent International Style taste for artificial lighting in art galleries in favor of the traditional skylighting techniques of the European museums of the nineteenth century.

Brown liked the spirit of what he saw but, like Jonas Salk and Rodney Armstrong before him, felt that major alterations were required. His most serious concern was size. He thought the proposed building was too big, and even after Kahn had responded by reducing it to 400 feet on a side, Brown was worried about the message that would be sent by such a mass. "Four-hundred feet square is a hell of a big square, and it might seem, in the setting, the city, and in relation to neighboring institutions, etc., just plain ostentatious," Brown observed.[17] Apologizing for assuming the role of "Richard the Chickenhearted,"[18] the director reminded Kahn that the biggest pictures in the collection measured roughly 2 feet by 4 feet, and that some items were a mere 12 inches wide. He also noted that the average museum-goer is "generally about five and one-half feet high" and has a preference "for intimacy of space rather than expansiveness." Brown asked Kahn to accept the fact that his building should be comfortable for "a little old lady from Abilene" looking at "our fifteen-inch Giovanni di Paolo."[19]

If traditional architecture of the Indian subcontinent was infusing Kahn's work there and at Exeter, the echoes of his experience in Rome returned in the concept for the Kimbell. "My mind is full of Roman greatness," he said, "and the vault so etched itself in my mind, that, though I cannot employ it, it's there always ready."[20] The Kimbell gave him the formal opportunity he had been waiting for. "The basic structural and space-creating idea did not emerge from our discussions at all," remembered Richard Brown. "That was already in Lou Kahn's mind and had been for a

Kahn reviewing documents in the finished building with engineer Frank Sherwood (far left) and Marshall Meyers, who played a major role in solving problems with both the form of the museum and the innovative lighting system that has become its most admired feature. KIMBELL ART MUSEUM, FORTH WORTH, TEXAS. PHOTOGRAPHER: BOB WHARTON

long time, I think. And when he was commissioned to do this particular job, he reached for that structural idea as ideal for it."[21]

In the summer of 1967, Marshall Meyers, who had worked for Kahn from 1957 to 1965 but had left for two years to attend to family matters, rejoined Kahn's office to oversee the Kimbell commission. As Meyers remembered the Kimbell director's reaction to Kahn's original angular design, "Brown liked the initial schemes, but he felt that the shape of the roofs made the space too lofty. He wanted the museum to have the sense of a large house or villa and not that of a palace, which he felt was too intimidating."[22]

Kahn had already rejected the V-shaped profile of the first vault scheme, which would have produced galleries with 30-foot ceilings. In its place, Meyers suggested a cycloid curve, a flattened arch form that would be supported by concrete columns at its four corners and create galleries only 20 feet in height. He cited a book by Fred Angerer, *Surface Structures in Building*, as a source for the cycloid scheme, but whatever the inspiration, it fulfilled Kahn's original intent in a graceful, less "lofty" way than the original proposal.

Although the architect would continue to refer to the roof form as a vault, it was more accurately a concrete shell, and it was structurally highly complex. To explore just what was involved in building it, Meyers called on Nicholas Gianopulos at Keast & Hood, the Kahn firm's usual engineers. Gianopulos discussed the form with Meyers and concluded that it was more than his people could handle. "Call Gus," Gianopulos said, meaning August Komendant.[23] Kahn's collaborator on Richards and Salk was duly contacted, and when he had studied the idea, he warmly endorsed the vaults because of their light weight and ability to span a large area with minimal support. He also approved of the plan to locate most of the mechanical services in the channels separating the individual vaults. But Komendant was certain that he could improve on the scheme. As he later recalled the development of the first design: "The arch shape confused [Kahn] and so he considered a shell primarily an arch and not a beam, which it actually is. . . . From a structural as well as from an architectural point of view, the roof design was dishonest and the elegance of a shell system was entirely missing. I changed the shell shape and layout so it would work structurally. Kahn accepted the changes after my explanations."[24] The tendency of the shell sections to collapse across the slot cut for sunlight was countered by inserting small struts of concrete at 10-foot intervals, and a "diaphragm," a thin arch or beam of concrete, was added at the ends of the vaults to stiffen them further.

Whatever the extent of Kahn's precise technical understanding of the structure as Komendant had refined it, the architect felt strongly that the concrete columns be understood as the support for the roof, rather than the infill walls, which were made of concrete block and faced with travertine. He was concerned that the vault and the walls touching each other might suggest otherwise, so he provided a narrow strip of Plexiglas (later changed to glass) between them. The strip—or "lightband," as Kahn called it—was originally intended to be of uniform width through its arc, but Kahn decided to make it wider at the point where the vaults met the columns, and more narrow at the apex, to symbolically reflect the force of the vault pressing down on it, as if the vault were "squeezing" the glass at the top of the curve. As at Exeter, the goal was to provide visitors with a visual explanation of the structure, even if it was somewhat exaggerated for effect. But the device also permitted an additional measure of natural light to enter the galleries in a way that would not threaten the art. Another thin strip of glass was inserted along the exterior walls between the walls and the bottom of the shell, adding both to the natural illumination, and to the illusion that the ceiling was "floating."

The long open spaces spanned by the vault-beams fulfilled one of Brown's original desires, for gallery spaces that were not interrupted by load-bearing walls. But the plan worked out by Kahn and Komendant ran afoul of the Geren organization, which insisted that the shells would be too difficult and costly to build and suggested instead a flat slab for the roof. According to Komendant, Kahn exploded to him and said, "August, what shall I do with this ignorant bunch?"[25] After heated conversations with Brown, a deal was struck according to which Komendant would take over the engineering, while Geren would do the foundations and basement. Komendant would handle the museum level and the roof shells, while serving as peacemaker between Geren and Kahn. Komendant wrote in his autobiography that "Dr. Brown later told me, if I had not taken charge, the trustees would have sued the architects, and the contractor would have sued the Kimbell foundation for damages. He himself probably would have been fired and the museum he visualized would have remained a dream."[26] Kahn took Komendant's rough ways in stride, later kidding him about his oft-repeated admonition in Estonian-accented English, "Never don't trust nobody!"[27]

The final design presented sixteen rectangular shells measuring 104 by 24 feet on the exterior, and 100 feet by 20 feet on the interior. The shells were arranged in three sections. There were six shells at either end, and four in the center section, the recess marking an entrance court. Three light courts pierced the composition in the second, third, and fourth rows of

The final plan was considerably smaller than the earlier ones, which Brown thought might be considered "ostentatious." He reminded the architect that the building should be one in which "a little old lady from Abilene" would feel comfortable. © THE ARCHITECTURAL ARCHIVES, UNIVERSITY OF PENNSYLVANIA. PHOTO BY MARSHALL D. MEYERS

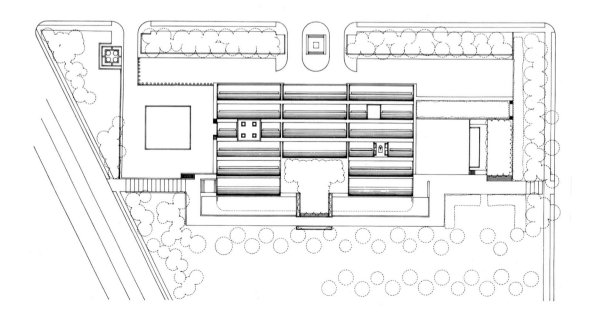

shells. One of the light courts penetrated to the lower floor, providing natural light for a conservation studio. Although the repetition of the vault form might have been expected to produce predictable, even boring, spaces on the interior, the light courts and the relatively small scale of the galleries promised to fulfill the ambition for an intimate ambience that Brown had sought from the beginning.

Because the site sloped downward, the public was intended to enter the upper floor from the park and entrance court to the west, while parking lots at the lower level provided access from the east. Unlike the Exeter library, Kimbell had a "proper" front door, unmistakable from the arrangement of the reflecting pools on either side of the approach, and the flanking porches of the building itself. But Kahn, who had never come to terms with the automobile and still did not drive, made no accommodation for arrival by car, with the result that most visitors entered by what Kahn considered the "back" door.

If the concrete had received special attention in La Jolla, in Forth Worth it was ennobled even further. The vaults were constructed using an innovative series of reusable plywood forms coated with plastic that could

Workers casting the cycloid "vaults." These were in fact structurally complex concrete beams slotted at the top to admit light to the galleries below. While crisply modern in execution, they communicated irresistible associations with the Roman ruins Kahn had long admired. KIMBELL ART MUSEUM, FORT WORTH, TEXAS. PHOTOGRAPHER: BOB WHARTON

be moved along the track of the structure on dollies. Kahn had hoped to have Fred Langford, who had served so effectively on the Salk commission, do the Kimbell concrete work. But the Geren firm insisted on its own people. Nevertheless, the final product set a new standard for elegance in the use of architectural concrete.

The finish of the concrete did much to complement the greatest achievement of the Kimbell, the mechanical manipulation of sunlight. Kahn had been refining his approach to the use of natural light ever since beginning work on the First Unitarian Church, where he brought illumination in through towers and bounced it off the main ceiling. He had made further use of sunlight in the Salk commission, admitting it indirectly to the courts and passages outside the laboratories. And at Exeter he had again used indirect sunlight by diffusing it against the concrete beams beneath the roof. But in Fort Worth, the sun was especially powerful, and there was no question of allowing its direct rays to reach the works of art in the collection, especially the sort of paintings and works on paper that formed the core of the Kimbell collection.

The concrete at Kimbell was treated like fine stone and given a high finish. Such attention to the material endowed forms that could have appeared heavy with an uncharacteristic lightness. KIMBELL ART MUSEUM, FORT WORTH, TEXAS. PHOTOGRAPHER: BOB WHARTON

Although Kahn had envisioned the use of natural light coming through slots in the vault from the start, he had not resolved how to diffuse it. Meyers went to work on the problem, invoking his knowledge of the way the partially mirrored prism in a single-lens reflex movie camera distributed light to both the camera's eyepiece and the film. The result was what Meyers came to call a "beam-splitter," a reflector that would separate the light coming through the roof openings and direct it up and down the undersides of the vaults on either side. Meyers's collaborator in the execution of the beam-splitter was Richard Kelly, the distinguished lighting designer who had first worked with Kahn on the Yale gallery, and became an essential member of the Kimbell team. He was assisted at Kimbell by Edison Price, a fabricator of lighting fixtures. Price's computer consultant, Isaac Goodbar, also took part in the extraordinarily detailed research. Kelly suggested using a perforated aluminum employed in the manufacture of commercial lighting fixtures.

After numerous calculations to confirm the angle for placement, the team settled on a curved screen of polished anodized aluminum pierced by

Although from the outside the building appeared to be merely a series of repeated identical forms, the interior provided an unexpected variety of spatial experiences. KIMBELL ART MUSEUM, FORT WORTH, TEXAS

tiny holes. The strongest light came through the slot, struck the main body of the reflector, and was bounced up on the silky concrete ceilings, while a small amount of light was allowed to filter into the gallery itself through the holes. As the testing proceeded, Kahn took to calling the reflectors "natural-light fixtures."[28] He predicted that they would produce an effect that would "give a glow of silver to the room without touching the objects directly, yet give the comforting feeling of knowing the time of day."[29] His prediction was borne out with extraordinary effect. The light in the Kimbell galleries assumed an almost ethereal quality, and has been the distinguishing factor in its fame ever since.

The execution of the lighting reflectors was yet a further example of the Kahn office's attention to detail, but also of the singularity of purpose and the receptivity of all the participants to new ways to solve a problem. As Meyers recalled the process: "Here were all these people who believed in something in their own way coming together: Kahn the Architect, his helper and the client and the builder. And all were moving in the same direction at different speeds, by different routes and by different means of locomotion."[30]

The attention of the architect and his associates to the way in which the user would experience the building extended to the most personal level. One example was the metal handrail designed for the main staircase. While at Salk the exterior staircases had been equipped with an extruded railing that was both functional and elegant, the one at the Kimbell flowered into a curved piece of steel that was matched to the shape of the human hand and qualified as a piece of sculpture in its own right. Kahn even insisted on taking a personal role in the design of the stainless-steel details of the public telephone booths. According to Frank Sherwood, "Kahn didn't want to use anything standard. He spent hours with Marshall Meyers deciding on the selection of the screw heads used to secure the stainless panels in the public spaces. The last thing we got was the drawings for the water fountain. Brown tolerated it."[31] The stainless steel was "sandblasted" with ground pecan hulls.

Brown's tolerance was often stretched to the limit, and, like Rodney Armstrong at Exeter, the director had to pacify trustees who were less patient. But Kahn would not be changed, even when it came to the job site. "Listen to the man who works with his hands," Kahn told Brown. "He may be able to show you a better way to do it."[32] At the same time, Kahn was comfortable bringing workmen around to his way of doing things. A supervisor on the job remembered Kahn inspecting some stainless-steel panels that were being installed near the museum offices. They had been shaped at the factory to create a rounded surface at their edges, and Kahn found a workman trying to polish out the stress marks that had been created by the process. As he had with the handrails at Salk, Kahn patiently explained that the marks were evidence of how the panel had been made, and that they should not be touched. The workman was puzzled, but ultimately convinced, and the "break marks" remained.[33]

Not surprisingly, such time-consuming attention to detail, not to mention the chronic delays in producing construction drawings, produced added friction between Kahn and the Geren firm. The problems were amplified by a steady rise in construction costs nationwide, which at the time were going up by roughly 1 percent a month. Making matters worse was the concern on

The silvery light that washes the underside of the vaults is the result of drawn-out experimentation with the reflectors suspended beneath the central slots. The final version admitted sunlight, but bounced most of it onto the highly polished concrete. KIMBELL ART MUSEUM, FORT WORTH, TEXAS. PHOTOGRAPHER: MICHAEL BODYCOMB

the part of the Kimbell board members about the impact on the museum's construction schedule of the work about to begin on the new Dallas-Fort Worth airport, which was expected to drain the local labor force. The Geren firm, which was now being run by the son of the founder, interpreted the original agreement with Kahn to mean that the architect's involvement would end when the design process ended, allowing Geren to take over the execution of the building. For Kahn, of course, the design process never really stopped, and he assumed that changes could be made even after construction had begun. At one point, he explained to Brown that "the building gives you answers as it grows and becomes itself."[34]

This was hardly the way the younger Geren saw things, and in early June of 1970, he refused to send Kahn final working drawings for his review, insisting that the architect's job had ended and threatening to terminate his agreement with Kahn on August 1. In September, the contract was altered by means of a document dubbed a "clarification" so that Geren would henceforth report directly to the Kimbell board of directors rather than to Kahn. The clarification did, however, give Kahn continued authority over the final design, with the understanding that any changes would have to be approved by Brown. In a gesture reminiscent of the cutbacks at Salk, Kahn's team responded to the crisis by trimming almost 25 percent of the building's projected cost.

Although he was working for Geren, Sherwood was impressed by how civil Kahn remained even under such great pressure. "Unlike most architects, who have pretty strong egos," Sherwood said, "Kahn did not project himself that way." During a drive through Dallas, Sherwood pointed out a building by Paul Rudolph that had gone up recently, but did not tell Kahn who had designed it and asked the architect for his opinion. Kahn responded with a story about his boyhood in Philadelphia. As Kahn told it, he had been walking down a street when two attractive girls passed him. A moment later, Kahn heard one of them say to the other: "They all look good at a distance." According to Sherwood, "That was the worst he would say about another architect."[35]

If Kahn shied from criticizing (or praising) his competitors, he was surprisingly miserly when giving credit to his collaborators. August Komendant was so angry that his name had been left out of a local newspaper supplement piece on the Kimbell that he refused to attend the opening ceremonies. "It was typical of Kahn not to give credit to any one of his associates, regardless of how great or extensive their contribution to a project was," Komendant wrote later. "He would have felt challenged and overshadowed by such a person."[36]

Someone who deserved credit, but was not about to demand it, was Harriet Pattison. Having been frustrated by the cancellation of her contribution to the landscaping of the Exeter library, Pattison got a measure of satisfaction from carrying her work on the Kimbell through to completion (even though she was not invited to the opening). Although now working for the Philadelphia landscape architect George Patton (with whom Kahn had traveled through Europe in 1951 when they were both at the American Academy in Rome), she took the lead role in the design of the setting for the museum. As Pattison recalled her contribution: "I soon took exception to Lou's imposing plinth and eased his building into its site, persuading him to incorporate the paired porches at the garden entrance. In my mind, they were 'Kahn ambulatories,' an alternative way to experience his building, the ambiguous middle ground that tied the museum to nature and lent the same dignity to live forms that sculpture had within."[37] Pattison's involvement also included the more traditional aspects of landscape design. "I chose groves of trees and water—reflecting, tumbling, purling—to temper the climate, animate a featureless site, and attract the public," she said.[38] The result was a subtle procession of grass, gravel, and water that created a psychological transition from the plainness of the surrounding park environment into the tranquility of the museum's galleries.

Even before the Kimbell opened, *Art Forum* was predicting that it would be "the best museum building in the country."[39] The finished product only strengthened the claim. A series of celebrations was held over the first week of October 1972, including one for the workmen, and one for the local cabdrivers so that they would know where to bring the first visitors. Richard Brown declared that the Kimbell was "what every museum man has been looking for ever since museums came into existence: a floor uninterrupted by piers, columns, or windows, and perfect lighting, giving total freedom and flexibility to use the space and install art exactly the way you want."[40] Years later, Frank Sherwood agreed, but observed that "it took a firm like Geren to get it done."[41]

When Brown died, in 1979, his successor concluded that the museum needed more space and embarked on expansion plans. A proposal was

The open porches flanking the main entrance were added at the suggestion of Harriet Pattison. Although not necessary as functional units, they created a stately transition into the galleries from the adjacent park.

KIMBELL ART MUSEUM, FORT WORTH, TEXAS. PHOTOGRAPHER: MICHAEL BODYCOMB

As at Dhaka, although on a smaller scale, the pools at either side of the entrance set off the museum as a "citadel," this time devoted to culture rather than government. KIMBELL ART MUSEUM, FORT WORTH, TEXAS. PHOTOGRAPHER: MICHAEL BODYCOMB

Although Kahn used no overt ornamental devices on the façade, his subtle variation of materials, textures, and colors animated the repetitive shapes. KIMBELL ART MUSEUM, FORT WORTH, TEXAS. PHOTOGRAPHER: MICHAEL BODYCOMB

drawn up by Romaldo Giurgola, who had been a member of the Penn architecture faculty with Kahn, and presented in 1989. (Giurgola had turned down an opportunity to design the Mikveh Israel synagogue in Philadelphia after the client fell out with Kahn. Giurgola, according to Sue Ann Kahn, said, "You already had the best. Don't come to me.")[42] The expansion plan, which would have added two wings to the north and south ends of the original building, caused a firestorm of protest in the architectural community and was eventually withdrawn. The critics' most powerful argument was Brown's own directive in the original program for the Kimbell that the building be complete unto itself and render additions both unnecessary and inappropriate.

After the Kimbell was finished, Kahn spoke about it with Sue Ann. As she remembered the conversation, he said that when he had been designing the museum, he felt that "another hand was doing the drawing."[43] Kahn's client clearly agreed. In a book about the building published a year after Kahn's death, Brown, speaking for "concrete workers, carpenters, trustees, engineers, draftsmen, foremen, curators, and contractors," wrote of the Kimbell that "in the making of it we all had one of the grand privileges and opportunities of our lives, for it was not simply making, it was creating." He went on to pay tribute to the architect for "leading us, through his character and his art, to a fuller appreciation of why life is worth living."[44]

With the Kimbell, Kahn had achieved something unique in the history of modern architecture, a building that engaged an element of nature—sunlight—with unprecedented skill and combined it with a contemporary program in a structure that also called upon the most advanced engineering while invoking the monuments of the past. The combination of materials—concrete, travertine, metal, wood—brought a potentially bunkerish feel into concert with the organic in a way that ennobled all of them. The result was a dynamic tranquility that approached the otherworldly. It is no surprise that, just as the Kimbell trustees had made pilgrimages to the great museums of the past to help them select Kahn, trustees and curators alike have since required their donors to visit the Kimbell to inform their decisions about the museum architecture of the future.

But for all he had accomplished in Fort Worth, Kahn was by no means done with his pursuit of ways to bring art and architecture together in a collaboration that would enrich both. His next, and final, design marked a consolidation of all that had gone before.

FACING PAGE The forms were apparently simple, but Kahn emphasized the points of connection both to create visual interest and to document the process of assembly. KIMBELL ART MUSEUM, FORT WORTH TEXAS, PHOTOGRAPHER: MICHAEL BODYCOMB

THE MOTH AND THE BUTTERFLY

THE YALE CENTER FOR BRITISH ART
1969–74

In an especially resonant coincidence, the last building Louis Kahn would build was just across the street from the one that launched his career. The Yale Center for British Art was, like the Yale Art Gallery, a mixed-use building. It was intended to include not only exhibition and teaching space, as the 1953 building had, but also a collection of rare books, a research library, an auditorium, and conservation facilities. As such, it brought together two of Kahn's most revered "institutions"—library and museum— and reconnected him with the kind of urban environment that he had loved since childhood. It also consolidated virtually all the aesthetic lessons that Kahn had learned since the 1950s and, more important, gave him an opportunity—so rare in life—to return to his professional beginnings and to improve on them.

The main purpose of the building—originally named the Paul Mellon Center for British Art and Studies—was to house the personal collection of a highly sophisticated art patron and philanthropist. Paul Mellon was the son of Andrew Mellon, the powerful banker who served as secretary of the treasury, ambassador to Great Britain, and patron of the National Gallery of

The Yale Center for British Art. © NORMAN MCGRATH

Art in Washington, D.C. Although his father was considered by some to be little more than a robber baron, the younger Mellon grew up to be the closest thing to an American aristocrat as was possible. After attending Yale College, where he became vice chairman of the *Yale Daily News* and wrote for the *Yale Literary Magazine*, Mellon spent time in England at Cambridge University's Clare College. He was smitten by it. As he remembered, "I loved the grey walls of Cambridge, its grassy quadrangles . . . the busy, narrow streets full of men in black gowns . . . the coal fire smell."[1] He was captivated by the surrounding countryside, and by just about everything else English. In 1936, Mellon bought his first English painting, of an eighteenth-century racehorse named Pumpkin. By the 1960s, he was collecting British art seriously, distributing paintings and sculptures throughout a mansion—The Brick House—on his 4,000-acre estate in the horse country of Upperville, Virginia, as well as in his houses in Washington and on New York City's Upper East Side.

Mellon was also a patron of architecture. He had already championed I. M. Pei to design an arts building for the Choate School, where Mellon had been a student, as well as the magisterial East Building of the National Gallery in Washington, begun in 1968.

Although Mellon was generous to many institutions, he remained especially devoted to Yale. The license plate on his silver-gray Mercedes read "1929," reflecting his Yale College class, and emblazoned on the tail of his private jet was "N1929Y". His largesse to his college was staggering. At the time of the Mellon Center commission, he had already funded the construction of two of Yale's residential colleges, designed by Eero Saarinen and completed in 1962, and had endowed the undergraduate college deanships, a freshman honors program, and special tutorials in writing, among scores of other gestures of support. Reflecting his aversion to self-promotion, none of these bore the Mellon name.

By the 1960s, Mellon's collection of British art was widely considered the finest—public or private—outside England. It included sporting paintings, landscapes, urban and maritime views, and genre scenes, as well as portraits. Mellon had announced in 1966 that he would give his collection to Yale, and with it he planned to provide funds for the acquisition of a site and the construction and endowment of a building. He also planned to provide enough money so that the Center would never have to charge admission.

The president of Yale at the time was Kingman Brewster Jr. With his prominent jaw, thick head of hair, and patrician bearing and background, Brewster was the model of an Ivy League university president, and a fitting companion to Mellon on the project for the Center. But Brewster surprised (and shocked) many members of his elite circle by becoming an unconventional steward of his institution in turbulent times. He would be remembered best by many for his willingness, during the trial in New Haven of a Black Panther accused of murder, to question the "ability of black revolutionaries to achieve a fair trial anywhere in the United States."[2] Provocative as he was, Brewster was able to keep Yale relatively calm during the demonstrations that were spreading across the nation.

For all his admirable qualities, Brewster was no aesthete. A rather windy, legalistic speaker, he enjoyed going on weekend picnics in an English roadster equipped with panniers of shrimp and martinis, but he was not drawn to art. To his credit, when it came to the Mellon Center, Brewster deferred to someone with impeccable aesthetic credentials. He was Jules David Prown, then a thirty-eight-year-old member of the Yale art history department, specializing in American eighteenth-century painting. Like

The art historian Jules Prown (far left) represented the client along with English professor Louis Martz (rear). Prown's ability to convey the concerns of Yale's president, Kingman Brewster (third from left) and the donor, Paul Mellon (right) to the architect was crucial to the building's success. ARCHIVES, YALE UNIVERSITY ART GALLERY

Richard Brown, Prown had been trained at Harvard's Fogg Art Museum. When plans for a building to house Mellon's collection were set in motion in 1968, he was appointed director. But beneath his civilized demeanor, he would be, like Brown and Rodney Armstrong, a fierce defender of innovative architecture at an institution that was steeped in tradition. When Prown asked Brewster to define his role in the Mellon project, the president replied, "You are the client. Yale is the owner."[3] Prown's own interpretation of his assignment was that "I was responsible for the soul of the building, the physical plant department was responsible for the body."

The hopes for the Center were ambitious, and in January of 1969, Prown presented Brewster with what he described as his "preliminary thoughts" on the building. The document characterized British art as one of "places, and human activities. It relates to the real world, and what goes on there." Prown went on to insist that the "building must be humanistic," and that it recognize the "relationship to the University and its relationship to the City."[4] Sounding remarkably like Brown in Fort Worth, Prown declared: "The building should not awe or overwhelm by its monumentality. It should welcome the visitor, arouse his interest and curiosity, evoke a desire to enter."[5]

In doing so, the Center would be in good company. The arts at Yale had long ago begun to cluster in a group of buildings along Chapel Street. The university's School of the Fine Arts—the oldest in the country—was estab-

The site for the British Art Center was diagonally across from Kahn's Yale Art Gallery addition, which had made no concessions to the life of the street. This time, the university insisted on including retail shops on the ground floor, but the architect accepted this "intrusion" with enthusiasm.
© THE ARCHITECTURAL ARCHIVES, UNIVERSITY OF PENNSYLVANIA. PHOTO BY MARSHALL D. MEYERS

lished in 1866 in Street Hall, which had since been turned over to the art history department. With its completion in 1928, the Tracy & Swartwout art gallery further established the arts in the area, and Kahn's own addition expanded that presence. The cultural flavor of the neighborhood was enriched even more in 1963 with the completion of Paul Rudolph's Art and Architecture Building, and the Yale Drama School had recently taken over a disused church adjacent to the intended site for the Center.

But however noble such a concentration may have appeared to Yale, it struck New Haven officials as a growing encroachment on the city's fragile tax base. The departure of major manufacturers in the 1950s had eroded municipal funds, and a proposal for two Yale dormitories fell afoul of the city because they would have replaced a number of taxpaying commercial properties. The tensions between town and gown had been aggravated by the widespread divisions across the country over the Viet Nam War and civil rights. It was, in short, a time of troubles, and when a fire broke out in the A&A Building in June of 1969, virtually everyone leapt to the conclusion that it had been started by students disgruntled with the university administration and American "imperialism" in general. There was no evidence to support the claim of arson, but the A&A and its fire were received in "anti-establishment" quarters as symbolic of everything that was wrong with the country at the time.

In this supercharged atmosphere, Jules Prown began the search for an architect for a building that was to house some of the most refined examples of "establishment" art in the world. The leading candidates included Philip Johnson and I. M. Pei. Johnson was taken off the list; the director found his work at the time "fussy" and "decorative."[6] Pei was busy with the early stages of the design of the East Building of the National Gallery, which Mellon was already paying for. Vincent Scully, by now a powerful figure on Yale's architectural scene, had "discovered" Kahn in the 1950s, but had more recently taken a strong interest in the work of Kahn's former student and employee, Robert Venturi, who in 1966 had published a provocative book entitled *Complexity and Contradiction in Architecture*. The book urged a new appreciation of the American vernacular, including the ordinary buildings of the American "Main Street," as a way to connect high-design architecture with current reality. Scully urged that Venturi, who had designed a deliberately populist building for the National Football League, be given the Mellon commission. Responding to Scully's proposal, Prown said, "You know it's not going to work. Just compare Venturi's Football Hall of Fame and Paul Mellon's collection of British art."[7]

Scully was not the only campus source of advice. Yale's architecture students, then among the most radical in its professional schools, "summoned" Prown to the A&A Building. One asked if Prown would consider having a student design the Mellon building. Prown responded that he would not, "for the same reason that I would not have my gall bladder removed by a medical student."[8]

All but persuaded of his ultimate choice, Prown proceeded to make the circuit of the Richards laboratories, Exeter, and Kimbell. "What moved me most was the way Kahn handled light," he said.[9]

Returning to New Haven, Prown received an impromptu visit from Edward Larrabee Barnes, the university's official architectural adviser who, like Pei and Johnson, had trained at Harvard's Graduate School of Design under Walter Gropius. Despite his credentials and urbane manner, Barnes had lost out to Kahn in the competitions for the Exeter library and the Kimbell museum. When Barnes rhetorically asked Prown, "Do you know whom you should have?" the director expected the answer would be Barnes himself. But Barnes, rising above his losses to Kahn in earlier competitions, recommended Kahn and offered to call him to expedite the process.

Prown then made a trip to Philadelphia, where, like all of his predecessors on this pilgrimage, he was struck by the modesty of the Kahn office. He noticed that the clock on the wall was about half an hour fast. He learned that this was done deliberately so that Kahn would not be late for appointments.[10] Prown also noticed a drawing across from Kahn's desk for the Palazzo dei Congressi, an enormous—and ultimately unsuccessful—plan Kahn had developed for Venice. "It made me uneasy," said Prown. " We knew we did not want a monumental building."[11]

In the summer of 1969, following a delay caused by an operation to remove Kahn's gall bladder, Prown and Kahn made a plan to see Mellon's collection in Washington, and also the Phillips Gallery, which Prown considered a place where "art looks just the way it should within a domestic kind of environment."[12] On the way to the meeting with Kahn in Washington, Prown had an unsettling experience. His plane collided with a flock of birds, which shut down one engine, and the pilot had to make a forced landing. "When I caught up with Lou," remembered Prown, "I told him what had happened, and we went to a bar and had a long heart-to-heart talk about life and death."[13]

Perhaps encouraged by the conversation about such elemental matters, Prown in the fall of that year wrote to Kingman Brewster saying that he considered Kahn to be "the greatest American architect of our time," but also described him as "a remarkable human being, sensitive both to the inner world of art and the external world of everyday existence."[14] The commission was awarded in October of 1969. Paul Mellon committed $10 million to its execution.

The challenge of matching the Center's design to Mellon's collection was not unlike the one that had faced Richard Brown and Kahn at the Kimbell. Mellon's works of art depicted the tranquil dominance of a secure—if vanished—imperial culture, one that could sustain enormous country houses for the benefit of wealthy individuals who spent their time racing horses and hunting foxes. The Mellon culture would have puzzled Kahn, who had had scant exposure to such a way of life. But it could also have intrigued him. He once told an interviewer, "I believe the wish and the fairy tale is the beginning of science."[15] Although the Mellon Center was about art rather than science, one might speculate that if a disfigured, poverty-stricken immigrant had not come to distrust the trappings of class and wealth (as his early socialist activities might have suggested), he might well have embraced them as a way to validate himself in a world that must have struck him as something out of a fairy tale.

In any case, by this time Kahn had become a celebrity—able to rise above prejudice, or any other form of criticism—so much so that some of his supporters were beginning to wonder if he was starting to believe his own press notices. "He developed an ego as he got older," said his cousin Leonard Traines. "One day, my wife and I were at Louie's house, and he took out all the architecture medals he had won and spread them out on the bed. He said, 'You know, I would only do this for *meshpocheh* [Yiddish for "family"].'" The incident has a slight ring of false modesty. Traines also noted that "by then Louie was not a man to take criticism."[16]

Whether or not there was some subconscious appeal to the new Yale commission, Kahn realized that the Mellon collection demanded a feeling for domestic space reminiscent of the English country houses that had sheltered these works of art when they were created. He told an interviewer in 1972 that, while he was still not an enthusiastic reader, "I love English history . . . I have many volumes of English history."[17] And indeed, his office bookshelf included a number of multivolume histories of the British Isles.

For all of its high artistic and academic aspirations, however, the building was shaped by some extremely mundane urban considerations. One of the assumptions was that the Center would include street-level shops. The first suggestion for such a radical idea had come from George Kubler, a member of the Yale art history faculty, who even suggested adding residential units on top of the museum. It was, after all, the 1960s. More influential was that the museum would be crossing the "moat" of Chapel Street, which had long marked the boundary between the university and the city. (The Yale salient on the city side was the Waldorf Cafeteria, the neon-lit diner where Kahn had spent many hours with students during his teaching days at the architecture school, and was a part of the proposed site for the Center.) New Haven did not want to lose more tax revenues to the university.

Kingman Brewster and Irwin Miller, a powerful member of Yale's governing body and himself a major architecture patron, were at first shocked by the idea of including shops in such a refined structure, but Kahn had no such reservations. The university soon came around, but insisted on keeping the idea quiet so that it could be used as a bargaining chip with the city of New Haven if problems arose. In due time, Yale announced proudly that the shops would generate more tax revenue than the retail space that would be lost to clear the site.

A number of meetings were held in Kahn's 1953 art gallery to discuss issues of light and the future location of work areas in the Center, but Prown recalled that whenever he and Kahn entered the older building, "he never looked left or right. It was clear that he was deeply unhappy with the changes that had been made to his original. He also never mentioned Rudolph's Art and Architecture Building."

Early thinking about the need for a building of 150,000 square feet suggested a three-story rectangular structure extending a full block from High Street on the east to York Street on the west. Prown was worried that such a long building would create "museum fatigue" in visitors forced to walk through long galleries, and the next proposal retained the adjacent church and was four stories high.

Construction costs had risen by a staggering 42 percent between the time of Paul Mellon's gift and the completion of the initial design. As the price tag continued to grow, Yale representatives went to Mellon to see if more money was available. Mellon, who also was watching the National Gallery's costs balloon, said, in effect, "I gave you $10 million. You will have to build it for that."[18] For the building to go forward, Yale concluded that it would have to be reduced by one-third, or 50,000 square feet.

Throughout the development of the design, Mellon, who never warmed to Kahn personally, remained involved. "He was the ideal donor," said Prown, "because he was very hands-off."[19] That is not to say that Mellon did not have strong views, but he expressed them in a characteristically self-effacing way, usually by asking questions. An early proposal included a parking garage in the basement. Mellon's comment was, "Do you think it is a good idea to put automobiles under my paintings?"[20]

The final design was remarkably sober, and essentially symmetrical in its organization. As at Richards and Exeter, the main entrance was muted, located under a corner of the building. The focal points were two interior courts, recalling but doubling the main organizing element at Exeter. One of the courts was located off the main entrance, extending four stories from the ground floor to the roof, and was surrounded by gallery space. The second, larger by a third than the first, rose three stories from the second floor above

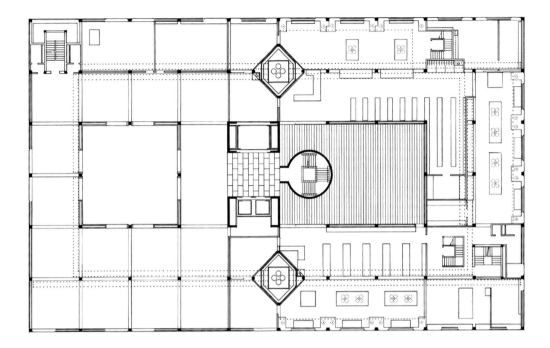

an auditorium and was surrounded by more galleries, offices, and study areas. Although the mechanical services were integrated into the structure, they were not called out as vigorously as they had been in earlier designs. The rigidity of the served and servant ideology was being absorbed into a more subtle accommodation. Nevertheless, Kahn still opposed any conspicuous cosmetics. Wherever possible, he avoided wallboard and paint, and there were no hung ceilings to conceal the air-handling ducts or other conduits.

Such shunning of artifice often required lengthy explanations to the Yale people responsible for the building. But by this time, Kahn had developed some heightened social skills. Prown recalled that at meetings with his colleagues, the architect would burst out, "I like your jacket; I'll have to get one just like it." At dinners with Yale officialdom, he would say to his host, "I'll have what you're having." Prown said he felt that "Lou was different in the 1960s from what he had been in the fifties or even the forties. He had developed a certain smoothness in dealing with clients."[21] Although the people who worked closely with Kahn on the design were invariably impressed by his levelheadedness in solving practical problems, the communication took another form around Mellon and Brewster, with whom Kahn would lapse into word clouds.

The second-floor plan of the BAC shows Kahn's familiar distribution of services around the periphery of the building, but here he has used two open courts. One (left) welcomes visitors on the ground floor through an entrance at the corner; the second forms a more private setting for the art they have come to see.

Kahn's language may at times have been fuzzy, but his imagery was often acutely evocative. He described the structural system of the Center as "the bones of an elephant." For that system, he turned to Henry Pfisterer, the engineer and Yale professor who had played such an important role in the Yale Art Gallery commission. But because of ill health, Pfisterer had to turn the majority of the Mellon work over to his partner, Abba Tor, an Israeli engineer who had worked with Eero Saarinen. Tor admired Saarinen, but had been amused by the way he used more material than was necessary to create a visual effect, only to "palm it off" as functionally necessary. Tor remembered in particular Saarinen explaining away the use of large amounts of steel on the short façade of the John Deere building in Moline, Illinois, as structural, when it was in fact decorative. "When you go around back, the steel disappears," Tor said.[22]

Not surprisingly, Tor was attracted to Kahn's expressed interest in the authentic. Having paid a visit to Kahn's Philadelphia office, he was "transfixed by the architect's views on the realms of art and architecture, and his worldviews." But he found himself on the way out trying to remember what Kahn had actually said. Tor said it "was a curious experience, something that a piece of metal would feel (if it could) when suddenly removed from a strong magnetic field which gave it direction and an inner flow of current."[23] While Tor recognized Kahn's own willingness to blur the line between "honest" expression of structure and theatrical effect—as Kahn had throughout his career, whether with the Yale Gallery ceiling slab or the X-bracing for the Exeter clerestory—Tor admired the architect's fundamental desire to tell an architectural story in plain terms that lay people could understand.

Whether or not a common heritage had anything to do with it, the relationship between Tor and Kahn was unusually warm. "My parents came from the same part of Europe, and maybe because of that Lou and I had a compatible sense of humor," recalled Tor. "He liked to be self-deprecating, but he practiced the arrogance of humility. He could get me to do things I would not have done for another architect."[24] As an example of Kahn's persuasive ways, Tor cited a call from the architect asking him to come to Philadelphia on a weekend. Tor protested, but eventually gave in, arriving late on a Friday when Kahn was the only person in the office. "He didn't really need me there," Tor said, "he just wanted someone to talk to about all kinds of things that had nothing to do with the job. But then he left the room and came back with bread and cheese and olives and declared, 'Abba, tonight you are my son.' "[25] It was hard to resist that kind of blandishment, even if Tor knew that he was being seduced.

But Tor was careful not to become a "disciple." In working with Kahn, Tor said, he realized it was important "not to be in awe of Lou. You had to argue with him, and if you did it the right way, he would respect you for it. One day, Lou said to me that he considered engineers to be the people 'who sliced the salami.' I told him it wasn't that way at all. I said, 'An engineer is like the male dancer in a classical ballet: He catches the ballerina in mid-jump, turns her around, and keeps her from falling on her face.' Lou got a laugh out of that."[26] Having endured one too many Kahn perorations about asking bricks what they wanted to be, Tor once asked him, "Lou, what was it the wall said to you the last time you spoke to it?"[27]

Even though many of Kahn's colleagues could be impatient with his abstractions, they all respected his devotion to detail. As a result of the work on the Salk Institute, and even more on the Kimbell museum, Kahn's attention to architectural concrete at the Mellon Center was more concentrated than ever. But in this case, because the interior of the building was supposed to be domestic in feeling, he insisted that the material used for the formwork leave no residual marks from the wood grain, and that only the largest plywood panels be used so that joints would be kept to a minimum. So high was the quality of the wood used for the forms that some of the contractors took used sheets home with them, not as souvenirs, but to make furniture.[28]

The attention to the finish was the same throughout the building, and made a powerful impression on Kenneth Borst, Yale's director of buildings and grounds. Borst had trained as a civil engineer at Syracuse University and worked with Mies van der Rohe on the Seagram Building before moving to New Haven to oversee the construction of the Beinecke Rare Book and Manuscript Library, designed by Gordon Bunshaft of Skidmore, Owings & Merrill and finished in 1963. When the Mellon project began, Borst realized that he would have to monitor the architect carefully. "If you were working on a project with Lou, you knew that you were going to be dealing with changes and negotiations all the way through the job," he said.[29] The experience exceeded his expectations. As the usual pattern of delays took hold, Borst was sent to La Jolla to talk with Jonas Salk, and then to Fort Worth to see Richard Brown for guidance. His question to both former Kahn clients was simple: "How in God's name do you get a building done with this man?" Borst was also worried about the money. "How many owners are willing to keep paying when the design process never ends?" he asked.[30]

Slow as the process was, the results seemed to be worth the effort, integrating many of the successful aspects of earlier buildings, but in an even more refined way than had been evident at Kimbell. On both the exterior and the interior of the Center, the architect evoked his tapering brick piers at Exeter, slimming and recessing the concrete columns slightly as they rose to signal the diminishing load. In the galleries, the open spaces were subtly divided into separate zones by connecting the columns at the floor level with strips of travertine, thus creating a sense of "rooms" without creating actual limits on the space. The walls of the court were faced with white oak; panels of beige linen were spread across the gallery surfaces on which the paintings were to be hung. The combination of concrete, travertine, wood—and now cloth—was skillfully modulated to convey a sense of repose underpinned by solidity.

Kahn and Tor struggled with the structural system, eventually settling on a variation of the Salk and Kimbell devices of locating utility conduits in the concrete beams. In doing so, they made some of the mechanical systems part of the aesthetic experience. Indeed, the exposed air supply ducts became pieces of sculpture in themselves. Tor described Kahn as having a "unique talent to study, learn, and understand in depth the possibilities and constraints of the structural and mechanical systems, and integrate them in a most organic way with his architectural concepts."[31] He said later, "To make order out of chaos is hard. Lou was like a virtuoso traffic cop."[32]

Few details escaped the architect's scrutiny. Not surprisingly, Kahn resented the safety code requirements to include light switches, thermostats, and electrical outlets on his pristine walls. He derisively referred to the hardware as "fraternity pins."[33] So he artfully grouped them all on the vertical oak members, where they would not interrupt the surfaces devoted to the art, but made a composition of their own.

Surely the most powerful—and improbable—gesture in the building is the cylindrical concrete "silo" that houses the main stair. It dominates the three-story library court with an alien force verging on the shocking. Of course, the form had its sources in the stair enclosure for the 1953 gallery and was originally designed as a diamond-shaped tower. But while he had used a similar form before, Kahn this time was apparently tapping into additional influences. In his investigation of the English country house, Kahn

By gradually slimming and recessing the exposed concrete columns, Kahn subtly reminded the visitor of the diminishing structural load they were carrying as they rose.

had been struck by the prominence given to large fireplaces, which were not only sources of heat for their chilly surroundings, but also sculptural statements and visual anchors for extended groupings of rooms. Even a small fireplace was out of the question in an art museum, but Kahn seems to have concluded that the stair tower might honor the "memory" of a manorial hearth. As one scholar has observed, the tower can be seen "as a massive stone chimney, commanding the focus of the room and giving it both directionality and intimacy."[34] Left unembellished, the massive form would have been intrusive if not overwhelming. But Kahn had discovered in Dhaka what a welcoming effect a few incised lines could have on a large geometric form. The scribing of the Center's stair tower was arguably an echo of the cylinders of the prayer hall at Dhaka. In this otherwise thoroughly domestic environment, however, the major incisions, which occur at the level of the adjacent floors, combined with "V" joints derived from Salk, tether the

The use of white-oak panels, linen wall coverings, and wool carpeting created a hospitable contrast with the exposed concrete, and produced a surprisingly domestic atmosphere that accommodated Mellon's highly refined works of British art. © JEFF GOLDBERG/ ESTO. ALL RIGHTS RESERVED

abstract solid to the intimate details of the rest of the building and the delicate scale of the paintings that face the tower on three sides.

The lighting for the Center posed a new set of challenges. Working again with Richard Kelly, Kahn early in the process experimented with a system similar to the Kimbell vaults, but the changeable New England climate made a recycling of that solution impractical. To study the problem, a full-scale mock-up of one 20-foot bay of the Center was constructed on the roof of the building that housed Yale's buildings and grounds offices.

Although the final lighting system was not executed during Kahn's lifetime, the complex of roof skylights and incandescent interior fixtures that was eventually installed fulfilled the original intention that the amount of daylight coming into the building would remain as constant as possible, regardless of time of day or season of the year.

One aspect of the design that Kahn hesitated to commit to was among the most important: the treatment of the façade. The architect repeatedly avoided questions from Prown about what materials he planned to use to clad the building, and revealed his decision only reluctantly, and as late in the process as he could. Kahn had been pleased by the effect of the brushed stainless-steel panels he introduced on the interior of the Kimbell, and now boldly decided to use the same material on the exterior of the Mellon Center. Such a use of steel was virtually unprecedented in museum design, and getting it right was not easy. Kahn insisted on inspecting the samples produced by the fabricator and immediately ran into trouble. He wanted the steel to be installed just as it had come off the rollers, without any applied finish to conceal imperfections. The fabricator was not used to such demands, and declared to the architect, "Your whole order isn't worth the cost of one day's rolling!"[35] Kahn eventually found a manufacturer who could produce what he wanted, but even so, Mellon was skeptical of the idea, and so was Prown. The director asked Kahn bluntly if he had ever seen a metal-clad building that he liked. Kahn replied that he had not. Prown then said, "But you are going to give us one?" Kahn reassured Prown that, "On a gray day, it will look like a moth; on a sunny day, a butterfly."[36] And it did. Subtle variations produced by acid-washing the steel, as well as the slight discoloration in the surface produced by subsequent weathering, made the façade infinitely varied as the light struck it. As never before with such effect, Kahn had taken the aging process and profited from it.

As usual, Kahn considered the design process to be never-ending. When Tor discovered that the location of the staircase conflicted with the

structural demands of a supporting column, he asked Kahn if he could move the stair about ten inches. Kahn studied the drawings and promptly relocated the stair to another part of the building. Tor shot back, "You can't do that! The foundations have already been poured!" The stair was returned to the desired spot. To avoid such problems in the future, Tor went so far as to ask other members of the Kahn office, who always clustered around his drafting board, to put their elbows on areas of the drawing that might attract Kahn's interest in alternate solutions.[37] Even Prown was annoyed when, after he and the architect had agreed to some detail, he discovered that Kahn had subsequently reverted to his own version, or come up with a new one. "For Lou, redesigning was never a problem; that's what he loved," Prown said, "but sometimes, I had to say, 'No more!' "[38]

In a development reminiscent of the Salk Institute—when Jack MacAllister was given oversight of the building's execution, and the Komendant situation at the Kimbell—Marshall Meyers was retained independently by Yale in the summer of 1973 to make sure that the construction would go forward with a minimum of further delays. After finishing his work on the Kimbell, Meyers had left Kahn's office to set up his own practice with a colleague, Anthony Pellecchia, who had also worked in Kahn's office, on the Performing Arts Theater of the Fine Arts

Center in Fort Wayne, Indiana. In New Haven, Meyers was assigned to act as liaison between the Kahn office and the contractor, and was given authority to make "field" decisions. Patricia Cummings Loud, an architectural historian who had come to know Meyers while he was working on the Kimbell, thought "Marshall was someone who could get things done; he had ideas, he was a doer." Loud also felt that Meyers played a crucial role in Kahn's communications with others. And because the architect was frequently away on other work, communications with Yale were becoming strained. "Marshall was so articulate," Loud said. "He could interpret for Kahn."[39]

Kahn would have been fortunate to have someone in his Philadelphia office with the day-to-day authority accorded to Meyers in New Haven. The accumulated inefficiencies of the firm were building toward a financial crisis. Indeed, the debts to members of Kahn's staff and to subcontractors were moving into the hundreds of thousands of dollars. Abba Tor, who at one point was owed $100,000 for his services, finally had to confront Kahn and explain that he could not afford to keep making changes for which he was not being paid. Kahn responded that he was not charging the client for his *own* time. Tor by then had come to know Kahn's ways, and was sending his invoices for the Mellon Center to Philadelphia with a notation that he was "billing through" the Kahn office. As a result, Tor was eventually able to recover his fees from Yale, even though his financial agreement was with the architect. Leonard Traines, Kahn's cousin who ran a successful electronics business in Philadelphia and was close to the architect, grew alarmed at the situation and began to ask him about it. "Louie said he wasn't interested in the money," Traines remembered, "so I said to him, 'Louie, you *have* to be interested in the money.' Finally, I told him I would be willing to retire from my own company and run the business end of his firm for him. But he wouldn't have it."[40]

Just as he persisted in pursuing his architecture at the expense of financial demands, Kahn maintained a precarious balance between his personal life and his work. Anne Meyers, Marshall Meyer's widow, remembered that he would appear unexpectedly at her house with her husband for "whatever was on the table." After dinner he would proceed to talk with the Meyers's ten-year-old daughter about her drawings, in one case focusing on a still life of fruit and talking to the youngster about the "essence of grape."[41] Anne Meyers said that Kahn "was wonderful with children." But Harriet

Kahn resisted as long as possible revealing how he planned to clad his building. The brushed stainless steel was unprecedented in Kahn's work for an exterior surface, but still responded to his fondness for materials that would show their natural properties and age in a visually intriguing way.
© NORMAN MCGRATH

was raising Nathaniel alone in the Philadelphia suburb of Chestnut Hill, and Kahn spent little time with them. Leonard Traines remembered that "Louie kept Alex and Nathaniel in the background; he wasn't much of a father to them."[42] But according to Meyers, what time Kahn did spend with them was important. "He may not have been parental, but he was a devoted father," she said.[43] Sue Ann was well established as a musician and teacher, and Alexandra, born in 1954, was looking forward to a career as an artist. But Nathaniel, who had been born in 1962, was still at a very vulnerable stage of life and was confused about what role his father played in it. He first realized that there was a second parent in his life when his mother announced to him at age three, "We have a special guest for dinner. Your father is coming."[44]

Discovering his father was a revelation to Nathaniel, who became a filmmaker, and in his 2003 documentary *My Architect* he expressed warm feelings about the times when Kahn would spend afternoons with him, painting watercolors and once drawing a "book of crazy boats." He knew that other fathers spent more time with their sons, but he considered them "just dads. I looked down on them."[45] On the other hand, Nathaniel also remembered the strange feeling he had when his mother would put him and his father in her car to drive the architect from Chestnut Hill back to his house in central Philadelphia, dropping him some distance from the front door so that he could walk the final blocks and not be seen by Esther with his other family. Although Nathaniel would receive postcards from his father from exotic locations addressed to "Dearest Boy of Mine" and signed "With all my love, Daddy," the messages could be mixed. In one letter to his son, Kahn wrote cryptically, "Someday I hope to teach you to be a better man than I."[46]

Esther continued to tolerate the situation. "He was devoted to her, and never would have left her," said Anne Meyers. "When he said he was going home, he meant Esther." Indeed. He never left so much as a bow tie behind in Harriet Pattison's house. It was, said Nathaniel, as if he had "never been there."[47] And Kahn did not support his other families financially. Kahn's personal priorities must have been clear to Esther, and, according to Meyers, she remained "devoted to him. They both looked at the bigger picture."[48] Leonard Traines had a slightly different interpretation of the relationship at this stage. "Esther was bitter," he said, "but she lived with the situation. She never mentioned Louie's other women, or the children."[49]

Rosella Sherman, the widow of Kahn's brother, Oscar, who had died in 1947, felt that "she didn't want to know."[50] In his cousin's defense, Traines recalled that "Louie used to work into the wee hours of the morning. When there are attractive, smart women around, the hormones probably got going, even at his age. And the women came on to him. It was a weakness in Louie, but he loved Esther."[51] According to Sue Ann, "they shared the same double bed for their entire marriage."[52]

The ability to carry on several simultaneous relationships—whether romantically with women or professionally with women and men—at last may have been waning. Anne Meyers was struck by the way Kahn was able to keep his personal and professional relationships "of a piece in the service of the work," and insisted that "there was no conflict between them."[53] But Kahn was now past seventy, and even a man of his capacities could be expected to behave erratically on occasion. Abba Tor remembered Kahn at this stage as "mercurial. When he loved you—you could do no wrong. When he fell out of love—he just looked past you. Some people were hurt by this alternately hot and cold treatment."[54] Several employees remembered Kahn

The architect with his son Nathaniel, whose mother, Harriet Pattison, persevered in her relationship with Kahn even though he remained married. © HARRIET PATTISON COLLECTION, THE ARCHITECTURAL ARCHIVES, UNIVERSITY OF PENNSYLVANIA airily reminding them that he was "a one-man office," making it clear that no one was going to succeed—or even challenge—him in the lead role. "There aren't going to be any partners," Jack MacAllister recalled Kahn saying. "When I die, it's over; there will be no crumbs." [55] Some have speculated that Kahn's insistence on an attitude of *"après moi, le déluge"* persuaded many talented designers to leave his office for work that might give them more of the limelight, or more security for the future.

In New Haven, troubles with the Center began to mount as the project moved forward. A potentially crippling problem emerged when the New Haven fire marshal balked at Kahn's plan to surround the building's two interior courts with unprotected openings to the galleries. Mindful of the 1969 fire in Rudolph's Art and Architecture Building, which had been made worse by the "chimney" effect of its multistory central atrium, the marshal insisted that Kahn enclose his balconies with glass that contained wire mesh. Borst recalled that Kahn, rather than make a scene, as some architects Borst had worked with might have, met calmly with the fire marshal and "charmed him out of the chicken wire" by proposing fireproof screens that would descend automatically in an emergency.[56] Another problem was the quality of the workmanship. According to the regulations at the time, Yale had to employ between 10 and 20 percent of its workforce from minority groups. They were not always the best trained, and many learned on the job. As he had in Ahmedabad, Kahn would spend hours with the workmen showing them how to use their tools to create a particular effect. (As a result, the details got better as the building rose.) "Lou's buildings were very hard to build," said Borst. "There was no place to hide anything."[57] When the exposed air-handling ducts were installed, the workers had to wear white gloves to avoid leaving fingerprints on the stainless-steel surface.

Despite the problems with budget, workers, and schedules, the experiments and investigations of a lifetime were coming together with a special power and subtlety. Here was an architect who was drawing on the entire history of his craft and yet seemed determined to absent himself from his art. There was no signature to this architecture. It stood alone, and on its own. If Exeter had penetrated to the core of the "idea" of a library, and the Kimbell had redefined the role of natural light in an art museum, the Mellon Center synthesized everything that had gone before. Here was a building laid out with a Classical rigor that would have pleased Paul Cret. Yet it embraced the messy realities of urban life and modern economics without apology. It provided a setting for its historical contents that was deeply respectful, yet also clearly modern. If the Center was less appealing to the camera than Salk, less monumental than Dhaka, less accessible as an ideal form than Exeter, and less overtly welcoming than Kimbell, those apparent shortcomings constituted a remarkable advance. Here was a building the power of which did not reveal itself without repeated exposure and careful inquiry. And only after that power became manifest was a visitor likely to ask, "Who *did* this?"

The man who did it was not to see the finished building. On March 17, 1974, on a flight back to the United States from Ahmedabad, Kahn had to change planes in London's Heathrow Airport. There he ran into Stanley Tigerman, a former student whom Muzharul Islam, a Yale classmate of Tigerman's, had brought to Bangladesh to design a number of vocational schools after Kahn had begun work on the capital. Tigerman recalled that Kahn did not look well, and that their conversation was uncharacteristically dark. "We met in the international transit lounge while each of our flights was delayed and had lunch," remembered Tigerman, who was on his way to Dhaka. "Lou looked beat, and unhealthy. If I had not known he was Lou Kahn, I would have thought he was a homeless person." Although the conversation was friendly, Tigerman remembered Kahn criticizing Muzharul Islam for dividing his time between architecture and politics. "Kahn devoted his life to architecture, and Islam did not," said Tigerman. "Lou could not accept that."[58] When they parted, Kahn proceeded on to New York. After landing, he called Esther to tell her that he had missed the connecting flight to Philadelphia and would be taking the train. He took a cab to Penn Station, where he stopped to use the men's room, and died suddenly of a heart attack. Because Kahn's papers listed only his office phone, and the office was closed on Sundays, the police were unable to contact the family until Monday. The body was taken to the city morgue and not identified until two days later, after Esther had retraced her husband's itinerary.

Kahn's death left many details of the Mellon Center unresolved. Meyers and his partner Anthony Pellecchia were assigned by Yale to complete the design, a task that included the final version of the skylights, the commercial space for the sunken courtyard adjoining the museum, and the interior millwork as well as the handrail for the main staircase. All involved were dogged by the question "What would Lou have done?" No one could be sure. One example was the stair rail. As Abba Tor recalled: "Everyone wanted to do what 'the master' would have done. But the rail that Marshall designed was not stable. We finally compromised, and it's pretty good."[59] Meyers honored Kahn's memory in his dedication to detail, perhaps to a fault. "Marshall proved to be just as much of a fussbudget as Lou had ever been," said Borst.[60]

At this point, Paul Mellon asked that his name be taken off the building and that it be renamed the Yale Center for British Art. The request reflected no dissatisfaction with the architecture. On the contrary, Mellon in his autobiography wrote, "As things turned out, I think the building and in particular the interior have been a resounding success."[61] Mellon was, in his deferential yet practical way, hoping that the institution would draw a wider base of financial support in the future if it did not bear the name of such a conspicuously wealthy patron.

Ironically, the financial situation of the BAC, as the institution quickly became known, actually improved over time. Yale had invested Mellon's original $10-million gift well, and because of the extended delays in finishing the building, the amount had appreciated enough so that the increase in value actually covered the rise in costs. So while the building exceeded the original budget, it did not exceed the total amount of money that became available.

The completion of the Center was clouded by Prown's decision in 1975 to step down as director and return to full-time teaching. Prown was succeeded as director of the Center by Edmund (Ted) Pillsbury, a 1965 graduate of Yale who had done his graduate work in art history at the University of London. Although Paul Mellon supported the choice, and later praised Pillsbury's brief tenure as director, many of those more intimately involved with the project felt that Pillsbury was a bad fit. "He was not good with people," remembered Kenneth Borst. "He and his staff were at war."[62] Anne Meyers was harsher, insisting that Pillsbury "was not interested in what was required to complete the building according to Lou's design. He just wanted to get it done." Finally, Meyers appealed to Kingman Brewster, who backed him against the new director. "Marshall and Ted were like oil and water," said Anne Meyers.[63] (Ironically, Pillsbury went on to succeed Richard Brown as director of the Kimbell, and was the author of the ill-fated plan to expand the Texas museum.)

For all the disputes over the Center's final details, the building at its dedication in 1977 arguably reflected more than anything in the architect's work his sense of fundamental values in architecture. Or, as Prown described it, "morality." The BAC, Prown insisted, was "all about morality—in the way it reveals the structure, in the way it uses natural materials, in its basic proportions." In that sense, the Center is all about Louis Kahn. From his humble beginnings to his ascendancy to membership in the architectural pantheon, he had always been drawn to essentials, to sources, to essences—"what had always been" as a key to what would be.

Louis Kahn's approach to morality in his personal life left an extraordinary amount of pain. As his widow said somewhat cryptically eight years after his death, "We were married forty-four years and never one minute of being bored. A lot of problems, yes, but never bored."[64] For all their time together, she conceded that "his first love was architecture and everything else came second."[65] Harriet Pattison came to the same conclusion. In 2004, she said, "Like anyone who came within his sphere, I was a minor player."[66]

Esther and Harriet could have been speaking for so many others—students, admirers, lovers, coworkers, and children—who had hoped for more from this man. Whether Louis Kahn's failure to satisfy those personal hopes should color the appreciation of his work is a question like those surrounding so many great artists, from Michelangelo to Pablo Picasso, from Frank Lloyd Wright to Willem de Kooning. But personal pain passes. Monuments in art endure. In this, Louis Kahn joined the roster of the great.

If the British Art Center consolidated Kahn's stature as an artist, it also served as something of a metaphor for the architect as a man. Its exterior is uninviting, even homely to some eyes. But the interior is richly complex, growing more satisfying the more one examines it. In the end, though, the signature of the maker is elusive. As Kahn said so often, he never liked finishing a building, because with completion came the end of creation.

At Kahn's death, the BAC and the buildings at Dhaka were still incomplete. And several others designs were in various stages of development, including a memorial to Franklin Delano Roosevelt that was intended for an island in New York City's East River and the hugely ambitious Hurva synagogue project for Jerusalem. But that lack of resolution might be seen as an appropriate legacy. What Kahn left was a body of work for the ages, but one in which the creator has stepped aside. Louis Kahn seems to have done so with a profound understanding that the marks of his hands would ultimately mean little compared with what those hands had made: forms and spaces that transcended time and style.

EPILOGUE

Between the time Louis Kahn received his degree in architecture in 1924 and his death, he designed more than two hundred buildings. Of them, fewer than seventy were built, and those included such minor jobs as renovations to his own office. For all practical purposes, Kahn's most productive phase did not begin until he was fifty. Just twenty-four years later, he died, suddenly and ignobly, short of the years granted to Frank Lloyd Wright, Mies van der Rohe, and Le Corbusier, the architects with whom he is now ranked.

When Kahn's body was reclaimed from the New York City morgue, plans for a funeral were set in motion. Normally, Jewish law requires that the dead be interred within a day, but this was not possible. Under the circumstances, there was no alternative to a ceremony well past the deadline—a condition Kahn himself might have appreciated.

The arrangements had to be made quickly. When Esther learned of her husband's death, she called Anne Meyers, and together they confronted the details. A notice was released to the newspapers. The news sent shock waves through the architectural community in the United States and abroad,

and many of those who had known, or even known about, Kahn were determined to pay him homage.

Several of those people were on a train that left New Haven's Union Station early on the morning of Friday, March 22. The weather was bad, raining and windy, and the regular commuters filled most of the seats. On this day, however, there was another group. Having risen early, a cluster of Louis Kahn's former students and colleagues at Yale had hurried to the station in order to get to Philadelphia in time for the ceremony.

As the train was moving south from New Haven, it stopped in Stamford. One of the passengers getting on there was John Morris Dixon, the editor of *Progressive Architecture* magazine, who had covered Kahn's work for years. Dixon remembered being surprised by how many people took the train so early in the morning, but he was also struck by how many of them he recognized. When the train stopped in New York City, the Kahn group grew. At Philadelphia's Thirtieth Street Station, Peter Blake, the longtime editor of *Architectural Forum*, joined the throng getting off what had become a funeral train.

The rites took place at the Oliver Bair funeral home, at 1820 Chestnut Street, the favored location for funerals of prominent Philadelphians. Ornately decorated in a Renaissance-Baroque style, Oliver Bair was one of the largest funeral homes in the country, and the entire building was taken over for the occasion. The majority of the guests were arranged in three tiers: the family in front, behind them Kahn's office staff, and then faculty from the University of Pennsylvania. Esther was there with Sue Ann. So were Anne Tyng and Harriet Pattison. Anne Meyers had asked Esther how to accommodate the other mothers, and Esther said that she wanted them and their children treated "with respect and dignity." But she also said that she did not want them "in her line of sight." [1] Anne Tyng and Alex arrived late and sat with the office group. Alex, who had hoped to be celebrating her twentieth birthday that day, moved up to the second row, taking a seat directly behind Sue Ann. Nathaniel chose to stay with his mother at the back.

Kahn's casket was of unfinished Swedish oak. The crowd of more than 1,000 who had come to view it included supporters and critics, and many in between. Among them was Holmes Perkins, who had brought Kahn back to Penn from Yale but had then found him more talented than he had expected. There was Edmund Bacon, who had planned to make a lifelong partnership with Kahn but found him too formidable.

In addition there were legions of admiring colleagues, including Bill Lacy, head of the architecture program for the National Endowment for the Arts. "Anybody who was anybody in architecture wanted to be there," remembered Lacy. "Just having your feet in the door made you feel good. It was like a state funeral." [2]

Many who arrived late could not find room in the funeral home, and were obliged to stand outside, chilled by the early-spring weather. One of these was Theodore Liebman, an idealistic young architect who had driven down from New York City with his boss, Edward Logue. A combative Yale-trained lawyer and World War II veteran, Logue had become president of the enormously powerful New York State Urban Development Corporation, established by Governor Nelson Rockefeller. As such, Logue had been Kahn's client for a memorial to Franklin D. Roosevelt planned for Roosevelt Island in New York's East River.

The presiding rabbi, Ivan Caine, from the Society Hill Synagogue, had never met Kahn but spoke at length about the architect's achievements, comparing him to Moses and quoting texts in several languages, including Hebrew and Italian. Caine made an awkward reference to the fact that Kahn had always pronounced his first name in the French fashion and declared that Kahn was "more royal than the French kings who carried that name on the throne." Caine was joined in the observances by the Rt. Rev. Msgr. John G. McFadden, pastor of St. Rose of Lima Roman Catholic Church, who had been a friend of the architect's. Leonard Traines was surprised by the ecumenical representation, but he recalled that "Louie was a man of the world."[3] In words that might well have amused Kahn, McFadden observed that "as quickly as his genius put together exquisite buildings of light and beauty, so God, the master builder, called him to his rest."

Norman Rice, Kahn's classmate from Central High School, spoke. The engineer Abba Tor was standing next to Esther, and at one point spoke what he considered to be some "heart-felt words" to the widow. "She gave me a stony look in return," Tor remembered, "and I thought, 'What did I say wrong?'"[4] Like many in the room, Tor knew about Anne Tyng and Alexandra but not about Harriet and Nathaniel. The official pallbearers included Rice, Traines, David Wisdom, and David Zoob, the lawyer who would have to tell Kahn's many creditors that they would have to "get in line" to recover their debts.[5]

The cortege extended for seven blocks and was some fifty cars long. "The city of Philadelphia was all tied up," remembered Traines. The line wended its way slowly to Montefiore Cemetery in northeast Philadelphia. At the gravesite, when the moment came to throw in the ritual handful of earth, Alex was not sure what to do. Sue Ann took her by the hand, and they did it together.[6]

After the ceremony, Edward Logue told Liebman that before driving back to New York he would like to make a stop at the Richards laboratories. When they arrived, Logue got out of the car, walked to the entrance, and stood mutely for several minutes, head bowed, rain splashing off his umbrella. Finally, he returned to the car and told Liebman that he wanted to go to Bookbinder's, one of Philadelphia's most venerable watering holes and a favorite of Kahn's. "I'm Irish, you know," explained Logue. Liebman's reaction was that Logue was "having his own private funeral for Lou."[7]

Many did the same in their own ways, in many places beyond Philadelphia. Whether through his buildings or the force of his personality and his teaching, Louis Kahn had reached thousands of people at some indefinable level. Many of them later in life confessed to never having had again an experience to equal that of working with Kahn.

In the years following his death, some who had been close to the architect may have felt that they alone had known who Louis Kahn really was, and might have contributed something essential to his art. No doubt each had a claim on some part of Kahn's legacy, but his greatest ability was to draw on every source he encountered—men, women, students, colleagues, books, music, history, buildings—and reconstitute what he found into a unique whole. But Louis Kahn—born poor, disfigured in childhood, an immigrant with no advantages other than his genius for architectural form, space, materials, and light—was the one who put it all together.

NOTES

CHAPTER ONE
ARRIVAL
ESTONIA, THE NORTHERN LIBERTIES, AND PENN
1901–24

1. I am grateful to Susan R. Behr, producer of Nathaniel Kahn's 2003 *My Architect*, Alexandra Tyng, and Patricia Loud of the Kimbell Art Museum, as well as Ingrid Mald-Villand of the Union of Estonian Architects and Jelena Polovceva of the Latvian State Historical Archives, for Kahn's early biographical details, many of which were documented only in 2006.

2. See Alexandra Tyng, *Beginnings: Louis I. Kahn's Philosophy of Architecture* (New York: Wiley, 1984), 3.

3. Quoted in Richard Saul Wurman, *What Will Be Has Always Been: The Words of Louis I. Kahn* (New York: Access Press and Rizzoli, 1986), 123.

4. Ibid., 124.

5. Lewis Mumford, *The Brown Decades* (New York: Dover, 1955), 144.

6. Joseph A. Burton, "The Aesthetic Education of Louis I. Kahn, 1912–1924," *Perspecta 2* (1953): 204–17.

7. Quoted in *Louis I. Kahn, Drawings*, the catalogue for an exhibition of the same name at the Max Protetch Gallery, (Los Angeles: Access Press, 1981), 3.

8. For a discussion of the social strata of Philadelphia from Colonial times forward, see E. Digby Baltzell, *Philadelphia Gentlemen: The Making of a National Upper Class* (New York: Free Press, 1958).

9. Personal communication from Susan Behr, Oct. 4, 2005.

10. The certificate survives as part of Collection 255, Esther Kahn Collection, Architectural Archives, University of Pennsylvania (hereafter AAUP).

11. Quoted in Alessandra Latour, ed., *Louis I. Kahn Writings, Lectures, Interviews* (New York: Rizzoli, 1991), 344.

12. *University of Pennsylvania School of Fine Arts, Courses in Architecture Music*

and *Fine Arts, Announcement, 1922–23* (Philadelphia: The Press of the University of Pennsylvania, 1922), 15–16.

13. Author interview (hereafter AI), Mark Ueland, May 13, 2004.

14. Wurman, op. cit., 121.

15. Quoted in Latour, op. cit., 344.

CHAPTER TWO
TO CHANGE THE WORLD
THE LEAN YEARS
1924–47

1. Walter Gropius, *The New Architecture and the Bauhaus* (New York: Museum of Modern Art, 1936), 33.

2. *Architectural Forum*, Sept. 1924, 97.

3. Le Corbusier, *Towards a New Architecture*, trans. by Frederick Etchells (New York: Praeger, 1965), 7.

4. Ibid., 9.

5. Ibid., 89.

6. *Architectural Record*, June 1924, 587.

7. *Architectural Record*, July 1926, 6.

8. Letter from John Molitor to Kahn, Mar. 27, 1926, Collection 255, Esther Kahn Collection, AAUP.

9. AI, Rosella Sherman, Oct. 20, 2005.

10. Interview with Esther Kahn in Alessandra Latour, *Louis I. Kahn: L'uomo, il maestro* (Rome: Edizioni Kappa, 1986), 19.

11. Ibid., 8.

12. David B. Brownlee and David G. De Long, *Louis I. Kahn: In the Realm of Architecture* (New York: Rizzoli, 1991), 22.

13. Norman N. Rice, "I Remember Rue de Sevres," undated, Collection 255, Esther Kahn Collection, AAUP.

14. AI, Sue Ann Kahn, Mar. 22, 2004.

15. Letter dated Dec. 4, 1930, Collection 255, Esther Kahn Collection, AAUP.

16. Esther Kahn journal, collection of Sue Ann Kahn.

17. Reprinted in Latour, ed., *Louis I. Kahn: Writings, Lectures, Interviews*, 11.

18. Letter dated Jan. 8, 1932, Collection 255, Esther Kahn Collection, AAUP.

19. *Pencil Points*, Apr. 1932, 217.

20. "Architecture and Modern Housing, Lecture to be Delivered Before the Graduate Students in Architecture of the University of Pennsylvania, Monday, Jan. 9, 1933," Collection 255, Esther Kahn Collection, AAUP.

21. "Outline of the Principles and Policies of the Society for the Advancement of Architecture," undated typescript, Collection 255, Esther Kahn Collection, AAUP.

22. "A.R.G. Submits Slum Clearance Scheme to Better Homes Exhibit," draft of press release, undated (but probably Apr. 23, 1933), Collection 255, Esther Kahn Collection, AAUP.

23. "Design for a Monument to Lenin to Be Erected in the Port of Leningrad," undated typescript, Collection 255, Esther Kahn Collection, AAUP.

24. Letter from Kahn to State Board of Examiners of Architects, Collection 255, Esther Kahn Collection, AAUP.

25. Letter from State Board of Examiners of Architects to Kahn, Aug. 7, 1934, Collection 255, Esther Kahn Collection, AAUP.

26. Letter from Bernard J. Newman to Kahn, May 7, 1935, Collection 255, Esther Kahn Collection, AAUP.

27. Esther Kahn journal, collection of Sue Ann Kahn.

28. Catherine Bauer, *Modern Housing* (Boston: Houghton Mifflin, 1934), 214.

29. Ralph Adams Cram, *My Life in Architecture* (Boston: Little, Brown, 1936), 283.

30. Gropius, op cit., 80.

31. Anthony Alofsin, *The Struggle for Modernism* (New York: W. W. Norton, 2002), 141.

32. Anne Tyng in Latour, *Kahn: L'uomo*, 45.

33. See Brownlee and De Long, op cit., 14.

34. Letter from Leopold Kahn to Louis Kahn, Jan. 7, 1942, Collection 255, Esther Kahn Collection, AAUP.

35. Latour, *Kahn: L'uomo*, 24–25.

36. Sue Ann Kahn interview.

37. See Paul Zucker, ed., *New Architecture and City Planning: A Symposium*

(Freeport, NY: Books for Libraries Press, 1944).

38. Lewis Mumford, *Roots of Contemporary American Architecture* (New York: Dover, 1972), ix.

CHAPTER THREE

ACADEMIA AND EMERGENCE
THE YALE UNIVERSITY ART GALLERY
1947–53

1. Letter from Charles Sawyer to Elise Kenney, Mar. 1998, Yale Art Gallery Archives, 1.
2. Letter from Sawyer to author, Dec. 18, 2004.
3. AI, Leona Nalle, Apr. 27, 2004.
4. AI, Wilder Green, Sept. 27, 2004.
5. Ibid.
6. AI, Duncan Buell, Apr. 27, 2004.
7. William Huff, interview by Elise Kenney, May 29, 1999, Yale Art Gallery Archives, 6.
8. Green interview.
9. Quoted in Robert A. M. Stern, *George Howe: Toward a Modern American Architecture* (New Haven: Yale University Press, 1975), 213.
10. AI, Earl Carlin, Sept. 8, 2004.
11. AI, Robert A. M. Stern, Sept. 27, 2004.
12. Carlin interview.
13. Charles Sawyer, "Louis I. Kahn: Some Personal Impressions," unpublished manuscript, Feb. 1992, Yale Art Gallery Archives, 2.
14. Buell interview.
15. Quoted in Robert A. M. Stern, "Yale 1950–1965," *Oppositions* 4: 38.
16. Eugene Nalle, interview by Walfredo Toscanini and Estelle Margolis, June 10, 2003, courtesy Walfredo Toscanini.
17. AI, Earl Carlin, Apr. 27, 2004.
18. AI, Estelle Margolis, May 11, 2004.
19. James Stewart Polshek, *Context and Responsibility* (New York: Rizzoli, 1988), 21.
20. AI, Vincent Scully, Dec. 1, 2004.
21. Margolis interview.
22. Carlin interview.
23. Nalle interview.
24. Ibid.
25. AI, James Stewart Polshek, June 2, 2004.
26. Toscanini and Margolis interview.
27. Leona Nalle interview.
28. Quoted in Stern, *George Howe*, 223, n. 77.
29. Carlin interview.
30. Green interview.
31. Letter from Laurance P. Roberts to Kahn, box 76, Kahn Collection, AAUP.
32. Sawyer, "Kahn: Impressions," 3.
33. AI, Alvin Eisenman, Oct. 1, 2004.
34. Letter from Charles Sawyer to Sidney Davidson, Sept. 6, 1950, Yale Art Gallery Archives.
35. Susan B. Matheson and Elise K. Kenney, "Prologue to Kahn: The Philip Goodwin Design," *Yale Art Gallery Bulletin* (New Haven: Yale University Art Gallery, 2000), 98.
36. Quoted in Walter McQuade, "The Building Years of a Yale Man," *Architectural Forum*, June, 1963, 88.
37. William Huff, "Louis Kahn: Sorted Recollections and Lapses in Familiarities," *Little Journal*, Sept. 1981, 1.
38. Letter from William Huff to Elise Kenney, May 31, 1999, Yale Art Gallery Archives.
39. Quoted in Latour, *Kahn: L'uomo*, 75.
40. Alexander Purves, "The Yale University Art Gallery by Louis Kahn," *Yale University Art Gallery Bulletin* (New Haven: Yale University Art Gallery, 2000), 109.
41. Letter from William Huff to Patricia Loud, June 22, 1993, Yale Art Gallery Archives.
42. Anne Tyng, *Louis Kahn to Anne Tyng: The Rome Letters, 1953–1954* (New York: Rizzoli, 1997), 26.
43. Ibid., 28.
44. Ibid., 31.
45. Ibid., 34.
46. Carlin interview.
47. Anne Tyng, "Architecture Is My Touchstone," *Radcliffe Quarterly*, Sept. 1984, 6.
48. Tyng, *Louis Kahn to Anne Tyng*, 58.
49. AI, Sue Ann Kahn, Mar. 22, 2004.

50. Tyng, *The Rome Letters*, 64.
51. AI, Peter Millard, Oct. 14, 2004.
52. Quoted in Yale University News Bureau release no. 48, Aug. 27, 1952.
53. Carlin interview.
54. *Progressive Architecture*, Jan. 1953, 92.
55. Millard interview.
56. AI, Nicholas Gianopulos, Feb. 14, 2005.
57. Millard interview.
58. Sawyer, "Kahn: Impressions," 7.
59. Carlin interview.
60. Eisenman interview.
61. *Progressive Architecture*, May 1954, 16.
62. Frederick Gutheim, "Modern Architecture at Yale," *New York Herald Tribune*, Nov. 28, 1953.
63. Tyng, *Louis Kahn to Anne Tyng*, 81.
64. Ibid., 88.
65. Letter from Charles Sawyer to author, Dec. 18, 2004.
66. *Louis Kahn to Anne Tyng*, p. 70.

CHAPTER FOUR
BACK HOME TO PHILADELPHIA
THE RICHARDS MEDICAL RESEARCH BUILDING
1957–64

1. AI, Robert M. Kliment , Mar. 17, 2004.
2. AI, G. Holmes Perkins, May 13, 2004.
3. Ibid.
4. Robert Geddes, *Harvard Design Magazine*, Spring-Summer 2005, p. 135.
5. AI, Tim Vreeland, May 2, 2005.
6. AI, John MacAllister, May 6, 2005.
7. AI, Mark Ueland, May 13, 2004.
8. AI, Peter Clement, Feb. 28, 2005.
9. Charles E. Dagit Jr., unpublished manuscript, 2005, author's collection.
10. AI. Duncan Buell, June 14, 2005.
11. AI. Sue Ann Kahn, June 20, 2006.
12. AI, Charles Dagit, Nov. 29, 2005.
13. Perkins interview.
14. AI, Duncan Buell, Mar. 1, 2004.
15. Vreeland interview.
16. William S. Huff, "Louis Kahn: Sorted Recollections and Lapses in Familiarities," 10.
17. MacAllister interview.
18. Vreeland interview.
19. Ibid.
20. MacAllister interview.
21. August E. Komendant, *18 Years with Architect Louis I. Kahn* (Englewood, NJ: Aloray, 1975), 172.
22. Latour, *Kahn: L'uomo*, 115.
23. Dagit interview.
24. Latour, ed., *Kahn: Writings*, 58, 72.
25. Buell interview.
26. Vreeland interview.
27. AI, Edmund Bacon, Mar. 18, 2005.
28. Ibid.
29. MacAllister interview.
30. Buell interview.
31. Bacon interview.
32. Perkins interview.
33. MacAllister interview.
34. Quoted in Ellen Posner, "Paying Homage to Kahn's Bathhouse Beautiful," *Wall Street Journal*, Sept. 9, 1986.
35. Susan G. Solomon, *Louis I. Kahn's Trenton Jewish Community Center* (New York: Princeton Architectural Press, 2000), 49.
36. Vreeland interview.
375. Susan Braudy, "The Architectural Metaphysic of Louis Kahn," *New York Times Magazine*, Nov. 15, 1970, 86.
38. Vreeland interview.
39. Ibid.
40. Perkins interview.
41. UP Archives, 030.II.A.25.8.
42. David Allison, "Places for Research," *International Science and Technology*, Sept. 1962, 30.
43. Vreeland interview.
44. Quoted in "Form and Design," *Louis Kahn, Essential Texts* (New York: W. W. Norton, 2003), 72.
45. Quoted in Heiuz Ronner, Sharad Jhaveri, and Alessandro Vasella, *Louis I. Kahn, Complete Works 1935–74*, (Boulder: Westview Press, 1977), 114.
46. Vreeland interview.
47. Latour, *Kahn: Writings*, 317.
48. Huff, "Louis Kahn," *Little Journal*, Sept. 1981, 12.
49. *Architectural Record*, Sept. 1959, 238.
50. Komendant, op. cit., 7.
51. Ibid.

52. Quoted in Allison, op. cit., 23.

53. Letter from MacAllister to author, Oct. 14, 2005.

54. Allison, op. cit., 20.

55. MacAllister interview.

56. Quoted in Latour, *Kahn: L'uomo*, 77.

57. Reyner Banham, "The Buttery-hatch Aesthetic," *Architectural Review*, Mar. 1962, 206–8.

58. Ibid.

59. Romaldo Giurgola, interview by Kazumi Kawasaki, in Latour, *Kahn: L'uomo*, 161.

60. Wilder Green, "Louis I. Kahn, Architect, Alfred Newton Richards Medical Research Building," *Museum of Modern Art Bulletin* 28, 3.

61. Vincent Scully, *Modern Architecture* (New York: George Braziller, 1961), 39.

62. Vincent Scully, *Louis I. Kahn* (New York: George Braziller, 1962), 27–30.

63. Vreeland interview.

64. UP Archives, 030.II.A.57.107.

65. Robert Venturi, "Louis Kahn Remembered," in *Iconography and Electronics Upon a Generic Architecture* (Cambridge: MIT Press, 1963), 87–92.

66. Perkins interview.

CHAPTER FIVE

THE CLIENT CONNECTION
THE SALK INSTITUTE FOR BIOLOGICAL STUDIES 1959–65

1. Kent Larson, *Louis Kahn: Unbuilt Masterworks* (New York: Monacelli Press, 2000), 54.

2. AI, Peter Salk, June 22, 2005.

3. *Complete Works*, 143.

4. Wurman, op.cit., 131.

5. Op.cit., 291.

6. Richard Carter, *Breakthrough: The Saga of Jonas Salk* (New York: Trident Press, 1966), 29.

7. Ibid., 37.

8. Salk interview.

9. Carter, op. cit., 4.

10. Ibid., 51.

11. Wilfred Sheed, *Time*, Mar. 29, 1999, 168.

12. Salk interview.

13. C. P. Snow, *The Two Cultures and the Scientific Revolution* (New York: Cambridge University Press, 1959), 6.

14. Carter, op. cit., 406.

15. Ibid., 407.

16. Ibid., 410.

17. Jacob Bronowski, *The Ascent of Man* (Boston and Toronto: Little, Brown, 1973), 15.

18. Wurman, op. cit., 77.

19. AI, Sue Ann Kahn, Dec. 1, 2005.

20. "Kahn," interview, *Perspecta 7* (1961), 9.

21. Wurman, op. cit., 216.

22. Ibid., 117.

23. Alexandra Tyng, *Beginnings: Louis I. Kahn's Philosophy of Architecture* (New York: Wiley, 1984), 19–21.

24. Wurman, op. cit., 290.

25. Salk interview.

26. Letter from Jonathan Salk to Peter Salk, Nov. 17, 2005, author's collection.

27. AI, John (Jack) MacAllister, June 23, 2005.

28. Komendant, op. cit., 42.

29. Wurman, op. cit., 91.

30. Letter from John MacAllister to author, Oct. 13, 2005, author's collection.

31. Quoted in Latour, *Kahn: L'uomo*, 81.

32. MacAllister interview.

33. Ibid.

34. Ibid.

35. Schlosser in Latour, *Kahn: L'uomo*, 111.

36. Wurman, op. cit., 3.

37. MacAllister interview.

38. Ibid.

39. AI, Alexandra Tyng, Apr. 22, 2004.

40. Latour, *Kahn: L'uomo*, 63.

41. Alexandra Tyng interview.

42. Ibid.

43. Ibid.

44. Anne Tyng, *The Rome Letters*, 210.

45. AI, Sue Ann Kahn, Mar. 22, 2004.

46. MacAllister interview.

47. AI, David Rinehart, June 22, 2005.

48. Ibid.

49. MacAllister interview.

50. Rinehart interview.

51. MacAllister interview.

52. Ibid.

53. Rinehart interview.

54. MacAllister interview.
55. Ibid.
56. Letter from Peter Salk to author, Nov. 24, 2005, author's collection.
57. Letter from Peter Salk to author, Nov. 17, 2005, author's collection.
58. MacAllister interview.
59. Letter from Peter Salk to author, Nov. 23, 2005, author's collection.
60. AI, Peter Salk, June 22, 2005.
61. Ibid.
62. Peter Salk letter, Nov. 17, 2005.

CHAPTER SIX
"A DEGREE OF PURITY"
THE SUBCONTINENT
1962–83

1. Nathaniel Kahn, *My Architect*, 2003.
2. Quoted in "Form and Design," *Architectural Design*, Apr. 1961, 152.
3. AI, Balkrishna Doshi, Dec. 20, 2004.
4. Ibid.
5. Balkrishna Doshi, *Le Corbusier and Louis I. Kahn: The Acrobat and the Yogi of Architecture* (Ahmedabad: Vastu-Shilpa Foundation for Studies and Research in Environmental Design, undated), 23.
6. Quoted in Richard Saul Wurman, *What Will Be Has Always Been*, 272.
7. Doshi interview.
8. Doshi, op. cit., 13.
9. *Complete Works*, 265.
10. Ibid.
11. Doshi interview.
12. Quoted in Romaldo Giurgola and Jaimini Mehta, *Louis I. Kahn* (Boulder, CO: Westview Press, 1975), 109.
13. AI, Anant Raje, Dec. 21, 2004.
14. Ibid.
15. Undated summary, LIK Collection, 030.II.A.58.4, AAUP.
16. AI, Shamsul Wares, Dec. 16, 2004.
17. Quoted in Brownlee and De Long, op. cit., 86.
18. AI, Muzharul Islam, Dec. 14, 2004.
19. Quoted in Anupam Banerji, *The Architecture of Corbusier and Kahn in the East* (Lewiston, ME: Edwin Mellen Press, 2001), 116.
20. AI, Nathaniel Kahn, Apr. 11, 2003.
21. LIK Collection, 030.II.A.56.66, AAUP.
22. Ibid.
23. AI, Nicholas Gianopulos, Feb. 14, 2005.
24. Ibid.
25. August E. Komendant, "Architect-Engineer Relationship," in Latour, *Louis I. Kahn: L'uomo, il maestro*, 319.
26. August Komendant, *18 Years with Architect Louis I. Kahn* (Englewood, NJ: Aloray, 1975), 83.
27. AI, Nicholas Gianopulos, Feb. 1, 2005.
28. Gianopulos interview, Feb. 14, 2005.
29. AI, Henry Wilcots, Feb. 14, 2005.
30. Ibid.
31. Quoted in Wurman, op. cit., 51.
32. Wilcots interview.
33. Quoted in Latour, *Louis I. Kahn: Writings, Lectures, Interviews*, 218.
34. AI, Muhammed Rashid, Dec. 12, 2004.
35. AI, Muhammed Rashid, Dec. 16, 2004.
36. AI, Henry Wilcots, Mar. 2, 2004.
37. AI, Thomas Leidigh, Mar. 2, 2004.
38. Ibid.
39. Abdul Wazid, interview by Sujaul Islam Khan, unpublished manuscript, "The Making of Sher-E-Bangla Nagar," 1998, author's collection.
40. Quoted in Kathleen James, "Availabilities Abroad," unpublished text of address to symposium, Yale University School of Architecture, Jan. 23–24, 2004.
41. AI, Henry Wilcots, Dec. 14, 2005.
42. AI, Reyhan Tansal Larimer, Feb. 21, 2005.
43. AI, Reyhan Tansal Larimer, Apr. 16, 2004.
44. Wares interview.
45. AI, Sanaul Haque, Dec. 14, 2004.
46. AI, Nurur Rahman Khan, Dec. 17, 2004.
47. Quoted in Banerji, op. cit., 108.
48. Komendant, 18 Years, 85–87.
49. Lawrence J. Vale, *Architecture, Power, and National Identity* (New Haven: Yale University Press, 1992), 243.
50. Ibid., 255.
51. Doshi, *The Acrobat and the Yogi*, 31.
52. Doshi interview.
53. Raje interview.

54. Doshi interview.
55. Larimer interview.

CHAPTER SEVEN
"A TEMPLE FOR LEARNING"
THE PHILLIPS EXETER ACADEMY LIBRARY
1965–72

1. AI, David Rinehart, June 22, 2005.
2. Quoted in Myron R. Williams, *The Story of Phillips Exeter* (Exeter, NH: Phillips Exeter Academy, 1957), 8.
3. Ibid., 187.
4. Ibid., 190.
5. Ralph Adams Cram, *My Life in Architecture* (Boston: Little, Brown, 1936), 275.
6. Quoted in Williams, op. cit., 139.
7. AI, Rodney Armstrong, May 6, 2004.
8. Rodney Armstrong Papers, box 4, file 6, Philips Exeter Academy.
9. *PEA Bulletin*, Spring 2004, 26.
10. Unpublished remarks by Rodney Armstrong on the occasion of the Exeter Library's twentieth anniversary, Nov. 7, 1991, author's collection.
11. Armstrong interview.
12. Armstrong Papers, box 5, file 6.
13. Ibid.
14. *Memorial Minutes* (Exeter, NH: Phillips Exeter Academy Press, 2002), 40.
15. AI, Caroline Fish, Aug. 2, 2005.
16. Letter from Sidney Guberman to Alexander Purves, Dec. 12, 2005, author's collection.
17. Armstrong interview.
18. Fish to Day, Armstrong Papers, box 1, file 9.
19. Ibid.
20. AI, Rodney Armstrong, Nov. 17, 1991.
21. Fish interview.
22. Fish to Day, Armstrong Papers, box 1, file 9.
23. Ibid.
24. Ibid.
25. Armstrong to Day, Armstrong Papers, box 1, file 9.
26. Armstrong remarks, Nov. 7, 1991.
27. Ibid.
28. AI, James Gamble Rogers III, Feb. 27, 2004

29. Rodney Armstrong, Elliot G. Fish, and Albert C. Ganley, *Proposals for the Library at the Phillips Exeter Academy* (Exeter, NH: Phillips Exeter Academy, 1966), 1.
30. Quoted in Wurman, op. cit., 182.
31. Armstrong remarks, Nov. 7, 1991.
32. NOTE TO COME.
33. Armstrong interview.
34. Ibid.
35. Kahn to Armstrong, Apr. 17, 1968, Armstrong Papers, box 1, file 9.
36. Quoted in *Complete Works*, 371.
37. Quoted in Ada Louise Huxtable, "New Exeter Library: Stunning Paean to Books," *New York Times*, Oct. 23, 1972.
38. Wurman, op. cit., 178.
39. AI, Thomas Leidigh, Aug. 3, 2005.
40. Quoted in Wurman, op. cit., 180.
41. UP Archives, 030.II.A.57.107
42. Ibid.
43. Armstrong to Kahn, Armstrong Papers, box 9, file 5.
44. Armstrong interview, May 6, 2004.
45. Wurman, op. cit., 181.
46. Ibid.
47. Louis Kahn, *Conversations with Students* (Princeton: Princeton Architectural Press, 1998), 26.
48. Kahn to Day, Aug. 18, 1966, Phillips Exeter Academy collection.
49. Minutes of the Dining Halls Building Committee, Jan. 11, 1967, Armstrong Papers, box 4, file 6.
50. Letter from Robert Venturi to Stephen Van Dyck, quoted in, "A Plea to Preserve Louis Kahn's Phillips Exeter Academy Buildings as a Complex," unpublished manuscript prepared for "Kahn in Context," a course at the Yale School of Architecture, Apr. 25, 2003, 6.
51. Ibid., 5.
52. Quoted in *The Exonian*, Feb. 18, 1970, 1.
53. Armstrong Papers, box 8, file 5.
54. Armstrong to Kahn, Armstrong Papers, box 7, file 9.
55. AI, Nicholas Gianopulos, Aug. 24, 2005.
56. Rogers interview.
57. Quoted in *Complete Works*, 371.

CHAPTER EIGHT
LIGHT UNLEASHED
THE KIMBELL ART MUSEUM
1966–72

1. Louis I. Kahn, "Silence and Light," in *Louis Kahn: Essential Texts*, ed. Robert Twombly (New York: W. W. Norton, 2003), 229.
2. Ibid.
3. Quoted in Patricia Cummings Loud, "The Kimbell Art Foundation: Planning the Kimbell Art Museum," unpublished manuscript, author's collection, 2.
4. Quoted in Patricia Cummings Loud, *In Pursuit of Quality: The Kimbell Art Museum* (Fort Worth: Kimbell Art Museum, 1987), 3.
5. Quoted in Loud, "Kimbell: Planning," 16.
6. Patricia Cummings Loud, "The Kimbell Art Foundation: The Search for an Architect," unpublished manuscript, author's collection, 8.
7. "Policy Statement," Kimbell Art Museum, June 1, 1966.
8. Quoted in Loud, *Quality*, 9.
9. "Pre-Architectural Program," Kimbell Art Museum, June 1, 1966.
10. Ibid.
11. Quoted in "Kahn's Museum: An Interview with Richard Brown," *Art in America*, Sept.–Oct. 1972, 44.
12. Loud, "Kimbell: Search," 12.
13. Ibid., 23.
14. AI, Frank Sherwood, June 21, 2005.
15. "Talk at the Conclusion of the Otterloo Congress (1959)," in *Louis I. Kahn: Essential Texts*, ed. Robert Twombly (New York: W. W. Norton, 2003), 53.
16. AI, Tim Thomas, June 21, 2005.
17. Quoted in Thomas Leslie, *Louis I. Kahn: Building Art, Building Science* (New York: George Braziller, 2005), 187.
18. Quoted in Patricia Cummings Loud, *The Art Museums of Louis I. Kahn* (Durham and London: Duke University Press, 1989), 131.
19. Quoted in Loud, *Pursuit*, 43.
20. *Complete Works*, 344.
21. Quoted in "Kahn's Museum: An Interview with Richard F. Brown," 48.
22. Quoted in *The Construction of the Kimbell Art Museum* (Milan: Skira Editore, 1999), 18.
23. Ibid.
24. Komendant, *18 Years*, 117.
25. Ibid., 120.
26. Ibid., 121.
27. Harriet Pattison, "Engaging Kahn: A Legacy for the Future," a symposium at Yale University, Jan. 24, 2004.
28. Quoted in Marshall Meyers, "Masters of Light: Louis Kahn," *AIA Journal*, Sept. 1979, 60.
29. Ibid., 62.
30. Quoted in Latour, *Kahn: L'uomo*, 81.
31. Sherwood interview.
32. Quoted in *Light Is the Theme*, compiled by Nell E. Johnson (Kimbell Art Foundation: Fort Worth, 1975), 54.
33. Thomas interview.
34. Quoted in Loud, *Pursuit*, 58.
35. Sherwood interview.
36. Komendant, *18 Years*, 131.
37. Pattison, op. cit.
38. Ibid.
39. Peter Plagens, "Louis Kahn's New Museum in Fort Worth," *Art Forum*, Feb. 1968, 18.
40. "Kahn's Museum: Interview with Richard F. Brown," *Art in America*, Sept.–Oct. 1972, 44.
41. Sherwood interview.
42. AI, Sue Ann Kahn, Mar. 22, 2004.
43. Ibid.
44. *Light Is the Theme*, 7

CHAPTER NINE
THE MOTH AND THE BUTTERFLY
THE YALE CENTER FOR BRITISH ART
1969–74

1. Paul Mellon, *Reflections in a Silver Spoon* (New York: William Morrow, 1992), 118.
2. Quoted in "Brewster's 'Fair-Trial' Statement," *Yale Alumni Magazine*, May 1970, 23.
3. Jules Prown, "On Being a Client,"

Journal of the Society of Architectural Historians, Mar. 1983, 11.

4. Jules Prown, *Yale Center for British Art* (New Haven: Yale University, 1977), 12.

5. Ibid.

6. AI, Jules Prown, Apr. 4, 2005.

7. Ibid.

8. AI, Jules Prown, Apr. 9, 2004.

9. Ibid.

10. Prown in Latour, *Kahn: L'uomo*, 135.

11. Prown interview, Apr. 4, 2005.

12. Ibid.

13. AI, Jules Prown, Feb. 28, 2003.

14. Prown, *Yale Center for British Art*, 14.

15. *Pennsylvania Gazette*, Dec. 1972, 21.

16. AI, Leonard Traines, Oct. 18, 2005.

17. Interview with Patricia McLaughlin, *Pennsylvania Gazette*, Dec. 1972, 20.

18. Prown interview, Apr. 9, 2004.

19. Prown interview, Apr. 4, 2005.

20. Ibid.

21. Prown in Latour, *Kahn: L'uomo*, 135.

22. AI, Abba Tor, Oct. 25, 2005.

23. Abba Tor, in Latour, *Kahn: L'uomo*, 123.

24. Tor interview.

25. Ibid.

26. Ibid.

27. Ibid.

28. Abba Tor, unpublished notes for a presentation at the Yale Center for British Art, Apr. 11, 2005, author's collection.

29. AI, Kenneth Borst, Oct. 31, 2005.

30. Ibid.

31. Tor notes, Apr. 11, 2005.

32. Tor interview.

33. Quoted by Marshall Meyers in Latour, *Kahn: L'uomo*, 83.

34. Sarah David, "British Art in Context at the BAC," unpublished manuscript, Yale School of Architecture, Apr. 11, 2003, author's collection.

35. Borst interview.

36. Prown interview, Apr. 4, 2005.

37. Tor interview.

38. Prown interview

39. AI, Patricia Cummings Loud, Oct. 14, 2005.

40. Traines interview.

41. AI, Anne Meyers, Oct. 13, 2005.

42. Traines interview.

43. Meyers interview.

44. Tim Madigan, *Fort Worth Star-Telegram*, Feb. 1, 2004.

45. AI, Nathaniel Kahn, Apr. 11, 2003.

46. Quoted in *My Architect: A Son's Journey*, film by Nathaniel Kahn, New Yorker Films Artwork, 2003.

47. Nathaniel Kahn interview.

48. Meyers interview.

49. Traines interview.

50. AI, Rosella Sherman, Oct. 20, 2005.

51. Traines interview.

52. AI, Sue Ann Kahn, Feb. 1, 2006.

53. Meyers interview.

54. Tor in Latour, *Kahn: L'uomo*, 127.

55. AI, John MacAllister, Apr. 6, 2005.

56. Borst interview.

57. Ibid.

58. AI, Stanley Tigerman, Jan. 18, 2006.

59. Tor interview.

60. Borst interview.

61. Mellon, op. cit., 324.

62. Ibid.

63. Meyers interview.

64. Quoted in Latour, *Kahn: L'uomo*, 27.

65. Ibid.

66. Pattison, op. cit.

EPILOGUE

1. AI, Anne Meyers, Oct. 13, 2005.

2. AI, Bill Lacy, Nov. 19, 2005.

3. AI, Leonard Traines, Oct. 28, 2005.

4. AI, Abba Tor, Oct. 25, 2005.

5. Ibid.

6. AI, Alexandra Tyng, Nov. 18, 2005.

7. AI, Oct. 21, 2005.

ACKNOWLEDGMENTS

I am indebted to many people for help on this book. My agent, Sterling Lord, supported the project from its beginnings many years ago. Nancy Green, my editor at W. W. Norton, stood by the idea during a long interruption. Joan Davidson of Furthermore was most generous in the funding of the artwork, as was Arvid Nelson.

Members of Louis Kahn's family, especially his children—Sue Ann Kahn, Alexandra Tyng, and Nathaniel Kahn—were extraordinarily open with their recollections and insights. I owe further thanks to Rodney Armstrong, Susan R. Behr, Nicholas Gianopulos, John E. MacAllister, Patricia Cummings Loud, Peter L. Salk, and Robert A. M. Stern, for their comments on the manuscript, and to Julia Moore Converse and William Whitaker at the Architectural Archives of the University of Pennsylvania for their support of my research and their personal hospitality.

I am also grateful to Edmund Bacon, Peter Blake, Kenneth Borst, Donald Briselden, Duncan Buell, Earl Carlin, Helen Chillman, Peter W. Clement, Andrea Costella, Charles Dagit, John Morris Dixon, Balkrishna V. Doshi, Alvin Eisenman, Jean France, Rosalie Genevro, Wilder Green, Sanaul Haque, Muzharul Islam, Marshall Alan Kahn, Augustus Kellogg, Elise Kenney, Nurur Rahman Khan, Robert M. Kliment, Bill Lacy, Reyhan Tansal Larimer, Thomas Leidigh, Theodore Liebman, David Macy, Estelle Margolis, Anne Meyers, Peter Millard, Adnan Morshed, Caroline Murray, Eugene Nalle, Leona Nalle, Harriet Pattison, I. M. Pei, G. Holmes Perkins, Nancy Platukis, George Pohl, James Stewart Polshek, Jules David Prown, Alexander Purves, Anant Raje, David Rinehart, Charles H. Sawyer, Vincent Scully, Winton Scott, Rosella Sherman, Mason Smith, Frank H. Sherwood, Erica Stoller, Abigail Sturges, Jacquelyn Thomas, Stanley Tigerman, Abba Tor, Walfredo Toscanini, Leonard Traines, Anne Griswold Tyng, Thomas Vreeland, Shamsul Wares, Fred Wiemer, Henry Wilcots, the MacDowell Colony, and my students in the Yale University School of Architecture course 777b, "Kahn in Context," 2003–2006.

INDEX